# ASE Science Teachers' Handbook

Edited by

John Nellist and Brian Nicholl

Hutchinson

London Melbourne Sydney Auckland Johannesburg

Hutchinson Education

An imprint of Century Hutchinson Ltd

Brookmount House, 62–65 Chandos Place, Covent Garden,
London WC2N 4NW

Century Hutchinson Australia Pty Ltd
PO Box 496, 16–22 Church Street, Hawthorn, Victoria 3122
Australia

Century Hutchinson New Zealand Ltd
PO Box 40–086, Glenfield, Auckland 10, New Zealand

Century Hutchinson South Africa (Pty) Ltd
PO Box 337, Bergvlei 2012, South Africa

First published 1986 by Hutchinson and Co. (Publishers) Ltd
Reprinted 1986, 1987


Typeset in 10 on 12 point Times by
Mathematical Composition Setters Ltd., Salisbury, UK

Printed in Great Britain by
Anchor Brendon Ltd, Tiptree, Essex

British Library Cataloguing in Publication Data
The ASE science teacher's handbook.
1. Science – Study and teaching – Great Britain
I. Association for Science Education
507'.1 LB1585.5.G7

ISBN 0–09–156340–2

# Contents

# Acknowledgements

The following people have contributed in various ways to this handbook:

Sarah Brock; Gerry Davis; Ken Dobson; Val Emmett; Bob Fairbrother; Jan Harding; Giles Job; Alan Jones; Sheila Martin; Bryan Milner; John Nellist; Brian Nicholl; Bob Osborne; Betty Preston; Pat Rowlinson; Linda Scott; Peter Scott; Jenny Selfe; Kabir Shaikh; David Tawney; S. Tomlinson; Ken Wild; and last but certainly not least Cathy Wilson.

Kind permission has been granted by the following for use of extracts in this book:

The Assesment of Performance Unit, the DES and the Controller of Her Majesty's Stationery Office for the use of APU and DES material; The English Centre for material from *The English Department Book*; The GCE and CSE Boards' Joint Council for 16+ National Criteria and the Controller of Her Majesty's Stationery Office for extracts from the *National Criteria for Science* (draft proposals); Heinemann Educational Books for extracts from *Towards a Science of Science Teaching* by M. Shayer and P. Adey; ILEA for the use of material from *Units and Unit Credits* by D. Hargreaves; Joint Matriculation Board for the use of an A-level Physics Examination question; Macmillan Publishers for material from *This is Science: Teachers' Guide* by K. Dobson; SCDC Publications for tables from *Girl-Friendly Science: Avoiding Sex Bias in the Curriculum*, Longman, York, 1985; SCDC Publications/ASE for extracts from *Decisions in the Science Department*; SCDC Publications/SSCR for extracts from *Towards a Statement of Minimum Entitlement: Brenda and Friends*; The Schools Council for material from the *Schools Council Modular Course in Technology, Teachers' Master Manuals*, published by NCST/Oliver and Boyd, 1981; SSCR for material from *Primary Science, Secondary Science: Some Issues at the Interface*; University of London Institute of Education for extracts from *Science in Schools: Which Way Now?* Studies in Education 8, by Ingle and Jennings, Heinemann Educational Books for the Institute of Education, University of London.

# Introduction

Science teachers are busy people caught up in a rapidly changing educational scene. Pleas for a time of consolidation, heard since the early days of the Nuffield projects, go unheeded, and there are few signs that we are moving into calmer waters. Local and national developments point clearly to a changing science curriculum and signal something of a new view of the profession. For many years the science teacher has not been seen solely as the purveyor of set bodies of knowledge, defined by an external and remote examinations industry, and recent perspectives give greater weight to an extended professional role. We are, for example, rightly expected to know something of management, more of the intricacies of assessment (an increasingly school-based activity) and to have a growing familiarity with those aspects of learning theory which seem to underpin our pupils' success in effectively acquiring science concepts. Alongside these important areas of knowledge there sits too the requirement to justify the inclusion of science as a core component in the educational programme of all pupils and properly to work in science with all other curricular components.

Despite the enhanced importance now given to such issues, more familiar priorities still remain. The effective management and deployment of both physical resources and the people who man our schools remain of the utmost importance. Arguably, such considerations bulk even larger in these straitened times.

Advice on all such issues is not in short supply, liberally spread across a wide range of publications – policy statements, periodicals and pamphlets. This book attempts to ease the access problem by collecting together within one set of covers views, information and advice on a spectrum of issues relevant, in the extended professional sense, to the science teacher of today. It is not then a conventional handbook, stacked with scientific data, useful addresses, new ways into chromatography or design notes for string and sealing wax apparatus. That is not to say that useful and practical hints are not contained therein, but in general the accent is not on the subject specific minutiae of the catalogue or data book. Rather, the text concentrates on discussing a set of broadly based issues and in bringing together extracts from and references to a range of publications and papers important to teachers and departments concerned to review their policies and practice.

The book has been written for all science teachers but directed particularly to those teaching youngsters in the 7–16 age range. It is not the work of a single author but contains a series of contributions from experienced science educators, teachers and others, each offering something of their particular expertise and enthusiasm. The length and depth of treatment is deliberately varied from chapter to chapter; it is a book which can be dipped into and used to visit and revisit topics of particular interest. The intention too is to encourage the reader, in the best traditions of participative learning, to try out in a practical way many of the messages in her or his own school context. To this end, Chapters 2 to 6 contain suggested activities – pointers to purposeful discussion, investigations or enquiries which can be carried out by individuals or departmental teams.

At a time of profound change in science curricula, in examination structures and styles, and as we struggle to come to terms with 'science for all' in practice, this book, collecting together as it does much of relevance to these and other issues, is seen as helping the busy science teacher the more effectively to tackle an evermore complex job.

*J. Nellist*
*August 1985*

# 1 Why teach science and why to all?

**Bryan Milner**

★ Science education can be justified because it contributes distinctive skills, concepts and perspectives.

★ Education in science can be regarded as having five dimensions, each producing one category of the aims of teaching science:

a content dimension;
a process dimension;
a context demension;
an affective dimension;
a meta-scientific dimension.

★ Scientific knowledge is established and developed through the use of distinctive skills, which include:

thinking skills;
practical skills;
communication skills.

★ It is theoretically possible to meet all the aims of science education within any structure, but a particular structure will lend itself better to achieving some aims than others.

★ Check-lists from different sources can help teachers to formulate their own philosophies of science education.

## Introduction

At any gathering of science teachers there will be considerable divergence of opinion on how best to teach some aspects of science, or even whether it should be taught to some particular groups of children. One suggestion which is likely to receive more or less unanimous support, however, is that all children should study science throughout the period of compulsory schooling. (It is increasingly agreed, too, that all are entitled to a broad, balanced and relevant education in science.) We might, of course, cynically attribute this support to the desire – conscious or unconscious - of science teachers to stay in business at a time of sharply falling secondary school rolls were it not for the fact that such support is also being given by the DES, members of HM Inspectorate, and LEAs. Given the degree of consensus on this matter within the education service (and to a considerable extent outside of it, too), it might appear wholly unnecessary to devote this initial chapter to a detailed consideration of the issue. It is important to do so, however, for two reasons: firstly, because the consensus view itself should only be accepted in so far as it is based on sound reasoning; and, secondly, because explicit formulation of the reasons for providing science education is essential for resolving those questions about which science teachers do not agree, i.e. what science to teach, to whom and in what style.

These initial pages provide the broad framework within which questions relating more immediately to the practice of teaching science can be discussed in subsequent chapters. This first chapter is intended also to help departments to establish their own philosophy of science, both as an aid to presenting the case for science within their own schools and to help them to look critically at the style and kinds of courses they offer.

## Can science education be justified?

In attempting to justify education in science it is helpful to begin by considering the justification for having a system of compulsory formal education at all. There are, it is argued, skills, concepts and perspectives which it is important for children to possess and which they are unlikely to acquire incidentally, i.e. simply by living in our society. It is necessary, therefore, deliberately and systematically to expose children to experiences which are likely to result in their acquiring these important competencies. If we are to justify including science within such a formal education, we need to show:

1 that science contributes distinctive skills, concepts and perspectives, i.e. different from those afforded by other areas of experience or forms of knowledge;
2 that the acquisition of these distinctly scientific skills, concepts and perspectives is greatly facilitated by structured formal education;
3 that it is important for children to acquire the skills, concepts and perspectives of science.

We shall deal with each of these points in turn.

1 There exists a very strong basis for regarding science as a distinctive form of knowledge. There is, in the natural sciences, an impressive body of knowledge expressed in terms of concepts which initially arose out of everyday language but which have developed in both scope and precision to a much more sophisticated level. The various sciences which can, on the face of it, be separated in terms of their subject matter and the sets of concepts they employ are, nevertheless, properly regarded as belonging to the single activity, science. There are two reasons for this view:
   (a) explanations in one science often depend on the concepts and principles of another (e.g. cellular biology in terms of chemistry, or meteorology in terms of physics), and the case for strict separation of sciences in terms of content does not, therefore, survive close scrutiny;
   (b) the manner in which knowledge is (provisionally) established – facts, principles, explanations and theories – arises out of, and is continually put at risk by, observation and experiment. The *process* of science is common to all the sciences.

The argument for regarding science as a single activity applies not only to the three most commonly taught sciences, biology, chemistry and physics, but also to the less frequently taught sciences like geology, meteorology and astronomy.

It is with these *natural* sciences that this handbook is primarily concerned. The behavioural (or human or social) sciences, e.g. psychology, sociology and economics, are also in some senses scientific and, though this issue is too complex to go into here, it is important in any overall consideration of breadth, balance and relevance in education.

2 It is because the body of knowledge (provisionally) established via the scientific process by many generations of scientists is so comprehensive yet, at the same time, tightly structured, that deliberate initiation into selected aspects is the most economical way of achieving an understanding of science that has reasonable breadth and depth. Furthermore, the process dimension of science – the capacity to think and act in a scientific way – is more likely to be achieved by apprenticeship than by precept.

TABLE 1.1 **Reasons for which an education in science might be regarded as important**

| *Science for interest (intrinsic justification)* | *Science for use (instrumental justification)* |
|---|---|
| 1 As with any other form of human activity, many people find the distinctive subject matter of science(s), the patterns and relationships which develop and the scientific processes interesting and rewarding. Everyone should have the opportunity to engage in the activity to a sufficient extent to appreciate what it has to offer and to be able to continue with it if they so choose. | 2 Both scientific knowledge and science processes enable individuals:<br>(a) to cope more adequately with everyday life in a society permeated by technology,<br>e.g. to make/develop/use/maintain bodies/homes/gardens/devices for basic needs/income/leisure;<br>(b) to make a positive contribution to that society as workers and as citizens having an informed opinion on, for example, matters of environmental importance. |
| 1 and 2 justify the provision of a broad, basic science education for everyone. | |
| 3 Those finding particular areas of science especially interesting should be allowed to develop their interests as far as resources allow. Maintaining and developing the activity of science as an area of potential interest (and utility) is of benefit to society also. | 4 More advanced and/or specialized studies of science (and/or its applications) for specific purposes is of benefit to individuals, in terms of employment, and to society, which needs scientists, technologists and technicians (whether we subscribe to a future of high technology or of alternative technology). |
| 3 and 4 justify the provision of more advanced or specialized science education for those who want it or need it. | |

3 Even if we are satisfied that science is a distinctive activity, competence in which is best facilitated via structured experiences, we cannot justify educating children in science unless we can also show that it is important for them to acquire the skills, concepts and perspectives of science. The crucial questions hinge on the word 'important'. One question we should certainly ask is, 'Important to whom?' In a relatively open and democratic society, the needs of individuals who have to live their lives in the context of that society, and the needs of society itself for individuals who are adequately equipped to maintain it and develop it further, should be regarded as being of equal importance. Ideally, therefore, an education in science will be of value both to the individual and to the society in which she or he lives. This, then, raises the further question of the reasons for which an education in science might be regarded as important. It is convenient to present a set of reasons in tabular form (Table 1.1).

## Aims of science education

The justification outlined above for providing all children with a broad basic science education (together with more advanced science education for those who want it or need it) must next be developed into a statement of the basic aims of science education. We shall concentrate on the aims of the broad basic science education for all since any additional science, for some, will have its own specific purposes and, hence, more specific aims.

Education in science may be regarded as having three main dimensions:

1 a content dimension;
2 a process dimension;
3 a context dimension.

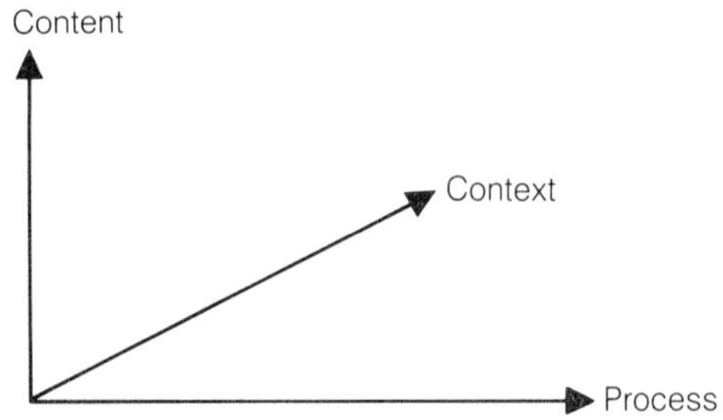


These three dimensions of science education provide us with three categories of aims. Each dimension can itself, however, be broken down into several components, and there are two further aspects of science education ( somewhat different in nature both from the three listed above and from each other):

4 the affective dimension;
5 the meta-scientific dimension.

Because these dimensions of science education form a complex matrix, attempting to derive from them a statement in linear prose of the basic aims of science education will inevitably be somewhat untidy. In fact, having considered aims in the order listed above, it will be necessary to reconsider content in the light of the other four aims.

## 1 Aims related to content

Scientific endeavour by many individuals over a long period of time has resulted in an impressive body of established knowledge (albeit provisional and always open to revision and modification). A basic aim of science education is, therefore, to enable children to understand a broad range of important scientific concepts, facts, principles and theories.

It is worth noting that the word 'important' has, once again, been used without being explained. Because the three main aims form a complex matrix it is convenient to defer consideration of the criteria for selecting content until something has been said about the other two aims.

## 2 Aims related to process

Much scientific knowledge is established and developed through the use of distinctive ways of thinking and distinctive practical activities, and by the communication of ideas and discoveries to others. The development in children of these skills constitutes a further important aim of science education. Three groupings of skills will be described briefly.

### (a) *Thinking skills*

The capacity to think in a scientific manner:

to make hypotheses;
to devise situations to test hypotheses;
to draw conclusions from evidence;
to explain phenomena (in terms of appropriate principles or theories);
to solve problems;
to evaluate claims in relation to evidence.

### (b) *Practical skills*

The ability:

to make careful and systematic observations and measurements;
to carry out experiments and practical assignments confidently, competently and safely;
to improvise sensibly when circumstances demand it.

### (c) *Communication skills*

The ability:

to communicate orally/present, in an appropriate form, observations, investigations, insights, solutions and explanations;
to comprehend (and, where necessary, initially evaluate) the instructions, descriptions and explanations of others, both orally and in printed form;
to seek out, select and apply knowledge and data from a variety of written and other sources.

The cumulative effect of the development of these skills should be the ability to integrate them in carrying out appropriate investigative work involving the identification of problems, the design, execution and evaluation of suitable experiments and the communication of results and conclusions in appropriate forms.

Once again it is worth noting that a little more will need to be said about the process aim after consideration of the context aim.

## 3 Aims related to context

It is important for children to be capable of deploying their understanding of science and their mastery of science process appropriately in a number of different contexts:

(a) in the context of establishing the patterns and relationships in science just because of the satisfaction afforded by such a comprehensive and coherent understanding, i.e. in the context of pure science;
(b) in the context of solving practical everyday problems and successfully accomplishing practical everyday tasks, i.e. in a technological context (where this term is liberally interpreted to encompass all activities where science facilitates successful manipulation of equipment and materials to achieve required ends. It thus includes, for example, first aid, growing vegetables and brewing beer as well as more commonly recognized technological tasks like maintaining and repairing motor cycles);
(c) in the context of reaching informed and considered views on matters of public concern relating to the impact of certain developments of science or technology, i.e. in an environmental context (this term again being liberally interpreted to include social and economic implications as well as implications which are environmental in the stricter or more narrow sense of the term).

Two important points emerge from this categorization of contexts. Firstly, the pure science context (which was, incidentally, tacitly assumed in the way that the content and process aims were formulated) relates primarily to the intrinsic justification for science education (Section I in Table 1.1) whereas the technological and environmental contexts relate mainly to the instrumental justification for science education (Section II in the same table). Secondly, adequate thought and action of a technological nature depends to varying degrees on the integration of knowledge and skills from science with knowledge and skills from other areas of activity. Similarly, reaching balanced judgements on environmental issues requires such integration to a very considerable extent. The question of the nature and extent of the liaison needed between science and other curriculum areas is considered in detail in Chapter 7(c). It is important to note here that the capacity to select and apply knowledge and skills from science and to integrate them with knowledge and skills from other areas to arrive at a solution to a complex problem or to reach a tenable point of view about a complex issue is a further, and significant, component of the process aim.

## 4 Aims related to attitudes

The content, process and context aims of science are themselves most likely to be achieved if children find their science education interesting, rewarding and worthwhile in its own right. Enjoyment of science should also help to develop in children a positive attitude towards it, enabling them:

to value the practical benefits afforded by a scientific understanding and a scientific approach, while at the same time being aware of the limitations of science;

to have sufficient familiarity with, and confidence in, their handling of scientific knowledge to be not only able, but also willing, to contribute to the public discussion of scientific issues of interest to society as a whole. Many children will, it is hoped, develop and maintain in their private lives and/or their jobs an active lifetime interest in science.

As well as attitudes towards science there are many attitudes that are important in science. Such attitudes, or dispositions to think, act or respond to situations in certain ways, include:

| | |
|---|---|
| adaptability | tolerance |
| commitment | empathy |
| cooperation | consideration for others |
| reliability | curiosity |
| self-confidence | honesty |
| self-discipline | integrity |
| perseverance | |

(This list is taken from *Curriculum 11–16: Towards a Statement of Entitlement* (DES, 1983).)

None of these attitudes is, of course, exclusive to science: they are important in many activities in which we engage and in many situations which we encounter. It is, nevertheless, important to note that science education provides many excellent opportunities for their further development.

## 5 Aims related to the meta-scientific

An explicit understanding of the different dimensions of science set out below should also be included as part of everyone's general education. (This will, incidentally, contribute to an awareness of the value and limitations of science and of the inherently provisional nature of 'established' scientific knowledge.)

(a) The nature of science (i.e. of the subject matter, the concepts, and the processes which make science a distinctive form of knowledge).
(b) The way in which scientific understanding can be developed and valued for its own sake (i.e. as pure science).
(c) The way in which scientific knowledge and skills can be deployed and integrated with other types of knowledge and skills in technological and environmental contexts.

(d) The historical development of science and technology (including the crises and conflicts in science when accepted theories and ideas are challenged and overthrown).

Considerations of the kind outlined above are, of course, about science and are not, therefore, strictly speaking part of science itself: they belong rather to philosophy, history and sociology. It is for this reason that the aspect of science education discussed in this section is referred to as meta-scientific. It is, nevertheless, important that such aspects of education should be incorporated into school science schemes. The matter is further discussed in Chapter 7(c).

## Content aim: an amplification

Having considered the process, context, affective and meta-scientific aims in reasonable detail, we are now in a position to return to a question earlier left unanswered, namely, how to decide what science content is sufficiently important to be included in science education for all.

With such an extensive body of established scientific knowledge, this question of selection is crucial. In fact, a recurring theme in statements about science education in recent years is that of content overload. Science education, even when concentrating almost exclusively on biology, chemistry and physics, and within a predominantly pure science context, has encountered problems in keeping content to manageable proportions. If we are to extend the range of sciences from which content is drawn, and also to give due emphasis to the technological and environmental contexts as well as to the meta-scientific perspective on science, the issue must be squarely faced and adequately resolved. While there is no simple way of resolving the issue, it is possible to draw up some broad criteria.

Content should be selected from across the whole range of natural and applied sciences in relation to the process, context, affective, or meta-scientific aims as outlined in the following table.

---

Below are described the **Aims** and Criteria for selection of content.

**Process**
lends itself readily to the development of certain thinking, practical, or communication skills.

**Context**
*Pure science*
is fundamental to science (or to a specific science), i.e. it is one of the more powerful concepts or theories;
is an essential basis for further study.

*Technological*
is likely to be useful to anyone in their basic living, in their work, or in their leisure.
*Environmental*
contributes to an adequate understanding of socially important issues.

**Affective**
is an area of science that children (children in general or some children in particular) find interesting.

**Meta-scientific**
exemplifies, for example, the interaction between science and technology, the emergence and resolution of a crisis in the accepted framework of science, or the way science by itself can provide only part of the solution to many problems; provides an important perspective from which to see human existence, e.g. the scales of time and distance in cosmological, geological and evolutionary theories.

---

Happily, the same content often satisfies several of these criteria at the same time, thus making the problem of content selection not altogether intractable. Indeed, we should exploit this fact as far as possible. It should not, however, be made an absolute condition for content selection since this would mean arbitrarily ruling out material which, while satisfying only one criterion, satisfies that criterion superbly well.

## Aims and organizational framework

The fact that the aims for science education form a complex matrix creates problems not only for stating those aims concisely but also, and more importantly, for organizing the science curriculum so as to realize all the aims effectively. Though it is, no doubt, theoretically possible to do justice to all the aims of science education within any structure (e.g. separate sciences, integrated science, applied science etc.), in practice a particular structure will lend itself to achieving some aims better than others. Furthermore, the aims which tend to be emphasized by the very organization of a course will tend to be seen by pupils as the central aims of their science education (a problem which is exacerbated if this emphasis is also reflected in assessments and examinations). Though detailed consideration of this matter is undertaken in Chapter 2, it is appropriate to make two general points before concluding the present chapter.

Firstly, it is important not only to consider the strengths and limitations of different organizational frameworks but also to consider how these different frameworks may be combined, either concurrently during some particular phase of science education or consecutively during different phases of science education. Science education during the years 5–16 (or 4–19) should have continuity and progression and should, overall, be fully rounded and balanced in terms of the aims formulated in this chapter.

Secondly, it should be remembered that the technological, environmental and meta-scientific aspects of science education also involve other curriculum areas. We shall need, therefore, to examine the merits and demerits of organizational frameworks not only within science education but also across the whole curriculum at school level. This matter is taken up in Chapter 7(c).

## Summary

Having provided reasons supporting the view that there is a need for people to be *educated* in science (i.e. it is unlikely to be picked up incidentally), and that *everyone* needs to be thus educated, these reasons were themselves used to derive an analysis of what *counts* as being educated in science.

This analysis indicated that education in science has a content, process, context, affective and meta-scientific dimension, and that each dimension itself has several components.

The complex matrix of aims of science education thus produced points to the need for detailed consideration of the organization framework(s) required to realize these aims effectively. Whatever organization framework(s) is used, however, it is clear from both the range of the aims involved and the maturity many of them demand that children's education will need to include a significant science component at least up to the end of their compulsory schooling.

## Check-lists

The following check-lists, which have been drawn from a wide range of sources, are included here because, while they express a philosophy of science education broadly compatible with that articulated in this chapter, they use a different language, are organized in a different way and sometimes have a slightly different emphasis. They are intended to help teachers of science to formulate their own philosophies of science education.

That no material is quoted from *Science 5–16: A statement of policy* (DES, 1985) should not be taken to imply that this document is regarded as unimportant. On the contrary, it is assumed that all teachers will have ready access to a copy.

### 1 General statements of aims

(a) *Alternatives for Science Education* (ASE, 1979, pp. 40–41).
This statement is specifically about primary science:

We propose that all primary and, where appropriate, middle schools, establish as a matter of priority a science education policy across the curriculum based on the following essential characteristics:

(a) That what is undertaken under the heading of science 'should arise out of the spontaneous interests of the children and should not be imposed upon them with the aims of laying foundations', in a formal sense, for future science studies.

(b) That elementary scientific ideas should be derived from the exploration of the immediate environment and should involve 'the application of an attitude of enquiry and the establishment of personal patterns of understanding from first-hand experience'.

(c) That pupils should be encouraged through the careful management of their learning environment to make emergent generalizations of a temporary nature, and be given the confidence to accept that these will have to be modified in the light of further experience.

(d) That pupils, through individual and small group work, should be encouraged to speculate freely and creatively on the nature of objects and phenomena. In particular, a strong emphasis should be placed on the pupils' talking about, and discussing, science and on encouraging the creative expression of personal meaning in their own language and through modes other than formal writing.

(e) That all scientific work should arise within the context of an integrated curriculum. Science should not be separately timetabled, or be taught in a specialist room. Existing course materials should be available in all classrooms as part of the general stock of accessible resources.

(f) Finally, scientific phenomena should be freely used as the starting point for a wide range of creative work, e.g. poetry, story writing, drama, painting, model making, as part of the process of establishing a confident and open approach to science studies.

b) *National Criteria for Science* GCE and CSE Boards' Joint Council for 16 + National Criteria, 1985.

On educational aims:

2.1 To provide through well-designed studies of experimental and practical science a worthwhile educational experience for all pupils whether or not they go on to study science beyond this level and, in particular, to enable them to acquire sufficient understanding and knowledge;

2.1.1 to become confident citizens in a technological world, able to take or develop an informed interest in matters of scientific import;

2.1.2 to recognise the usefulness, and limitations, of scientific method and appreciate its applicability in other disciplines and in everyday life;

2.1.3 to be suitably prepared for studies beyond the GCSE level in pure sciences, in applied sciences or in science-dependent vocational courses.

2.2 To develop abilities and skills that

2.2.1 are relevant to the study and practice of science;

2.2.2 are useful in everyday life;

2.2.3 encourage safe practice.

2.3 To stimulate

2.3.1 curiosity, interest and enjoyment in science and its methods of enquiry;
2.3.1 interest in, and care for, the environment.
2.4 To promote an awareness that
2.4.1 the study and practice of science are cooperative and cumulative activities and are subject to social, economic, technological, ethical and cultural influences and limitations;
2.4.2 the applications of sciences may be both beneficial and detrimental to the individual, the community and the environment.

(c) *Education through Science* (ASE, 1981)

Education through science should enable the individual by the end of his or her period of compulsory education to have engaged in a study of science which has embodied all the following aims to an appropriate extent.

(a) The acquisition of a knowledge and understanding of a range of scientific concepts, generalizations, principles and laws through the systematic study and experience of aspects of the body of knowledge called science.
(b) The acquisition of a range of cognitive and psycho-motor skills and processes as a result of direct involvement in scientific activities and procedures in the laboratory and the field.
(c) The utilization of scientific knowledge and processes in the pursuit of further knowledge and deeper understanding, and the development of an ability to function autonomously in an area of science studies to solve practical problems and to communicate that experience to others.
(d) The attainment of a perspective or way of looking at the world together with some understanding of how it complements and contrasts with other perspectives or ways of organizing knowledge and inquiry.
(e) The attainment of a basic understanding of the nature of advanced technological societies, the interaction between science and society, and the contribution science makes to our cultural heritage.
(f) The realization that scientific knowledge and experience is of some value in the process of establishing a sense of personal and social identity.

(d) *Science Education 11–16: Proposals for Action and Consultation* (SSCR, 1983)

. . . to provide, at appropriate stages of a five year programme, adequate opportunities for all students to

(a) explore the nature of the biological and physical environment through observation, experiment and systematic inquiry;

develop the ability to design and carry out experiments, evaluate evidence and solve problems;

study the key concepts and principles of science that are essential to an understanding of science as a way of looking at the world;

study those aspects of science that are essential to an understanding of oneself, and of one's personal well being;

(b) use their knowledge of science to design and develop solutions to technological problems, to test and evaluate those solutions and to cost such exercises;

study the key areas of science and technology that relate to the world of work and leisure so that they are better able to participate in a democratic society;

study key concepts that are essential to an understanding of the part science and technology play in a post-industrial and technological society;

(c) gain some understanding of the historical development and contemporary cultural significance of scientific principles and theories;

appreciate that technologies are expressions of the desire to understand and control the environment and that technologies change in response to changing social needs;

appreciate that past scientific explanations were valid in their time and that early technologies are still valid in some cultural contexts;

(d) discuss, reflect upon and evaluate their own personal understanding of key scientific concepts, theories and generalisations;

explore topics or themes which exemplify the limitations of scientific knowledge as an explanation of the human condition.

The degree of emphasis given to the meta-scientific dimension of science education in both the ASE (1981) statement from *Education through Science* and the SSCR (1983) statement is perhaps best interpreted as reflecting the fact that this aspect of science education has hitherto been badly neglected rather than as indicating the relative weighting it should have in the science curriculum.

## 2 Suggestions about content

(a) *Science Education in Schools – a Consultative Document* (DES and Welsh Office, 1982)
This statement is about primary science:

The pupils need to grow accustomed from an early age to observing, looking for patterns, generalising, and testing their ideas. Much of the work in science should arise from the children's spontaneous interests. But they should also gain a progressively deeper understanding of the central concepts of science. Every primary school should aim to provide work which introduces at least the following:

(a) living things – eg life cycles, inheritance, adaptation, the human body;
(b) the weather, seasonal changes, the local environment;

(c) energy – eg energy conversions, conservation of energy resources;
(d) structures, materials and their properties - eg forces, pressure, particles, sand, clay, metals, plastics, chemical changes.

There are many interconnections within and between these broad themes, and most of the work on them arises naturally out of, or can be integrated with, other areas of the curriculum.

(b) *Curriculum 11–16* (DES, 1977)
No pupil should leave school without a usable understanding, based on observation and experiment but not bounded by the limits of his own capacity for any of the following

1 His own body and its functioning, with a reasonably clear notion of some of the many contributory causes of malfunctioning.
2 The nutritional needs of plants and of animals, the variety of ways in which they are obtained, and how they are turned to effect, both by the plants and animals themselves and by man. Matter and energy cycles.
3 The cell, and cell specialisation, each contributing to the harmonious functioning of the whole. The individual and the group.
4 Multiplication, replication, checks and balances in individuals and in communities.
5 Patterns of inheritance. Evolution as an observable phenomenon. Introduction to the lines along which the study of the causes of evolution is being pursued.
6 The concept of a pure substance and of how, by successive approaches to purity, it is possible to assert with some assurance the properties of the pure substance. Properties used in analysis. What is it we are handling, and in what quantity?
7 Extension of the usage of the words 'metal' and 'non-metal'.
8 New substances from old. Synthesis.
9 The significance of analysis and synthesis to the quality of life.
10 Chemical change and energy. The control of chemical change.
11 Atoms, molecules and indications of the lines along which study of what binds atoms together is being pursued. Introduction to the use of formulae and equations.
12 The widely dispersed substances and the localised ones. Some reasons why. Man the disperser. Re-cycling.
13 The various ways in which energy can be used. It cannot be used up, but the ways in which it can be used are reduced each time it is used, hence the need to use it economically.
14 What energy can do to matter.
15 How energy is transmitted.
16 Particles more fundamental than atoms.

The following list of words should be understood by pupils as a result of their school science course. It is not a complete list and pupils will vary greatly in both the breadth and the depth of meaning they attach to the words.

| | | |
|---|---|---|
| Absorption | Equation | Photosynthesis |
| Acceleration | Evolution | Plant |
| Acid | Fat | Potential energy |
| Activity | Fertilization | Power |
| Alkali | Food chain | Pressure |
| Animal | Force | Protein |
| Atom | Gas | Reaction |
| Base | Genetics | Reflection |
| Carbohydrate | Heredity | Refraction |
| Cell | Hormone | Reproduction |
| Change of state | Interference | Salt |
| Combustion | Invertebrate | Saprophyte |
| Conservation | Ion | Solid |
| Crystal | Kinetic energy | Sterile |
| Current | Liquid | Synthesis |
| Decomposition | Mass | Temperature |
| Density | Metal | Velocity |
| Digestion | Molecule | Vertebrate |
| Diffusion | Momentum | Vitamin |
| Electrolyte | Non-metal | Wave |
| Electron | Osmosis | Work |
| Enzyme | Parasite | |

(c) *Towards the Specification of Minimum Entitlement: Brenda and Friends* (SSCR, 1984)

**Content**
Through a study of the biological and physical characteristics of the natural and man-made environment the school will provide students with opportunities to develop a basic working knowledge and understanding of the following:

Change and rate of change
Chance and probability
Competition, balance and dynamic equilibrium
Communications
Ecology and communities
Energy
Evolution
Feedback and control
Growth, reproduction and replication
Interactions and forces
Health
Materials

Particulate nature of matter
Space
Systems
Time

These broad headings are then fleshed out in terms of an overall science education via a set of pupil biographies.

Content check-lists need to be given in detail if they are to be really useful in curriculum planning at the secondary level. A number of such check-lists have been published and mention must be made of the APU (1982) *Science Progress Report 1977–78*. The list of science concepts and knowledge, provided as an appendix to the report, represents a consensus of what was (then) regarded, in the light of current science education practices, as a reasonable concept base for the assessment of children's performance in science at ages 11, 13 and 15.

More recently, the Royal Society has produced its contribution in physics and biology in the publications *A Reduced-Content 16+ Syllabus in Physics*, (1984), and *A Reduced-Content 16+ Syllabus in Biology* (1985). At the time of writing, their proposals for chemistry were in preparation.

A third example is provided by Ingle and Jennings (1981) in *Science in Schools. Which Way Now*? This list, while not increasing the overall content, and possibly even reducing it, makes considerable progress towards:

including content relevant for its applications and implications, and not simply as pure science;
extending the range of science beyond biology, chemistry and physics.

The check-list is reproduced here in full.

It may be questioned whether content selected on technological and environmental criteria ( in the sense in which these terms have been used in this chapter) receives sufficient emphasis; content relevant to the meta-scientific dimension certainly does not.

(d) *Science in Schools: Which Way Now? (Ingle and Jennings, 1981): content check-list*

**Part A of a sample core – physics component**

| *Suggested core content* | *Some possible extensions (not in the core)* |
|---|---|
| 1 *Materials and measurement* | |
| Measurement of length, area, volume, time, mass, temperature. Measuring devices. | Density. Calculations on density. |
| Estimation (in co-ordination with mathematics department) | |
| Simple ideas on density of solids and liquids. Hydrometer, *use only* – as in car accumulators and beer making. | |

| *Suggested core content* | *Some possible extensions (not in the core)* |
|---|---|
| Force. Weight. Stretching of springs, wires and other materials. | |
| Gravity. | |
| Surface tension – bubbles, raindrops and detergents. | |
| Meaning of 'elastic' and 'plastic' in a general understanding of materials of various kinds (alloys, plastics, plasticine etc.) Deformation. | |
| 2 *Motion and forces* | |
| Speed (including measurement of), acceleration. Everyday examples such as in cars and bicycles. Braking distances – safety factors. | Velocity (a vector)<br>Calculations involving acceleration<br>Free fall; experimental measurement of g |
| Friction. Lubrication. | Newton's laws of motion. $F = ma$ |
| Strength of structures – girders, triangular frameworks | Momentum and its conservation |
| Inertia – safety belts | |
| Action and reaction – rockets | |
| Circular motion in the simplest terms; centripetal force – satellites | |
| The solar system (see Part D – Miscellaneous Component) | |
| 3 *Work and energy* | |
| Simple calculations on 'work done'. | Kinetic energy as $\frac{1}{2}mv^2$ |
| Various forms of energy. Energy change devices such as motors, dynamos, steam engines, turbines, brakes, light bulbs etc. | |
| Conservation of energy – idea that energy is 'countable' or conserved. Degradation of energy. The energy crisis. | Power |
| Levers – many practical applications. Simple numerical examples. | |
| Simple machines – everyday examples. Efficiency. Hydraulic systems – car brakes. | Calculations involving Heat Energy $= mc\,\Delta\theta$ and $ml$ |
| Specific and latent heat (qualitative only). | |
| Conduction, convection, radiation – examples of each. Solar energy panels. | |

| *Suggested core content* | *Some possible extensions (not in the core)* |
|---|---|
| Expansion and contraction. Thermometers, thermostats and temperature control. | |
| Energy 'saving' in the home. | |
| 4 *Kinetic theory* | |
| Molecular theory. | |
| Brownian motion. Diffusion. Evaporation. | |
| Pressure. Collapsing tin-can due to atmospheric bombardment. Manometer. Simple barometer. Water supply system. | |
| Change of volume of a gas with pressure (qualitative only) – bicycle pump, meteorological balloons. Explanation in terms of kinetic theory. | Calculations involving $\frac{P_1V_1}{T_1} = \frac{P_2V_2}{T_2}$ |
| Change of pressure of a gas with temperature. | |
| Change of volume of gas with temperature – hot air balloons. | |
| Basic principles of the working of the four-stroke internal combustion engine. | |
| 5 *Periodic motion: sound* | |
| Simple pendulum. Factors affecting period. | Wave explanation of light and sound; velocity = frequency × wavelength |
| Production of sound, including vibration of strings (guitars etc.) Resonance. | Wave forms, harmonics. |
| Propagation and reflection of sound. Echoes, echo-sounding with oscilloscope (see Section 8). | |
| Music, noise. | |
| Various forms of electromagnetic radiation (e.g. light, X-rays, infra-red). | Diffraction and interference. |
| 6 *Light* | |
| Propagation of light in straight lines. Shadows. Pin hole camera, Eclipses. | Focal length. |
| Reflection at plane mirror. Virtual images – car mirrors. | Calculations involving magnification |

| *Suggested core content* | *Some possible extensions (not in the core)* |
|---|---|
| Refraction at plane surface. Real and apparent depth. | |
| Magnifying glass. Camera, Projector. | $\frac{1}{u}+\frac{1}{v}=\frac{1}{f}$ (solutions by algebra or ray diagrams) |
| Total internal reflection – fibre optics. | |
| Eye. Spectacle lens. | $\frac{\text{Sin i}}{\text{Sin r}}$ = constant |
| Spectrum produced by a prism. | |
| Colour addition – colour TV. | |
| 7 *Magnetism and electricity* | |
| Simple magnetic effects. Compass. | Magnetism of the earth. Angle of dip. |
| *Using electricity to produce magnetism:* Electromagnets and their applications such as electric bell, loud speaker. | Factors affecting magnitude of electromagnetically induced current. |
| Simple direct current motor. Electric meters (ammeter, voltmeter). | |
| *Using magnetism to produce electricity:* Dynamo, moving coil microphone, car ignition system. | |
| Alternating current. Transformers and their uses, including in the 'National Grid'. | |
| Simple D.C. circuits, explanation perhaps on the basis of the water analogy. Effect of resistance on current. Short circuits. | Measurement of resistance. |
| Simplest meaningful understanding of potential (as 'push') and current (as 'flow'). | Ohm's Law. |
| Practice in handling simple calculations on *Volts* × *Amps* = *Watts*, and hence values for fuses. | Deeper understanding of electrical units. Calculations involving resistors in series and parallel. |
| Simple household electricity – ring main, fuses, earthing, wiring 13 amp plug, *safety factors*. | Transformer equation $\frac{V_1}{V_2}=\frac{N_1}{N_2}$ |
| The cost of electricity – 'units'. | |
| Electrostatics. Positive and negative charge. Examples such as paint sprayers, explosions in oil tankers, lightning. | Millikan's experiment to show the particulate nature of electric charge. |
| 8 *Electonics* | |
| Electron streams, Deflection in electric and magnetic fields. | Basic components in electronic circuits and what they do. Resistor, variable capacitor, transistor. Simple radio circuit. |

| *Suggested core content* | *Some possible extensions (not in the core)* |
|---|---|
| Cathode ray tube: oscilloscopes and TV tube. (See also in Miscellaneous section) | The function of amplifiers, oscillators, switching circuits and logic gates, treated as 'black boxes'. |
| 9 *Radioactivity* | |
| Simple model of atom (protons, neutrons, electrons). | Nuclear equations could be given, e.g. |
| A treatment in the simplest terms of radioactive decay; half-life. | $\frac{235}{92}\text{U} + \frac{1}{0}\text{n} \rightarrow \frac{140}{54} + \frac{93}{38}\text{Sr} + 3\,\frac{1}{0}\text{n}$ |
| Nuclear fission; basis of large scale generation of power. | |
| Biological effects of nuclear radiation, vital importance of safety factors. | $\Delta H \approx -2 \times 10^{9}\,\text{kJ mol}^{-1}$ |
| Problems involved in the storage of nuclear waste. | Calculations on half-life. |
| Nuclear weapons. | Fusion. |

**Part B of a sample core – chemistry component**

| *Suggested core content* | *Some possible extensions (not in the core)* |
|---|---|
| *1 Simple substances and mixtures* | |
| The earth's crust as the source of almost all chemicals. | |
| Separation of mixtures. | |
| Idea of a pure substance. | |
| Purification of crude materials using techniques such as filtration, crystallisation (see Section 2), distillation, etc. | |
| 2 *Crystals* | Allotropy |
| Their characteristic shape etc. | |
| Growth of crystals by cooling of saturated solutions. | |
| Purification by means of crystallisation. | |
| 3 *Elements and compounds* | |
| Meaning of, with examples. | |
| 4 *Air and water* | |
| Composition of air, burning. Water; formation by burning of hydrogen. Reaction of water with sodium, iron | Gravimetric and volumetric composition of water. |

**Part B of a sample core – chemistry component – continued**

| *Suggested core content* | *Some possible extensions (not in the core)* |
|---|---|
| and anhydrous copper sulphate. Biological and human importance of water. | |
| 5 *Atomic theory* | |
| A very elementary idea of the atomic theory. (An idea of the size of atoms might be conveyed by means of repeated steps of tenfold size decrease). | A more developed model of the atom involving electronic configuration. |
| The indestructibility of matter under ordinary conditions. | |
| 6 *Chemical change* | |
| Characterised by formation of new substances and accompanied by energy change. | |
| Adequately summarised in 'word equations', e.g. Zinc + Hydrochloric acid → Zinc chloride + Hydrogen. | May be more fully represented: $Zn + 2HCl \rightarrow ZnCl_2 + H_2$ *or* $Zn(s) + 2HCl(aq) \rightarrow ZnCl_2(aq) + H_2(g)$ *or* $Zn(s) + 2H^+(aq) \rightarrow Zn^{2+}(aq) + H_2(g)$ |
| Common types of chemical reaction, e.g. Combination and decomposition Neutralization Oxidation and reduction. | |
| Simple qualitative examples to establish the idea that chemical substances normally react in definite quantities by mass. | Chemical equations interpreted in terms of mass relationships |
| Simple quantitative examples to illustrate energy changes occurring during chemical reactions, e.g. experiment to find heat energy evolved by burning 1g of a liquid hydrocarbon (kJ per gram). | More sophisticated experimental methods to determine the *molar* heat of combustion ($kJ\,mol^{-1}$) |
| 7 *Electrochemistry* | |
| Electrolysis explained *operationally* as a process using electricity as a source of energy to bring about formation of new substances, *without* using the concept of the ion. Meanings of the terms: electrolysis, electrode, electrolyte, anode and cathode. | Electrolysis explained conceptually in terms of migration and discharge of ions. Faraday's laws of electrolysis. |
| Electroplating. | |
| Chemical change as a source of electricity. | |

**Part B of a sample core – chemistry component – continued**

| *Suggested core content* | *Some possible extensions (not in the core)* |
|---|---|
| 8 *Radioactivity*<br>(See Physics section) | |
| 9 *Metals and non-metals*<br>Characteristic properties of some metals and non-metals.<br>Extraction of iron and aluminium. | |
| Reactivity series of metals. | Electrochemical series of the elements. |
| Corrosion of metals and its economic effects. | |
| 10 *Oxidation and reduction*<br>In operational terms of gain and loss of oxygen, with illustrative examples. | In *conceptual* terms of loss and gain of electrons.<br>Oxidation number. |
| 11 *Acids, bases and salts*<br>Described in *operational* terms, e.g. 'an acid is a substance that contains hydrogen that may be replaced by a metal; that turns litmus red, etc.' | *Conceptual* understanding, e.g. 'acidic substances are proton donors'. |
| Characteristic properties and illustrative uses of acids, bases and salts.<br>Preparation of salts. Neutralisation. Indicators. | |
| pH as a convenient scale of acidity and alkalinity (omitting formal definition). | $pH = -lg_{10}[H^+]$ |
| 12 *Rates of reaction*<br>Knowledge that most precipitation reactions proceed almost instantaneously.<br>Some other reactions take place at a modest rate, e.g. action of zinc on dilute hydrochloric acid, others slowly, e.g. rusting of iron. | |
| The rate of a reaction may be speeded up by the presence of a catalyst, by increasing the temperature or the concentration (semi-quantitative study). | *Qualitative* studies of reaction rates; results illustrated graphically.<br>Activation energy. Theories of catalysis. |
| 13 *Structures of elements and compounds*<br>The structure of the following:<br>Gases, liquids and solids. Particulate | More sophisticated examples could be given, e.g. structure of sulphur, DNA. |

**Part B of a sample core – chemistry component – continued**

| *Suggested core content* | *Some possible extensions (not in the core)* |
|---|---|
| theory to explain differences | |
| Molecules (e.g. oxygen, water, ethanol, polythene). | X-ray analysis as a means of probing chemical structure. |
| Giant structures (e.g. diamond and graphite). | |
| Structure of metals and alloys; use in engineering. | Heats of vaporisation as an indicator of bond strength. |
| 14 *Some elements and their compounds* | |
| *Hydrogen* – Preparation and properties, including reducing action. | |
| *Oxygen* – Preparation by one common method, properties including oxidising action. | |
| *Carbon* – The role of carbon in synthetic materials and living things. | |
| Simpler properties and some uses of a selection of common metals such as sodium, calcium, iron and aluminium. | |
| Simple chemistry of a few other non-metals such as nitrogen (role in fertilisers), sulphur and chlorine. | |
| 15 *Chemistry in living organisms* (in co-ordination with Biology) | |
| Awareness that chemical processes occur in living organisms in e.g. digestion and respiration. | |
| 16 *Chemistry in the home* (in co-ordination with Home Economics) | |
| Food and cooking; drinks (including alcoholic ones); water (purity, hard and soft); detergents; household chemicals (labelling of, mixing of, e.g. *Harpic* and *Domestos*); plastics and elastomers; fabrics and textiles; cosmetics; fuels – natural gas, oil, coal (conservation and safe use of); fire extinguishers; building materials – bricks, mortar, cement, polyfilla; drugs and medicines; smoking; glass and ceramics. | Types of hardness of water. |

**Part B of a sample core – chemistry component – continued**

| *Suggested core content* | *Some possible extensions (not in the core)* |
|---|---|
| 17 *Chemistry in the environment*<br>Water resources; soils (chemical tests for); chemicals used in gardens and on the farm; the chemical industry; the motor car (illustration of alloys, plastics, elastomers, paints, glass, petroleum products, combustion etc.); conservation of resources; pollution; recycling. | |
| 18 *Health and safety*<br>Method of handling flammable and corrosive substances.<br>Importance of ventilation and safe working conditions especially in the home. Correct labelling of substances.<br>Corrective action. | |

**Part C of a sample core – biology component**

| *Suggested core content* | *Some possible extensions (not in the core)* |
|---|---|
| *1 Cells*<br>Living organisms are made of cells.<br>Plant cells – leaf epidermis, moss leaf.<br>Animal cells – protozoans, cheek cells, blood.<br>Cytoplasm, nucleus.<br>Chloroplasts. | Cell organelles.<br>Cell membranes.<br>Vacuolation.<br>Cell differentiation. |
| 2 *Conditions for life*<br>Living organisms can only survive in limited climatic conditions, especially temperature<br>Atmosphere.<br>Water. | Effects of pressure/altitude.<br>Osmotic conditions, freshwater/marine. |
| 3 *Diversity of life*<br>Introduction to the variety of living organisms, especially through visits to zoos, nature reserves, museums and ecological investigations.<br>Micro-organisms (see Miscellaneous Component 5 – Health Education) | Introduction to:<br>Algae, diatoms and seaweeds |

**Part C of a sample core – biology component – continued**

| *Suggested core content* | *Some possible extensions (not in the core)* |
|---|---|
| Simple plants.<br>Flowering plants.<br>Invertebrate animals, especially insects.<br>Vertebrate animals, especially mammals. | Fungi, mucor, yeast, mushrooms/toadstools<br>Ferns<br>Monocotyledons/dicotyledons<br>Radial and bilateral symmetry in invertebrates |
| 4 *Plant growth* | |
| Grow plants to show the conditions for growth, especially water, oxygen, light and carbon dioxide.<br>Effect of fertilisers. | Optimum conditions for growth.<br>Influence of temperature and day length.<br>Primary and secondary structure. |
| 5 *Plant nutrition* | |
| Simple structure of a leaf.<br>Outline of photosynthesis, equation in words.<br>Water + Carbon Dioxide + Light Energy → Food (sugar) + Oxygen<br>Food storage. | Stomata – opening and closing<br>Means of water uptake and gaseous exchange.<br>Transpiration. |
| 6 *Plant life cycle* | |
| Grow a plant from seed to maturity with production of fruit and new seeds, e.g. dwarf bean, alpine strawberry.<br>Need for pollination and fertilisation.<br>Different kinds of fruits.<br>Ways in which seeds dispersed.<br>Other means of reproduction. | Parts of the flower.<br>Comparisons of wind/insect pollination.<br>Compatibility for pollination as in fruit trees.<br>Vegetative and sexual reproduction in terms of pure strain and variation.<br>Sports and mutations. |
| 7 *Animal nutrition* | |
| Animals need a ready-made food supply.<br>Grazers – snails, cattle.<br>Flesh eaters – birds of prey, lions and tigers.<br>Mixed feeders – including man. | Energy flow through an ecosystem.<br>Pyramid of numbers. |
| 8 *Study of a habitat* | |
| Survey of a local habitat at different seasons to emphasise: | Further quantification by scientific approach to sampling and data recording. |

**Part C of a sample core – biology component – continued**

| *Suggested core content* | *Some possible extensions (not in the core)* |
|---|---|
| 1 dormancy, rapid growth and reproduction, cycle.<br>2 variety of life.<br>3 interdependence of organisms.<br>4 effect of man. | More detailed study to discover foodchains, population estimation, etc.<br>Parasites, commensals, symbionts. |
| 9 *Study of man as an animal* | |
| The systems of the human body and their maintenance in a steady state. | |
| *Food, digestion and nutrition.* | |
| The major food needs and a balanced diet. | Introduction to the chemical composition of foods. |
| The need to break down food by a physical and chemical means so that it can be used by the body. | Qualities of enzymes and conditions for enzyme action. |
| The alimentary canal as a tube with specialised regions. | Details of alimentary canal and enzyme secreting organs. |
| *Breathing and respiration* | |
| Simple structure of respiratory organs.<br>Breathing movements to exchange air in lungs. | Solubility of gases. Haemoglobin as oxygen carrier.<br>Tidal and residual air. |
| Respiration as a process in cells to release energy and expressed in words.<br>Sugar + Oxygen → Energy + Carbon Dioxide + Water | Further explanation of respiration including aerobic, anaerobic respiration.<br>Oxygen debt in muscles. |
| Effects of smoking on lungs. | |
| *Circulation* | |
| Simple properties of blood. | Erythrocytes, lymphocytes, granulocytes, etc. Blood clotting. |
| Introduction to the ideas of circulation, blood vessels, the heart as a pump. | Detailed structure of heart. |
| Pulse, pulse rate. | Blood pressure. |
| Warm blood. | Lymph and lymphatic system. |
| Consideration of heart disease. | Temperature regulation. |
| *Removal of waste* | |
| Concept of excretory materials. | Osmo-regulation in animals. |
| Effects of wastes on body. | Osmotic gradient. |
| Simple treatment of kidney. | |
| Removal of wastes through skin, lungs and urinary system. | Homeostasis. |

**Part C of a sample core – biology component – continued**

| *Suggested core content* | *Some possible extensions (not in the core)* |
|---|---|
| *Sensitivity and response* | |
| Exploration of some of the senses by concrete experience, e.g. width of field of vision in black and white and also in colour; ability to hear sounds of different pitch and loudness; ability to detect differences in temperature; reaction time. | Structure of the eye and ear.<br>Further quantification in experimental work.<br>The central nervous system.<br>Nervous and chemical co-ordination. |
| *Movement and support* | |
| The skeleton and muscles as a supporting, movable framework.<br>Muscles shorten and pull, and work in pairs.<br>Movement about a joint.<br>The protective function of the skeleton.<br>Ability of bones to repair. | Voluntary and involuntary muscles.<br>Kinds of joints.<br>Main parts of skeleton.<br>Growth regions of bones. Structure to resist stresses. |
| *Life cycle* | |
| Reproductive organs.<br>Slow development of sexual maturity, importance of hormones. Female cycle.<br>Mating, fertilisation and contraception.<br>Pregnancy.<br>Pre- and post-natal care. | Elaboration on influence of hormones in many processes.<br>Control of pregnancy by hormones.<br>Structure of placenta.<br>Transfer of materials through the placenta. |
| Body proportions at different ages.<br>Processes of ageing and death. | Rates of growth of nervous tissue, compared with reproductive tissues. |
| 10 *Evolution and genetics* | |
| Introduction to elementary ideas of genetics – like begets like.<br>Concrete experience of single gene inheritance in plants, idea of a hybrid.<br>Consideration of visible inherited human characteristics.<br>Continuity of inheritance between generations with reappearance of characteristics in succeeding generations.<br>Elementary notion of the gene.<br>Evolution in terms of change of life over long periods of time. | |

**Part C of a sample core – biology component – continued**

| *Suggested core content* | *Some possible extensions (not in the core)* |
|---|---|
| Historical, biographical approach to work of Darwin. | |
| Concrete experience through examination of fossils, museum visits and film. | |
| Melanism as an example of change. | |
| 11 *The effect of man on the environment* | |
| Local studies embracing local history on the changes man has effected. | |
| Consideration of selected contemporary issues using TV, film, etc., e.g. effects of deforestation. | |
| Local practical studies on environmental pollution. | |
| 12 *Natural cycles of materials* | |
| Simple treatment of the cycles of | Nitrogen cycle. |
| water. | |
| oxygen. | |
| carbon dioxide. | |

**Part D of a sample core – miscellaneous component**

| *Suggested core content* | *Some possible extensions (not in the core)* |
|---|---|
| *1 Geology* | |
| A study based in a local rock site exposed. | Identification and classification of rocks. |
| The concepts of a mineral, crystal and rock. | |
| Introduction to different kinds of rock. | |
| Weathering, soil formation. | |
| Erosion and sedimentation. | Physical sedimentation. |
| Fossils. | Chemical sedimentation. |
| Earthquakes, volcanic activity. | Means of dating rocks. |
| 2 *Astronomy* | |
| The solar system. | Phases of the moon. |
| Size of planets and distances from earth. | |
| Simple comparison of sun and moon. | |
| Eclipse of the sun. | |
| Comparison of distances of stars from earth with those of solar system. | |

**Part D of a sample core – miscellaneous component – continued**

| *Suggested core content* | *Some possible extensions (not in the core)* |
|---|---|
| Problems of space travel. | Prospects of life on other planets. |
| 3 *Meteorology* | |
| The atmosphere – composition, atmospheric pressure | Atmospheric pollution. |
| Water cycle – evaporation: clouds, fog, rainfall. | Types of cloud formation. Thermal air currents – gliding flight. |
| Movement of air due to heating and cooling. | More detailed study of a depression. Monitoring and forecasting the weather. |
| Reading a weather map. | |
| 4 *Microprocessors* | |
| As manipulators of information. | See Physics: Section 8 – Electronics. |
| Prestel and Oracle. | |
| Automatic washing machine controls; pocket calculators. | |
| 5 *Health education* | |
| Concept of health. | |
| Personal healthy living – exercise, rest, nutrition, hygiene, effects of smoking, alcohol and drugs, stress. | Culture and eating patterns. |
| Relationships with others, including peers and parents, long-term relationships. | Emotional needs of young children. Effects of loss and separation. |
| Sexual relationships. | |
| Education for parenthood. | |
| Community health provision. | Relative contributions of local authority and voluntary organisations. |
| Personal responsibility for a healthy environment. | Industrial environmental considerations. |
| Introduction to first aid principles. | |

(Ingle and Jennings, 1981)

## 3 Suggestions about process

(a) *Science Progress Report 1977–78*, Summary Report No. 9 (APU, 1982). Though originally designed for the purpose of monitoring scientific performance, the categorization of science processes is very pertinent to the formulation of aims for science education.

**Process List (Science activity categories)**

The process list's principal function is to set out categories of scientific activity which are recognisable by, and have validity for, those involved in science education. This list below is designed to serve the needs of those who set the questions for the monitoring tests. Nevertheless, its ultimate justification is that it defines the main aspects of school science teaching, so that a variety of audiences can benefit from the reporting of results in terms of its categories.

1 *Using symbolic representations*

Tasks in this category assess the ability of pupils to make use of standard forms of symbolic representations:

relating information to its representation in graphical forms;

relating objects, events and constructs to conventional representations (eg chemical symbols, formulae and equations,

circuit diagrams, sectional diagrams of apparatus).

2 *Using apparatus and measuring instruments*

These tasks will involve the pupils in some practical activities:

using apparatus and instruments to make measurements in a standard manner;

carrying out an unfamiliar and purposeful **sequence** of actions following instructions;

carrying out a **sequence** of actions following instructions that may include conventional representation or reference to standard procedures.

3 *Observation tasks*

In this category the tasks are those in which pupils have to decide for themselves what it is they should take notice of, in contrast to category 4, where the selection has already been made:

taking notice of features relevant to a presented problem or task;

inferring patterns in observations;

assessing the consistency between observations and possible interpretations;

making predictions based on patterns inferred in observations.

4 *Interpretation and application*

In these tasks a selection from observations has been made and is presented as data to pupils:

inferring patterns in data;

making predictions based on patterns inferred from data and/or accepted concepts;

suggesting one or more hypotheses consistent with presented data;

assessing the validity of conclusions and/or patterns in relation to presented data.

5 *Design of investigations*

These tasks involve planning or evaluating an investigation to tackle a presented problem. This may involve:

identifying amongst a set of specified variables those to be investigated and those to be controlled;

reformulating a presented problem in terms which can be investigated scientifically including the identification of variables to be investigated and those to be controlled;

planning or evaluating a sequence of procedures, including the consideration of equipment;
showing how information to be gained could be interpreted to solve the problem.

6 *Performing investigations*
Questions in this category will set pupils a complete investigation task, for which they may have to use processes in any or all of categories 1 to 5. Thus, the responses will be assessed in a holistic way.
Tackling an investigation or problem experimentally. This involves:
reformulating a presented problem in terms which can be investigated scientifically;
identifying those variables to be investigated and those to be controlled;
planning and executing a proper sequence of procedures for which the range of equipment is specified;
interpreting information gained in order to solve the problem.

The following more concise but less detailed formulation of APU science processes is often useful:

**Framework of categories and sub-categories used in the assessment of performance in science**

| | Main categories | | Sub-categories |
|---|---|---|---|
| 1 | Using symbolic representations *(Written tests)* | $\alpha$ | Reading information from graphs, tables and charts |
| | | $\beta$ | Expressing information as graphs, tables and charts |
| | | $\gamma$ | *Using scientific symbols and conventions* |
| 2 | Using apparatus and measuring instruments | $\alpha$ | Using measuring instruments |
| | | $\beta$ | *Estimating quantities* |
| | *(Practical tests)* | $\gamma$ | *Following instructions for practical work* |
| 3 | Using Observations | $\alpha$ | *Using an identification key* |
| | *(Practical tests)* | $\beta$ | Observing similarities and differences |
| | | $\gamma$ | *Interpreting observations* |
| 4 | Interpretation and application | $\alpha$ | Describing and using patterns in information |
| | (i) Not dependent on taught science concepts | $\beta$ | *Judging the applicability of a given generalisation* |
| | *(Written tests)* | $\gamma$ | *Distinguishing degrees of inference* |
| | | $\delta_{AB}$ | Applying biology concepts |
| | (ii) Dependent on taught science concepts | $\delta_{CD}$ | Applying physics concepts |
| | | $\delta_{EF}$ | Applying chemistry concepts |
| | *(Written tests)* | $\eta$ | *Generating alternative hypotheses* |

*Continued*

| | Main categories | | Sub-categories |
|---|---|---|---|
| 5 | Design of investigations *(Written tests)* | $\alpha$ | Identifying or proposing testable statements |
| | | $\beta$ | Assessing experimental procedures |
| | | $\gamma$ | *Devising and describing investigations* |
| 6 | Performing investigations *(Practical tests)* | | |

(b) *Curriculum 11–16* (DES, 1977)
The work should be presented in such a way that positive answers may be obtained to the following questions:

(a) Is the pupil observant? That is to say, does he see all that there is to see, or does he rely on being told what to see?
(b) Does he select from his observations those which have a bearing on the problems before him?
(c) Does he look for patterns in what he observes and is he able to tie in to his current observations others he has made earlier? That is to say, can he recall other observations which contribute to the pattern?
(d) Does he seek to explain the patterns? If he can offer more than one possible explanation, does he attempt to rank them in order of plausibility?
(e) Does he have an acceptable level of practical skills in the efficient and safe handling of apparatus and equipment?
(f) Can he devise, or contribute to the devising of, experiments which will put to test the explanations he suggests for the pattern of observations?
(g) Does he possess the verbal and mathematical skills adequate to allow him to interact with his classmates, his teacher and the written and other material to which his attention is directed?
(h) Does he respond to a novel situation by recalling and applying facts and generalisations previously acquired? Does he do this when the situation is outside the immediate content of the school science courses? That is to say, does he see the relevance of what he has learnt in the science lessons to situations outside the laboratory?

(c) *National Criteria for Science* (GCE and CSE Boards' Joint Council for 16+ National Criteria, 1985)
The full range of assessment objectives are provided for completeness though it should be noted just how many of them are concerned with processes (skills and abilities).

3.1 knowledge and understanding of:
3.1.1 scientific phenomena, facts, laws, definitions, concepts theories;
3.1.2 scientific vocabulary, terminology, conventions;

3.1.3 scientific instruments and apparatus, including techniques of operation and aspects of safety;
3.1.4 scientific quantities and their determination;
3.1.5 scientific and technological applications with their social, economic and environmental implications.
3.2 the skills and abilities to:
3.2.1 observe, measure and record accurately and systematically;
3.2.2 follow instructions accurately for the safe conduct of experiments;
3.2.3 communicate scientific observations, ideas and arguments logically, concisely and in various forms;
3.2.4 translate information from one form to another;
3.2.5 extract from available information data relevant to a particular context;
3.2.6 use experimental data, recognise patterns in such data, form hypotheses and deduce relationships;
3.2.7 draw conclusions from, and evaluate critically, experimental observations and other data;
3.2.8 recognise and explain variability and unreliability in experimental measurements;
3.2.9 devise and carry out experimental or other tests to check the validity of data, conclusions and generalisations;
3.2.10 devise and carry out experiments or other tests for particular purposes, selecting suitable apparatus and using it effectively and safely;
3.2.11 explain familiar facts, observations and phenomena in terms of scientific laws, theories and models;
3.2.12 suggest scientific explanations of unfamiliar facts, observations and phenomena;
3.2.13 apply scientific ideas and methods to solve qualitative and quantitative problems;
3.2.14 make decisions based on the examination of evidence and arguments;
3.2.15 recognise that the study and practice of science are subject to various limitations and uncertainties;
3.2.16 explain technological applications of science and evaluate associated social, economic and environmental implications.

(d) *Towards the Specification of Minimum Entitlement: Brenda and Friends* (SSCR, 1984)
The following are regarded as the skills and processes which constitute a minimum entitlement.

**Skills**

| | | |
|---|---|---|
| Listening | Numeracy | Searching |
| Talking | Estimating | Measuring |
| Writing | Small group skills | Manipulating |
| Drawing | Nonverbal communication | Graphicacy |
| Reading | Observing | Recording |

**Processes**

Communicating and discussing, which include

thinking
questioning
seeking help
negotiating

Processing of information, which includes

selecting
using relationships
controlling interacting variables
designing
drawing conclusions

Problem solving, experimentation and decision making, which include

predicting
inferring
formulating hypotheses
interpreting
modelling
evaluating
assessing
classifying
managing time

## 4 Suggestions about context

(a) *Curriculum 11–16* (DES, 1977)
Any scientific subject can have three components, namely, science for the inquiring mind, science for action and science for citizenship.

Science for the inquiring mind is concerned with the laws and theories – the disciplines of the subject. A great range of phenomena can be accounted for in terms of the nature of the particles of which all material things are made and of the forces between them which result in their being arranged in certain numerical and spatial configurations, and in terms of the laws of energy to be followed in all their transactions. It is more or less exact statements about all of these which form the disciplines of any natural science subject and which allow it to be asserted, with an increasing high probability of accuracy, how matter will behave in given circumstances. At school level we can sample only relatively simple instances, we frequently have to account for the behaviour of matter at a less fundamental level. This is especially true when we are dealing with the complexities of behaviour associated with living things. In biology, some explanations will be in terms of the adaptive usefulness of structures and processes to the whole organism and to the species of which it is part, and still further, in terms of ecological function, to the communities in which the species occurs. To these can be added historical explanations in terms of evolutionary development.

Science for action is concerned with the use of these disciplines in technology, in mastery of the environment, in the creative handling of materials and living things. Disciplines other than science contribute to the understanding of that technology, which is a central ingredient in modern societies. But technology must be grounded in sound science, and science teachers through their teaching should be making an important contribution to increasing the knowledge and awareness of our technological base. Information, discussion and activities such as the making of models, engineering projects, and plant and animal husbandry need to be included. Science for action should be able to set limits within which there is a probability of success, and will naturally lead on to controversial areas concerning the use of science in our society.

Science for citizenship is concerned with the role of science in the social, economic and political decision-making processes. Scientific general knowledge is increasingly an essential ingredient in the making of such decisions. Man's growing mastery of his environment also poses many ethical questions, and so an understanding is needed of the consequences of these decisions.

The components 'science for the enquiring mind', 'science for action' and 'science for citizenship' closely parallel 'the pure science context', 'the technological context' and 'the environmental context' as used in this chapter. (This particular use of the term 'context' appears to have been introduced into science education literature by APU – see 4c below.)

(b) *Alternatives for Science Education* (ASE, 1979) – directly used by SSCR (1982) *Advisers' Bulletin No. 1*

The personal and social aims of science education can be further explored by considering the variety of **contexts** within which scientific knowledge can be deployed. These may be conveniently classified as follows:

(a) *Science as science* The pursuit of scientific knowledge as an end in itself, as an intellectual activity leading to the creation of further scientific knowledge. In this context a science curriculum would seek to establish the essential foundations upon which higher education would build in order to equip the individual to undertake scientific research and development.
(b) *Science as a cultural activity* The more generalized pursuit of scientific knowledge including aspects of its history, philosophy, literature and social context to effect a greater understanding of the contribution science makes to society and the world of ideas.
(c) *Science and citizenship* The development of an understanding and appreciation of scientific and technological knowledge to enable active participation in the processes of democratic decision-making, especially in

areas relating to the utilization of scientific developments and their technological applications.

(d) *Science in the world of work* The development of an understanding of the way in which scientific and technological ideas are used to maintain an economic surplus and, in particular, the use to which science and technology are put in specific industrial, commercial and social situations.

(e) *Science and leisure* The appreciation that science and technology provide a basis for a wide range of leisure activities and pursuits, and the development of a creative knowledge and understanding in this area.

(f) *Science and survival* The development of an understanding of the role of science and technology in human survival interpreted in the broadest sense, but including aspects of self-sufficiency, the careful use of resources and the implications of alternative technologies.

Each of the above can be regarded as appropriate and legitimate contexts within which scientific ideas can be explored and developed; these aims should also be regarded as components of a sound science education programme. The problem for the curriculum planner is that of ascribing values and priorities across them whilst seeking to ensure that each is properly represented in a coordinated and balanced manner.

It is interesting to note a later, simplified version from *Education through Science* (ASE, 1981).

(i) *Science as an intellectual discipline* The pursuit of scientific knowledge as an end in itself which leads to an understanding of the essential principles and processes of science and allied disciplines.

(ii) *Science as a cultural activity* The more generalized pursuit of scientific knowledge and culture that takes account of the history, philosophy and social implications of scientific activities, and therefore leads to an understanding of the contribution science and technology make to society and the world of ideas.

(iii) *Science and its applications* The development of an appreciation and understanding of the ways in which science and technology contribute to the worlds of *work*, *citizenship*, *leisure* and *survival*. We would include under this heading an understanding of the way scientific and technological ideas are used to create and maintain an economic surplus, facilitate participation in democratic decision making in a technological society, enrich and sustain a wide range of leisure activities and pursuits, and enable the individual to utilize scientific ideas and technological processes in the context of increasing self-sufficiency, the conservation of resources and the utilization of alternative technologies.

(c) *Science Progress Report 1977–78* (APU, 1982)
Questions devised for the purposes of assessing children's competence in science processes were found by APU to be influenced not only by their science content,

i.e. by the science concepts involved, but also by the context in which they were asked:

Test questions could be located on a three-dimensional grid with each axis representing one of the three characteristics, as shown.

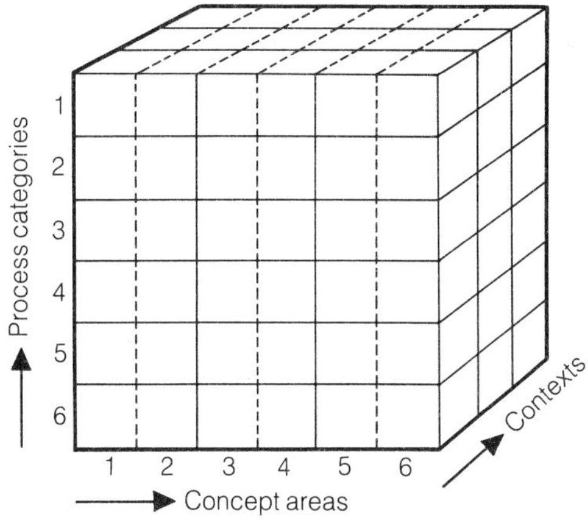


The context of a question is the setting in which ideas and processes are used and is represented on the oblique horizontal axis of the grid. Contexts can significantly affect performance: for example, it is frequently found that pupils who can calculate percentages in mathematics suddenly find the operation very difficult in chemistry. Therefore it is necessary to describe a question in terms of its context so as to ensure a balance of questions across the test. This will make it possible, eventually, to compare performance on the same processes but on questions set in different contexts. From the many possible categories of contexts three broad areas have been chosen: contexts of science teaching, contexts of teaching in other subjects, contexts of everyday or out-of-school situations. Thus, a question which involves the concept of keeping things hot or cold by insulation could be asked in the context of home insulation (an everyday context), or studying the conductivity of different substances (a science lesson context), or of ways people used for keeping food cool in pre-refrigerator days (a non-science lesson context).

This use of the term 'context', together with the idea of a complex matrix, was transferred into the literature on the aims of science education by ASE and SSCR (and subsequently adopted in the writing of this chapter). The context categories are, however, interestingly different.

## 5 Suggestions about attitude

(a) *Towards a Specification of Minimum Entitlement: Brenda and Friends* (SSCR, 1984)
It is useful to compare the following list with the DES list included in the text of this chapter.

Open-mindedness
Self-criticism
Independence of thought
Responsibility
Perseverance
Cooperation
Scepticism
Desire to be well informed
Confidence
Respect
Willlingness to be involved
Sensitivity
Enthusiasm
Tolerance
Persuasiveness
Questioning
Trust

(b) *Curriculum 11–16* (DES, 1977)
After producing a list of what are effectively process aims (see 4b above), the following statement is made:

A pupil who has been educated in this way in science should have four fundamental attitudes; curiosity, honesty in observation that, [sic] willingness to make predictions, and the readiness to record observations promptly, honestly and accurately, whether or not they support his predictions.

When considering education as a preparation for the world of work other important attitudes are mentioned:

Many attitudes traditionally valued by schools, such as appreciation of quality, a pride in work, a concern for accuracy, a willingness to cooperate, to take responsibility and to sustain the effort needed to complete a task are equally relevant to the world of work...

## 6 Meta-scientific suggestions

The most explicit statements relating to this dimension of science education are to be found in the general statements of aims from ASE and SSCR (1c and 1d above) and in the ASE categorization of contexts (4b above).

More extended statements of meta-scientific aims (and of relevant content) are to be found in the literature of curriculum projects specifically concerned with this aspect of science education, e.g. *Science in Society* (ASE, 1981) and *SISCON* (ASE, 1983). This area of science education will be discussed more fully in Chapter 7.

# Bibliography

APU, 1982, *Science Progress Report* 1977–78 (HMSO, London)
ASE, 1979, *Alternatives for Science Education* (Association for Science Education, Hatfield)

ASE, 1981, *Education through Science* (Association for Science Education, Hatfield)
ASE, 1983, *Science in a Social Context*‡
ASE, 1981, *Science in Society**
DES, 1977, *Curriculum 11–16, Working papers by HMI* (HMSO, London)
DES and Welsh Office, 1983, *Curriculum 11–16: Towards a Statement of Entitlement* (HMSO, London)
DES and Welsh Office, 1985, *General Certificate of Secondary Education. The National Criteria: Science* (HMSO, London)
DES and Welsh Office, 1982, *Science Education in Schools – a Consultative Document* (DES and Welsh Office, London)
DES and Welsh Office, 1985, *Science 5–16: A Statement of Policy* (HMSO, London)
Ingle, R., and Jennings, A., 1981, *Science in Schools: Which Way Now?* (Studies in Education 8, Heinemann Educational Books for the Institute of Education, University of London)
The Royal Society Institute of Biology, 1985, *A Reduced-content 16+ Syllabus in Biology* (The Royal Society, London)
The Royal Society Institute of Physics, 1984, *A Reduced-content 16+ Syllabus in Physics* (The Royal Society, London)
SCDC Publications/SSCR, 1984, *Towards the Specification of Minimum Entitlement, Brenda and Friends* (Secondary Science Curriculum Review, London)
SSCR, 1982 (June), *Science Advisers' Bulletin No. 1* (Secondary Science Curriculum Review, London)
SSCR, 1983, *Science Education 11–16: Proposals for Action and Consulation* (Secondary Science Curriculum Review, London)

*Science in a Social Context series includes a Teachers' Guide published by the Association for Science Education and edited by Joan Solomon and Sue Addinell, plus eight student books published jointly by ASE and Basil Blackwell and edited by Joan Solomon.
‡Science in Society publications include a Teachers' Guide and 16 Student Readers published jointly by Heinemann Educational Books and the Association for Science Education, plus eight simulation exercises published by ASE.

# 2 How is science teaching structured?

**Bryan Milner**

- ★ The science curriculum should emphasize processes and skills as well as content.
- ★ Science should both respect the internal structure of the separate sciences and clearly display the similarities.
- ★ Science should develop students' capacity to use the concepts and skills of pure science in solving real problems.
- ★ Each component of science should be developed to an appropriate level for each individual, starting from a common core.
- ★ A modular curriculum structure provides a middle course between the selection of full-subject options and following a core curriculum.

## Introduction

Chapter 1 of this handbook explored the reasons underlying the emerging consensus that all young people are entitled to a broad, balanced and relevant science education as an important component of a broad, balanced and relevant overall education. Satisfying these criteria was shown to require:

content drawn from across a wide range of sciences (i.e. breadth)

at least as much attention being given to the development of skills, processes and attitudes as is given to mastery of content (i.e. balance);

not only the acquisition of scientific knowledge, skills and processes and the development of appropriate attitudes but also extensive opportunity for their practical application and for critical appraisal of their implications (i.e. relevance).

A science education satisfying these criteria is likely to need very substantial experience of the whole constellation of activities which constitutes science, together with a reasonable maturity. Consequently science education will require a sizeable proportion of curriculum time throughout the period of compulsory schooling. Considerations of this nature underly the recent impetus towards 'science for all'. It is, however, important to realize that though everyone is entitled to a science education, 5–16, satisfying the above criteria, this does not imply identical provision for all at all stages. Where there are relevant differences in young people's abilities, interests or likely future needs, it would be irresponsible not to take these into account when deciding what form of science education is most appropriate.

Furthermore, as indicated at the end of the previous chapter, although one particular curriculum structure or organizational framework for teaching science might lend itself well to achieving particular aims, it may well be less effective in achieving others. It follows that in order to achieve a broad, balanced and relevant overall science education, a variety of different structures may need to be used consecutively and/or concurrently during the years 5–16 (or 4–19) and their precise phasing and balance to be nicely judged. Particular decisions relating to particular groups at particular stages will always need to be made in the context of an overall pattern of science education.

> How far, in your school, are
>
> science courses designed
> counselling services provided
>
> to ensure that, as far as possible, each young person receives a broad, balanced, relevant and appropriate science education?

## Structuring the science curriculum (11–16)

Some of the more important ways in which the science curriculum can be organised are conveniently stated as oppositions:

| | | | |
|---|---|---|---|
| 1 | an emphasis on process | as opposed to | an emphasis on content |
| 2 | integrated science | as opposed to | separate sciences |
| 3 | applied science | as opposed to | pure science |
| 4 | a common core of science | as opposed to | options/differential provision |
| 5 | a modular structure | as opposed to | a full-subject structure |

As each of these oppositions is examined in turn, the inadequacies of such crude polarizations will become apparent. The various dimensions will also be seen to be more interdependent than they might initially appear.

### 1 An emphasis on process as opposed to an emphasis on content

Science skills and processes cannot be acquired in a vacuum: some content is needed within which skills can be deployed and through which they can be developed. Furthermore, skills of all types – practical skills, thinking skills and communication skills – are best developed by being consolidated and extended in a wide variety of contexts and via a wide range of content. Acquaintance with a broad range of content is not only valuable in its own right, but can be essential for maintaining interest and motivation. Provided, therefore, that the development of skills does actually permeate all science education to a greater extent than has hitherto been common, and provided that this emphasis is reflected in schedules of assessment for certification (as in fact it will be by the National Criteria for Science at GCSE), the secondary science curriculum may well continue to be 'packaged' on a content basis for some time to come.

It is important to note that content need not be organized under conventional subject headings (biology, chemistry, physics etc.) and so taught in what was described in Chapter 1 as a 'pure science' context. Content can also be organized under task-centred or problem-centred headings and so taught in a technological or environmental context, again using the terminology of Chapter 1. It is in these latter contexts that there are often the greatest opportunities for genuinely open-ended discussion and problem solving, involving the deployment and integration of a wide range of knowledge, skills and attitudes. It is not infrequently possible for what is ostensibly the same task or activity to be pitched at different levels appropriate to the ages and abilities of the young people concerned.

> Do all science courses in your school (for all ages and all levels of ability) sufficiently emphasize the full range of skills and processes
>
> in the day-to-day teaching?
> in their assessment?

## 2 Integrated science as opposed to separate sciences

Each separate science has its own distinctive subject matter and, to a considerable extent, its own distinctive set of concepts, in terms of which phenomena are selected and described, questions asked, patterns and relationships established and explanations provided. On the other hand, the various sciences share a common approach to method (e.g. the formulation of hypotheses and testing them by observation and experiment). They also display considerable overlap of subject matter and associated sets of concepts. (Chemistry, for example, overlaps significantly with both biology and physics, whereas the latter two subjects overlap rather less.) Furthermore, problems and situations met in the world are usually complex and do not fall neatly into separate subject areas; they require for their understanding or solution the insights and perspectives afforded by several separate sciences. Any adequate science education must, therefore, both properly respect the internal structure of the separate sciences and, at the same time, clearly display the similarities between the sciences. It must also demonstrate how, taken together, they provide a more comprehensive understanding of the world at large than is possible via each science separately.

Teaching each science separately clearly allows the internal structure of that science to be brought out to the fullest possible extent. Very careful coordination is needed, however, to ensure that important connections and relationships across the separate sciences are effectively developed and to ensure that the phasing of content in each separate science area facilitates such development. The necessary coordination can be achieved, but it is a complex, time-consuming task and hence is often neglected. A separate subject structure also allows those staff with strong subject allegiances to work in the areas in which they are most confident and competent and in which they therefore teach best. It should be recognized, nonetheless, that it is hardly possible to do even reasonable justice to the integrative aspects of science education without a comprehensive grasp of the whole science curriculum, at least up to age 14 and preferably up to 16.

Science courses which are not formally differentiated into separate science components, and which are therefore – whatever their titles – in one sense or another 'integrated', obviously lend themselves well to bringing out what is common to all sciences. They also permit content to be drawn from several special sciences to provide a more complete understanding of some situations. Careful planning is needed, nonetheless, to ensure that key concept areas in the separate sciences are introduced and adequately developed at appropriate points. It is also important to check that, when staff are working in unfamiliar territory outside their main specialisms, appropriate help and support is provided by colleagues more familiar with the work in question. The general expectation that such help will be both sought and given, formally and informally, needs to be quite explicit within a departmental team. At its best, support of this kind constitutes valuable in-service training and professional development for all the parties concerned.

It is worth noting that 'science' courses are very common in Year 1 of secondary schools and fairly common in Year 2. Many such courses draw on materials from one, or more, published courses, such as Nuffield Combined Science, Scottish Integrated Science or ILEA's Insight to Science, often incorporating material produced at school level. By contrast, 'science' courses are very much less common in Year 3 and, while not uncommon in Years 4 and 5 for less able children, are rarely available to more able youngsters in these years. Explanations for these facts are not difficult to find. Teaching across the sciences in Years 1 and 2 does not present specialist teachers with the same problems as it would if continued through to Year 5 and to the top of the ability range. Looked at from another perspective, seeing a single teacher for 4/40 (or 6/40)

Re-examine the reasons underlying whatever decisions have been made in your school concerning when, and for whom, science courses are (or are not) 'integrated'.

For any integrated courses:

how effectively are separate science components introduced?
how effectively are teachers supported when working outside their specialist subject?

For any separate science courses, how effectively are links and relationships established:

between teachers?
in the actual teaching?

periods per week rather than two (or three) teachers each for 2/40 periods per week eases the transition for the youngster from the primary school to the secondary school. In addition to making greater demands upon teachers further up the school, an integrated approach is often thought, though not necessarily correctly, to lay a less good foundation for A-level studies than the separate sciences. However, using separate science courses to provide the basis for possible A-level studies, even in the three established sciences, requires at least 30 per cent of curriculum time, and this is increasingly being regarded as resulting in an unbalanced overall curriculum. A double-subject integrated science course offers one solution to this problem and is further explored in a later section. See box on previous page.

## 3 Applied science as opposed to pure science

Whether the sciences are taught separately or taught in a more integrated way, it is very common for the major emphasis to be on science as science rather than on the applications and implications of science. To put the same point using the terminology of Chapter 1, science is taught in what is a predominantly pure science context rather than in a technological or environmental context. The main aim of such teaching is to help young people to acquire key scientific concepts and skills rather than to develop their capacity to deploy those concepts and skills in solving technological problems or in reaching an informed point of view on environmental issues. It is, of course, possible, and indeed quite common, for young people to acquire their scientific concepts and skills via investigative learning and for some attention to be given to applications and implications. Nevertheless, whenever the main focus of science courses is on the acquisition of science concepts and skills:

(a) practical work is rarely genuinely open-ended or experimental. Its main purpose is seen as providing concrete, first-hand experiences in order that students can acquire concepts at a fully meaningful and operational level. Students and teachers alike are aware that their 'experiment' has a right answer. It is comparatively rare for much time or energy to be devoted to serious investigation of discrepancies between student's results and the 'official' answer;

(b) applications are usually treated in a much 'cleaner' way than they are met with in everyday life. Potentially complicating factors are stripped away in order to focus attention upon some particular concept or principle. Special apparatus may well be designed to achieve such simplification. Most real problems, on the other hand, are 'messy': their investigation, comprehension and solution usually involve chasing several 'red herrings' and eventually require drawing upon a range of scientific concepts and skills. Nor are solutions usually simply right or wrong, but they often lie somewhere on the scale from rather better to rather worse.

There is, then, a need for the application of science to be given a rather more prominent place at the focus of attention in science education. This should not replace the well established focus of acquiring key scientific concepts and skills, but complement it. More complex and sophisticated problems can be solved only from a well developed base of concepts and skills, in terms of which potentially relevant questions can be raised, plausible solutions conjectured and intelligent strategies implemented. Solving problems in this way will be of great value in consolidating the concept/skill base and may well develop it further. In principle, it might even be possible to develop a science education entirely through problem solving. In practice it is well nigh impossible to construct problem sequences providing sufficient continuity.

As argued earlier, the pure science approach is eminently well suited to developing related concepts in a structured, organized and systematic way. Similarly, precisely because the practical work involved in this approach is very directed in nature and limited in scope, it lends itself well to the development of component skills. Applied science courses – such as environmental science or technological science – on the other hand, supply the context within which content drawn from a wide range of concept areas can be selected and integrated with an array of skills in situations similar to those encountered in a person's everyday life. For an effective and efficient science education both approaches are needed. The precise balance and phasing of the approaches does, however, need relating to the ages, abilities and interests of the young people concerned.

Before turning to these issues of balance, phasing and differential provision, we must briefly consider the staffing implications of any shift in emphasis towards applied science. In many science departments there will be only a minority of staff with experience of an applied science approach and with the confidence and competence in the style of teaching involved. Not only does the 'applied' practical work often involve more variables and less clear-cut results – and make use of improvised equipment, sometimes outside the laboratory – but the content of the work is also selected and organized differently: relevance and applicability to a range of practical problems become important rather than the place of the content within the conventionally accepted academic structure of science. Any movement towards applied science must, therefore, proceed both at a pace and with a level of support which will allow the necessary confidence, competence and commitment to develop. In-service education and training will form an important part of the required support. This will need to cover a range from school-based courses involving, for example, preparation of teaching materials within schools, to externally-based courses of varying lengths provided by LEAs or the DES. Bringing outside advice into schools and the joint development of courses between groups of neighbouring schools are other potentially valuable strategies. The latter approach has been found both interesting and profitable by many teachers in the context of SSCR and TVEI working groups. Any shift towards applied science in Years 4 and 5 will also need careful presentation to parents and employees, who relate most readily to courses with which they are familiar, i.e. to separate and predominantly pure science courses.

Finally, it is important to underline the message of Section 1. Science skills and processes must pervade all science education. It is perfectly possible for science which has been selected for its relevance and applicability to be taught in a descriptive non-investigative manner. Human biology, for example, has sometimes tended to be taught in this way, and rural science courses can concentrate on teaching good practice without investigating the rationale underlying such practice.

> To what extent has your science department developed 'applied' science courses (e.g. rural science, environmental science, technological science) or included substantial elements of such work in other courses?
>
> How well is any such work distributed:
> with respect to age?
> with respect to ability?
> with respect to sex?

## 4 A common core of science as opposed to options/differential provision

The point was made at the beginning of this chapter that providing a science education for all to 16, which satisfies the criteria of breadth, balance and relevance, does not necessarily imply that all children's science education should be identical. The precise nature of the science education provided, and perhaps also its extent, should be matched to the abilities, interests and likely needs of the individuals concerned: each particular component of science should be developed to an appropriate level using appropriate means. In practice, however, in the early years of most secondary schools, all children in a particular school do follow a broadly common science curriculum. The broad, basic science education thus provided is increasingly likely to be built upon foundations laid in the primary school (a point taken up again later). It may also be presented somewhat differently to children of different abilities, particularly to the least able. Though detailed consideration of the case for different provision and the related question of setting or teaching in non-streamed groups is the concern of Chapter 5, it is worth noting that the greater the degree of differential provision in these early years, the more committed we are likely to be to continuing that differentiation for the very same groups of children throughout the secondary school.

As children become older, not only do their levels of attainment become more widely divergent, but there is also a similar divergence in their interests and aspirations. These divergencies, readily apparent both to the children themselves and to their parents and teachers, are commonly recognized in the curriculum by offering a choice of science(s) from a range of options in Years 4 and 5 (See Table 2.1). Young people are usually required to choose at least

TABLE 2.1 **Student subject choices in Years 4 and 5: England, Wales and Northern Ireland** (1980 data)

| | *Percentages* | | | |
|---|---|---|---|---|
| *Subject choices* | *Boys* | | *Girls* | |
| Biology, chemistry and physics | 14 | | 9 | |
| Total three subjects | | 14 | | 9 |
| Biology and chemistry | 3 | | 10 | |
| Biology and physics | 7 | | 4 | |
| Chemistry and physics | 14 | | 3 | |
| Total two subjects | | 24 | | 17 |
| Biology only | 7 | | 33 | |
| Chemistry only | 2 | | 3 | |
| Physics only | 18 | | 3 | |
| Total one subject | | 27 | | 39 |
| General science | 13 | | 10 | |
| Human biology | 2 | | 11 | |
| Other combinations | 12 | | 0 | |
| Total | | 27 | | 21 |
| No science | 7 | | 14 | |
| Total | | 7 | | 14 |

Source: Assessment of Performance Unit (1982, p. 19).

one science course in Years 4 and 5, thus retaining some semblance of breadth and balance in their overall curriculum. The range of science courses from which this choice can be made, however, together with the wide variation usually permitted in the overall amount of curriculum time devoted to science, seldom reveals much concern for the breadth, balance and relevance of the science education itself. (A similar situation is also obtained in other curriculum areas, e.g. humanities.)

There has been a significant move in recent years towards insisting that young people who pursue only one science course in Years 4 and 5, usually occupying 4/40 periods per week or 10 per cent of curriculum time, should take an integrated, combined or general science course. Regrettably, many such courses suffer acutely from information-overload, and they often fail to satisfy the balance and relevance criteria while satisfying the breadth criteria at a very superficial level only. Many Mode 3 science syllabuses have been designed to redress this problem. Young people pursuing all three separate science subjects, on the other hand, are likely to satisfy the breadth criteria tolerably well, though other areas of science are unlikely to feature very prominently. Certain aspects of the balance criteria will also be satisfied, but, despite devoting 30 per cent of curriculum time to science, there is no certainty that the student will have developed a full range of skills or will have adequately explored the process dimension. Nor will there have been anything like sufficient emphasis on the applications and implications of science. The National Criteria for Science (GCSE) should, however, go some way towards remedying both these deficiencies.

If schools continue to provide such enormous scope for choice in the science course(s) pursued in Years 4 and 5, it follows that all that is essential for the achievement of a broad, balanced and relevant science education has to be accomplished in Years 1–3. Since, however, some key concept areas, essential skills or important emphases are relatively complex, requiring for their effective acquisition a reasonable level of intellectual development and social maturity, they are unlikely to have been achieved by the end of Year 3. Consequently, any such concepts will need to be included in young people's science education in Years 4 and 5, whatever option choices they might make. One way to achieve this would be to continue with at least some common core science education through to 16, albeit pitched at different levels for different abilities. Alternatively, core components could be incorporated into different options targetted at different groups of young people.

We are now in a position to return to the question of how best to phase and balance the pure science and applied science emphases discussed in the previous section. In the primary school the science which is studied is often, though by no means always, selected because of its relevance or applicability to some particular problem or interest that has arisen, sometimes in some other area of the curriculum. Taking this problem or interest beyond a relatively superficial level will, however, often require stepping aside and more systematically providing a concept base which can then be brought back and applied to the interest or problem. Furthermore there will be some concern, even at the primary stage, about including a reasonable breadth of basic concept areas, whether or not they spontaneously arise. In the early years of the secondary school, although rather more continuity with the primary approach is desirable than is currently very common, there should, nonetheless, be rather more emphasis on covering a broad range of science concept areas. Though these areas will often be selected because of their general relevance and applicability, and though there will be frequent opportunity for their actual appplication in particular situations, such application will no longer be the major criterion for the selection and organization of content. Some content too will be selected not so much for its potential practical relevance and applicability but rather because of its theoretical relevance, i.e. its explanatory power and its importance in science as (pure) science.

By the time young people reach Year 4 (and, possibly, by the time they have reached Year 3), those with a real interest in and aptitude for science for its own sake (i.e. who take a delight in patterns and relationships and in explanations of a 'pure science' nature which unify apparently very different phenomena) may have identified themselves. Whatever other aspects of science such young people ought to study, they should certainly be given the opportunity to extend and develop their intrinsic interest in science, possibly with a view to progressing to A-level studies and beyond. But even such students as these also live in the real world, with its many technological problems and complex environmental issues. The implication is clear: all young people should continue to have a significant applied science component in their science education in Years 4 and 5.

There will be many other young people, however, who do not find the patterns, relationships and explanations of pure science at all easy to grasp or to appreciate. For them, science is far more likely to be enjoyed and valued through being applied in, for example, a technological or environmental context rather than in a pure science context. Within such an applied context there will be ample opportunity to consolidate and develop further the concepts and skills encountered in earlier years. Indeed, the more complete mastery of relatively elementary concepts, if they are being used to achieve some recognizable goal, may result in arousing a delight and satisfaction missing in earlier years. Nor need the possibilities of further studies in science be ruled out. A science education with an emphasis on application is at least as useful a basis for more vocational science studies beyond 16 as an education in pure science.

Of course, if we wish to 'fine tune' the science curriculum to provide just the right balance and emphasis, not only in relation to age but also with respect to ability and interest, it is important to show how such provision is logistically feasible. This task will be embarked upon after comparing the relative merits of modular and full-subject curriculum structures.

> At what point(s) does your department differentiate science provision to any significant degree with respect to ability?
>
> On how sound a basis is such differentiation made, and how irrevocable are the consequences?
>
> How far does any choice and/or differentiation in the nature and amount of science studied make it more difficult to ensure that everyone receives a broad, balanced science education, regardless of ability or sex?

## 5 Modular structure as opposed to a full-subject structure

So far in this chapter we have examined how different types of science course contribute in different ways to the overall aim of providing all young people with a broad, balanced and relevant science education. A separate science approach readily permits the distinctive conceptual structure of each science to be systematically developed. Integrated science schemes more clearly demonstrate how much all the natural sciences have in common. Courses in pure sciences, whether separate or integrated, lend themselves well to displaying science as a disciplined and demanding yet intellectually stimulating and rewarding activity. Applied science courses, on the other hand, provide young people with the opportunity to appreciate, through successful first-hand experience, how powerful scientific knowledge and scientific methods are in enabling us sensitively to shape the world to meet our needs.

Given the relative strengths and weaknesses of different approaches it is clearly unhelpful to ask whether we should teach science in an integrated way rather than as separate sciences, or whether our emphasis should be applied rather than pure. The important question is how best to combine the strengths of the different approaches to ensure that everyone receives a science education which satisfies the criteria of breadth, balance, relevance and differentiation, and which does not occupy an undue proportion of curriculum time.

Probably the biggest single obstacle to the satisfactory resolution of this problem is the established structure of the secondary school time-table and, in particular, the large blocks of time with which it usually operates. What is being questioned here is not the length of individual teaching sessions (indeed the trend in recent years towards double periods or even half-day blocking of time is a positive advantage to any subject which has, like science, an important practical component), but rather the assumption that courses should carry the same title and be taught in much the same style and with much the same emphasis across a period of one, or even two, school years. If the educational potential of each different approach – pure and applied, integrated and separate – is to be exploited to maximum advantage, it is essential to employ reasonably fine gradations in the balance and phasing of each style of science education. In developing this suggestion in more detail, it is convenient to consider the earlier years of secondary education separately from the science education provided in Years 4 and 5.

In Years 1 and 2 of the secondary school it is possible, and not uncommon, to provide 'integrated science' courses which include both integrated topics and units of work which belong to a separate science. A topic on air, for example, might include and relate atmospheric pressure (physics), oxygen and carbon dioxide (chemistry) and how and why we breathe (biology). Units of work on electrostatics or reproduction, on the other hand, will belong, more or less exclusively, to physics and biology respectively. By introducing both kinds of topic at appropriate stages, and by making them of an appropriate length, we can produce a science course which is genuinely integrated but which also provides that more systematic development in key concept areas which is an important strength of the separate sciences approach. Units of work, of either type, can also include elements concerned with the applications and implications of science. Too often, however, such elements tend to be somewhat incidental to the units and relatively brief in duration. More extended work of a technical nature can be provided by units which have this as their focus. The inclusion of such units will help to provide children in the early years of the secondary school with a more balanced (and more interesting) diet. Movement in this direction will also provide better continuity with the style of science with which children are familiar from their primary schools.

Before leaving the early years of secondary education it is worth raising a few issues, each related in one way or another with staffing. Integrated science courses of the type described above (i.e. incorporating significant units of separate science and applied science) are usually taught to a given group of children by a single teacher throughout a school year. Thus there need not be any constraints on the size of units: each can be as long, or as short, as is appropriate to its content and emphasis and its place in the overall scheme of things. Furthermore, although the sequence of units is important, it is usually possible to identify several different yet equally satisfactory routes through a scheme, thereby allowing sufficient flexibility to accommodate pressures on equipment and materials even when classes are simultaneously timetabled. Lastly, it is worth returning to a point raised earlier in this chapter about expecting specialist staff not only to teach those areas of 'pure science' with which they are relatively unfamiliar, but also to work in the much less tidy area of the applied sciences. While it cannot reasonably be denied that any aspect of science which is regarded as an essential part of anyone's science education should be within the competence of any professional teacher of science, it is still important to underline the need for adequate preparation time, for specialist support and for proper resourcing in terms of equipment, materials, teaching spaces and technician support.

Turning now to science provision in Years 4 and 5, it is worth noting how the education system has attempted to respond to perceived needs for particular focuses or emphases in science education. The tendency has been to generate new, full-subject science options, each occupying the standard 10 per cent of curriculum time for two full years. Thus, alongside courses in the 'big three', well established sciences of physics, chemistry and biology have grown, for example, Nuffield courses in each of these disciplines, together with courses in geology and human biology. The need for a more substantial technological or environmental emphasis has been met via courses in technical science, engineering science, electronics, control technology, agricultural and/or horticultural science, rural studies/science and environmental science. Courses of the 'science and society' type have also been produced to provide a historical, social and economic slant, though in fact such courses have mainly been taught to students over the age of 16. A similar range of courses is likely to be available under the aegis of GCSE commencing September 1986. The significant message emerging from the above is that the strategy of proliferating full-subject courses is not an appropriate solution to the problem of providing a broad, balanced and relevant science education for all young people to 16: locking up important components in full-subject courses merely exacerbates the difficulties. The hitherto common alternative solution of schools devising their own Mode 3 courses, specifically targetted at particular groups of young people, is also likely to prove a less attractive proposition under GCSE regulations. Mode 3 courses have always made heavy demands on teachers and these demands will be increased still further with the need to satisfy several sets of very stringent criteria.

An alternative strategy, albeit somewhat radical, is available; the altogether unhelpful proliferation of science options can be done away with and a science course provided, taken by all young people who, in effect, thus pursue a common core science curriculum to 16. Such a course conventionally involves 4/40 periods per week for all, with the possibility of extending this to 8/40 periods per week, thus matching recent policy statements. (The Nuffield 13–16 materials are being used in this manner by groups of schools in Hertfordshire.) Alternatively, it might involve 8/40 periods per week for all. Courses of this type, having a large compulsory component drawing upon a range of sciences, can certainly ensure breadth and balance far more effectively than can choices within the options jungle. There is, for example, no difficulty in extending the breadth of sciences beyond the usual biology, chemistry and physics. Similarly, it is readily possible to strike a balance between an integrated approach and units of work belonging predominantly to one of the separate sciences, or between pure, concept-centred science and applications-centred science. A common science curriculum might even make timetables easier to write.

A common science curriculum is, however, unlikely to be particularly strong in catering appropriately for young people having widely different abilities, needs and interests. While all young people should develop the capacity to apply their scientific knowledge and skills to solving technological problems, or to reaching informed points of view on environmental issues, for some this will be the predominant aim of their science education in Years 4 and 5. Such students may be making more secure a relatively elementary set of concepts, commonly included in courses for 11–14 year olds. There will be others, however, for whom an extensive widening and deepening of their concept base is seen as first priority. These pupils may well concentrate on the relatively abstract and 'pure' aspects of such which are widely – though perhaps erroneously – regarded as a better foundation for A-level studies.

There are topics which can be treated in a meaningful and worthwhile way at a number of different levels. Others demand complex and abstract conceptual thinking and are not appropriate for many young people. Many chemical phenomena, for example, if collected together as chemistry (rather than for their relevance in some applied science context) only make sense in the light of abstract, conceptually difficult and inter-related ideas such as periodicity, atomic structure and electron configurations. Many courses (which have been strongly influenced by Nuffield materials) – particularly those at CSE level – have been inadequate for just this reason. If the integrative cement is removed from a course on the grounds that it is conceptually too demanding, one is left with little more than a shapeless heap of stones. Shayer and Adey (1981), in *Towards a Science of Science Teaching*, argue that many developments in science education during the past 20 years, stimulating though they might be for the most able, have produced a largely inappropriate style of science education for the majority of young people. The widely used Nuffield Combined Science scheme is regarded by them as being pitched at too demanding a conceptual level for most of the children with whom it is used.

There is a middle course between the one extreme of selecting full-subject options, short on breadth and balance, and the other extreme of following a core curriculum, thin on differentiation. What is needed is a modular curriculum structure. Within this units of work can be drawn from across a wide range of sciences, some units drawn from particular sciences, others more integrated in nature; some units relatively pure in emphasis, others having a much more strongly applied focus; some well suited to developing certain skills, others providing a strongly social or economic slant, and so on. Within such a scheme it would be possible for schools to construct a range of science courses all of which satisfy the general criteria of breadth, balance and relevance, though not all in precisely the same way. Any core elements thought to be essential to all 14–16 year olds, if interpreted at an appropriate level, can be readily included, while variations in emphasis allow courses to be matched to the abilities, interests and needs of young people and to particular strengths of either staffing or local circumstances.

A modular approach is not, of course, without its problems. A modular structure permits very flexible course construction and can often aid motivation: young people are presented with units of work whose overall scope they can readily grasp and performance within which can be assessed on completion of the unit. But these very strengths are also potential sources of weakness. Modular courses can easily become fragmentary, lacking coherence, continuity and progression. It is, however, perfectly possible to build these features, coherence, continuity and progression, into a modular system. (A group of chemistry modules, for example, could be clustered into a 'pattern' or a 'package'.) Where the content of the modules within a package is closely inter-related it might well make little educational sense to allow them to be taken outside the complete package. Provided, however, the package occupies less time than a normal, full-subject course and is equivalent in duration to a whole number of modules, at least some of the flexibility of the modular structure will be retained. Within a package of this kind there is absolutely no reason why modules need to be the same length, a feature of modular courses sometimes perceived as a problem (especially for the separate sciences where a topic heading tends to create rather precise expectations of what should be included by the age of 16). Performance in such 'semi-specialisms' within an overall modular structure might also be indicated in the certification, thereby better informing potential end-users, such as parents and employers, who tend to favour that with which they are familiar. Promotional work explaining such novel ways of reporting performance would need to be undertaken at regional level by examination boards and at a more local level by LEAs and, indeed, by individual schools.

A well designed modular structure can, then, incorporate the advantages of all the various approaches discussed earlier in this chapter and combine them in a variety of ways to provide a broad, balanced and relevant science education appropriate to the needs of different groups of young people. Such a structure need not be regarded as an alternative to other forms of science curriculum structure; it can incorporate other approaches. It has, too, the capacity for evolutionary or 'organic' development. For example, a modular structure can accommodate staff preference for particular subjects (already noted) in the following way: it is possible for a school to select a set of predominantly familiar modules and to group these within the structure under familiar headings producing a largely conventional course. Over several years, as confidence, competence and commitment develops in hitherto less familiar areas, the centre of gravity of the courses covered can gradually shift, within the same modular structure, towards courses of a more radical nature. If it also proves possible for schools to use a Mode 1 modular scheme yet include within it some Mode 3 modules, this would not only allow innovation by individual schools – without the burden of undertaking a full Mode 3 course – but would also ensure the evolution and development of the overall scheme. An exciting Mode 3 module developed in one school could be adopted by other interested schools and eventually might become part of the Mode 1 structure.

Next, a brief word about logistics. An important strength of a common core approach to the science curriculum in Years 4 and 5 is its simplicity. A modular structure, by comparison, seems on the face of it to be immensely complex. In fact, this complexity is more apparent than real. The worst possible scenario for the operation of a modular science scheme is where constraints of staffing, accommodation, timetabling and student roll require young people to be taught science in unchanged groups for the full two-year period by the same teachers. Even within these constraints, however, a modular structure will allow courses to be constructed more adequately, providing a broad, balanced and relevant science education, than would selection from a conventional range of full-subject courses. Flexibility, leading to courses which can be more closely tailored to the needs and interests of students, is the key. The simultaneous timetabling of several groups, for example, will allow more possible combinations within a half-subject structure or, more radically, the partial exchange of students between groups at the commencement of new modules.

One particularly interesting possibility is that of working within 'half-subject' blocks rather than 'full-subject' blocks for the purposes of certification. The widely canvassed figure of 8/40 periods per week of science for all has much to recommend it if the only alternatives are either 4/40 periods per week or 12/40 periods per week. A very strong educational case can, however, be made for 6/40 periods per week being a more acceptable minimum, especially if significant components of environmental and technological material were included elsewhere in the curriculum. Similarly, 10/40 periods per week is an admirable maximum where a person's science education includes considerable environmental, technological and socio-economic components. The notion of some young people undertaking $1\frac{1}{2}$ or $2\frac{1}{2}$ full-subject equivalents of science does, of course, have implications extending into the overall curriculum of schools and indeed into the whole GCSE examination structure. The more widespread

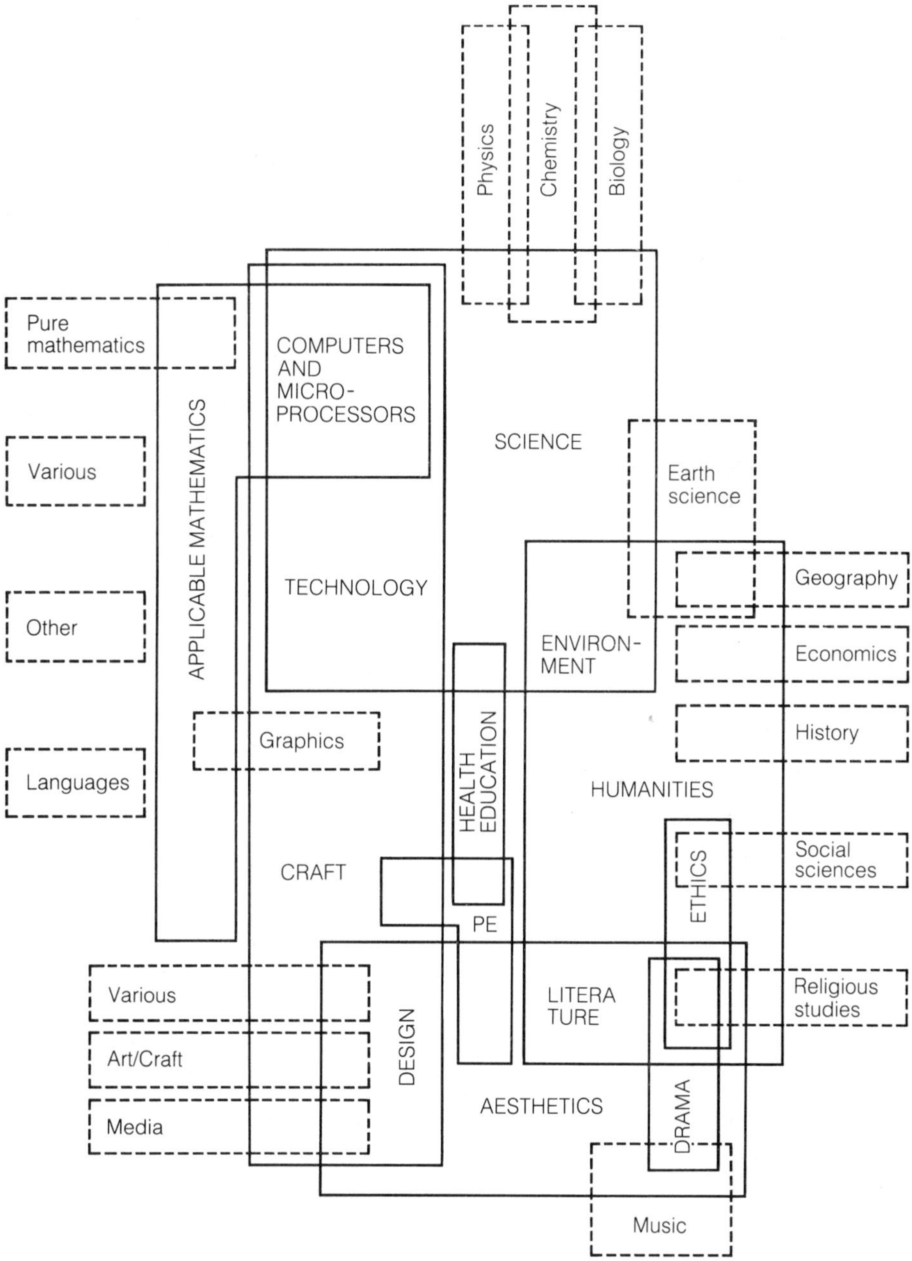
Physics
Chemistry
Biology
Pure mathematics
COMPUTERS AND MICRO-PROCESSORS
SCIENCE
Various
APPLICABLE MATHEMATICS
Earth science
TECHNOLOGY
Geography
Other
ENVIRON-MENT
Economics
Graphics
HEALTH EDUCATION
History
Languages
HUMANITIES
Social sciences
CRAFT
ETHICS
PE
Various
LITERA TURE
Religious studies
Art/Craft
DESIGN
Media
AESTHETICS
DRAMA
Music

FIG. 2.1

adoption of a modular approach across the curriculum as a whole immediately suggests itself as a possible solution. One outcome of this would be that it would become obvious whenever the same material was being covered in much the same way by different departments. The negotiation between departments needed to resolve this problem of unnecessary replication could also prevent the omission of topics which fall between departments. This applies, of course, to science subjects themselves as well as to science and other curriculum areas. What matters is that all children undertake what schools consider to be appropriate units of work concerning, for example, the environment, technology, health education or computer appreciation. Whether or not responsibility for them resides wholly, or in part, with science departments (or with geography, CDT, HE or mathematics departments) will depend upon the outcome of negotiations in individual schools. These will need to take into account the relative strengths, weaknesses, interests and, indeed, availability of the staff concerned. The diagram on p. 55 and the following notes show some of the more obvious departmental intersections and suggests some possible implications in terms of a core plus extension curriculum. Similar issues are also treated in a different, but complementary way in Chapter 7(c).

**Diagram Notes** for Figure 2.1 (p. 55)

Core (say 75%)

(a) has emphasis on knowledge and skills for application;
(b) is indicated by solid boxes and upper case letters.

Extensions (say 25%)

(a) emphasize the knowledge and skills intrinsic to the activities themselves;
(b) are indicated by broken boxes and lower case letters.

However:

(a) both core and extensions are developed from knowledge and skills laid down in primary schools, and in Years 1–3;
(b) for many young people, it will be most appropriate to devote all their curriculum time in Years 4 and 5 to studies with the emphasis on the applications of skills and knowledge.

If a modular structure were adopted across the curriculum, then material lying within the intersections between different areas could be taken under either heading (but not, of course, under both). This would help to ensure not only a more balanced educational provision for all young people, but more effective use of staff, especially in the context of falling rolls.

Since the English language pervades all other studies, it is not represented in the diagram. This, perhaps, suggests interesting implications for the curriculum!

Before leaving this section it is worth reiterating the point made earlier that specifically focused courses (e.g. in physics, chemistry, geology, rural science, technological science etc.), by occupying about 10 per cent of available curriculum time and hence a much greater proportion of science curriculum time, impose considerable constraints on the provision of a broad and balanced science education. Oddly enough, integrated science courses, even those occupying 20 per cent of curriculum time, and courses constructed of relatively short modules (of the order of, say, about 1 per cent of curriculum time), are each readily capable of producing breadth and balance. In fact, well designed courses of each type will include a sensible balance and sequence of components drawn from a range of separate sciences together with integrated and applied science components and will often be remarkably similar. Whereas integrated courses put a premium on coherence and continuity at the expense of flexibility, modular courses tend in the opposite direction. If, however, integrated courses are able to offer some choice, and modular schemes include a significant compulsory core, these differences can become small. Whatever structure is adopted, the most important consideration is whether or not it readily allows the provision of a broad, balanced and relevant science education appropriate to the needs of young people of all abilities.

> How far, if at all, would the possibility of offering a larger number of less than 'full-course' units of work in Years 4 and 5 better enable your department to provide broader and more appropriate science courses for all young people?

## 6 Continuity and progression: some additional considerations

There are two further matters requiring brief consideration before proceeding to the next section of this chapter. Firstly, while a broad distinction has been drawn throughout the chapter between science education in the early years of the secondary school and that in Years 4 and 5, virtually nothing has been said specifically about Year 3. Secondly, the question of ensuring continuity in science education beyond 16 needs to be considered, if only to the extent that brief reference has been made earlier to continuity across the primary secondary interface.

Year 3 has frequently been regarded as very much an in between year, partly aiming to complete the basic core science education provided in Years 1 and 2, and partly providing a clear basis on which to make more informed option choices for Years 4 and 5. In the context of a broad, balanced science education for all to 16, in which all science courses in Years 4 and 5 will include essential core elements and where much finer graduation of balance and emphasis will be possible, Year 3 courses can be an integral part of a continuing science education rather than a transitional period within it. There remains, nevertheless, the important question of the nature and extent of any differential provision in Year 3, i.e. whether this should mainly be in the form of treating core material at different levels, as is common in Years 1 and 2, or whether we should begin to provide more substantive differences in balance and emphasis along the lines argued above as being appropriate in Years 4 and 5. Precisely how this question is best resolved will depend to a large extent upon the details of the overall pattern of provision in particular schools. What should be common to all schemes is the avoidance at any stage of sharp discontinuities with all of their attendant problems.

Once a more appropriate structure has been established for science education in secondary schools, particularly in the 14–16 age range, it will become possible to ensure that provision beyond 16 shows continuity and progression relative to what has been done prior to 16. Though provision beyond 16 has in the past been even more complex than the range of options for 14–16 year olds, courses have in recent years been rationalized to quite a considerable degree and there are strong pressures towards further rationalization. A levels apart, there are definite trends in this rationalization process:

(a) towards more generic courses which only gradually tend to the more narrowly vocational (and hence less generally educative);
(b) towards a modular structure.

If the curriculum 14–16 develops along the lines envisaged in this chapter, we shall need to develop a clear system of prerequisites and exemptions so that it will be possible, beyond 16, to:

(a) undertake work which could have been (but, in fact, was not) done in earlier years;
(b) build further knowledge and skills upon work already accomplished.

To keep this task to manageable proportions, it may well be necessary (as it currently is in the context of TVEI) to negotiate local agreements on areas of study best left alone until after 16.

There is a direct parallel here to the way in which local groups of primary schools can negotiate, both between themselves and with the local secondary school(s) they feed, a common approach to science education. This might include agreement on whether certain content areas are to be covered and, if so, to what level. Perhaps the biggest problem of all beyond 16 is the great divide between A-level provision and what, for want of a better term, is often described as vocational education. (Though A-level courses could, not altogether unfairly, be described as the most narrowly vocational education of all, appropriate only to potential dons!) This is an enormous problem requiring for its resolution much political will and political skill at the highest level.

Something of the complexity of post-16 provisions is indicated by the following diagram (from 'Examinations: An Update' (1984) in *Education in Science*).

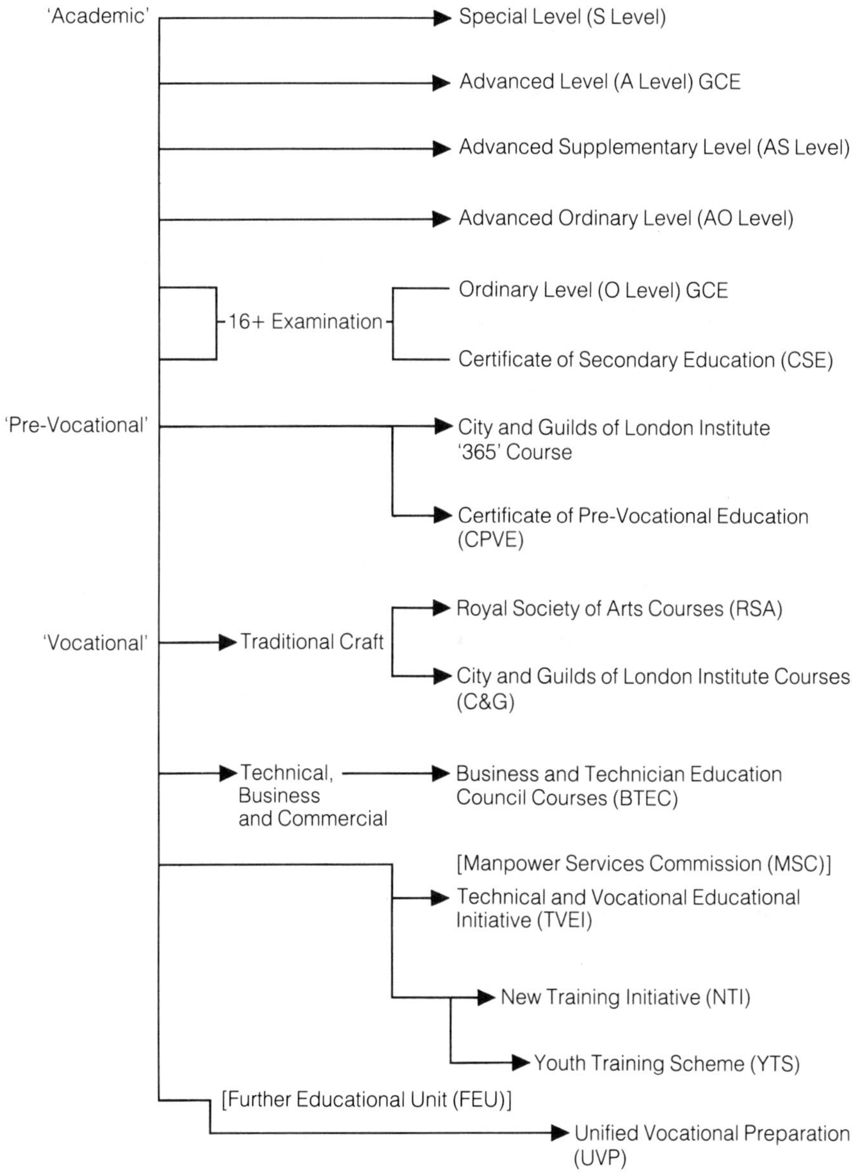
'Academic'
Special Level (S Level)
Advanced Level (A Level) GCE
Advanced Supplementary Level (AS Level)
Advanced Ordinary Level (AO Level)
16+ Examination
Ordinary Level (O Level) GCE
Certificate of Secondary Education (CSE)
'Pre-Vocational'
City and Guilds of London Institute '365' Course
Certificate of Pre-Vocational Education (CPVE)
'Vocational'
Traditional Craft
Royal Society of Arts Courses (RSA)
City and Guilds of London Institute Courses (C&G)
Technical, Business and Commercial
Business and Technician Education Council Courses (BTEC)
[Manpower Services Commission (MSC)]
Technical and Vocational Educational Initiative (TVEI)
New Training Initiative (NTI)
Youth Training Scheme (YTS)
[Further Educational Unit (FEU)]
Unified Vocational Preparation (UVP)

FIG. 2.2

> How far are you able, in your school, to build upon the science education children have received in their primary schools?
>
> How suitable are your science courses for 14–16 year olds as a basis for further studies in science other than A levels?

## 7 A (partial) summary via curriculum models

This section comprises two models, each in the form of a diagram with accompanying notes, and each of which is intended to highlight some important aspect of providing an appropriate broad, balanced and relevant science education within a wider curriculum context.

Model A displays how different emphases can be phased and balanced within an overall pattern of science education.

Model B embodies one possible solution to the problem of designing a range of GCSE science courses within which it is possible to complete everyone's broad, balanced and relevant science education while at the same time permitting adequate differentiation.

It should be noted that inevitably this summary is partial both in the sense of being incomplete and because the models exemplify approaches to key curriculum issues via particular, and therefore hardly impartial, solutions, each representing but one from among many possible points of view.

MODEL A **Balance and phasing within an overall pattern of science education.**

| *STAGE* | *STATUS* | *TIME* | *MAIN ORGANIZING PRINCIPLE** | *CONTEXT* |
|---|---|---|---|---|
| 5–11 | Core | 10% | PURE INTEREST and/or APPLICATIONS (i.e. simple technology) and/or IMPLICATIONS | INTEGRATED with any or all of curriculum (though often detaching itself for periods of time) |
| 11–14 | Core | 10% to 15% | Rather more systematic and sequential coverage of basic science CONCEPTS and PRINCIPLES | INTEGRATED mainly within science, though with substantial units of biol., chem., phys., earth sci., env. sci., techngy etc. |

MODEL A *(continued)*

| *STAGE* | *STATUS* | *TIME* | *MAIN ORGANIZING PRINCIPLE** | *CONTEXT* |
|---|---|---|---|---|
| 14–16 | Core | 5% | Social, economic, political and environmental IMPLICATIONS of science and technology<br>+ | LIAISON with HUMANITIES (e.g. first and second industrial revolutions, siting of industries, management of resources, protection of environment) |
| | | | APPLICATION of science concepts, principles and skills (together with knowledge and skills from CRAFT) to the successful accomplishment of TECHNOLOGICAL tasks | LIAISON with CDT, HE (and RS/AGRIC. if separate), e.g. design, build, test and evaluate an alternative energy device |
| | + | | | |
| | OPTION Either I | 10% to 15% | Further work of an APPLIED science nature to add a particular emphasis (e.g. TECHNOLOGY or RURAL STUDIES) to the balanced selection of topics covered in the core | |
| | or II | 15% to 20% | Focus on CONCEPTS and PRINCIPLES (at a more demanding level) N.B. (i) Applications/implications adequately covered in core (ii) Since achieving important aims in, e.g. craft and humanities, up to 25% of time to be available to science | PURE science: PHYSICS/ CHEMISTRY/ BIOLOGY or PHYSICAL SCIENCE/LIFE SCIENCE or INTEGRATED SCIENCE |
| 16–18 | I → B/TEC, CPVE<br>II → A LEVEL | | | |

(i) Process aims of science – practical and experimental skills, thinking skills, communication skills – to pervade all science education in appropriate forms
(ii) *Other emphases also to be present throughout.

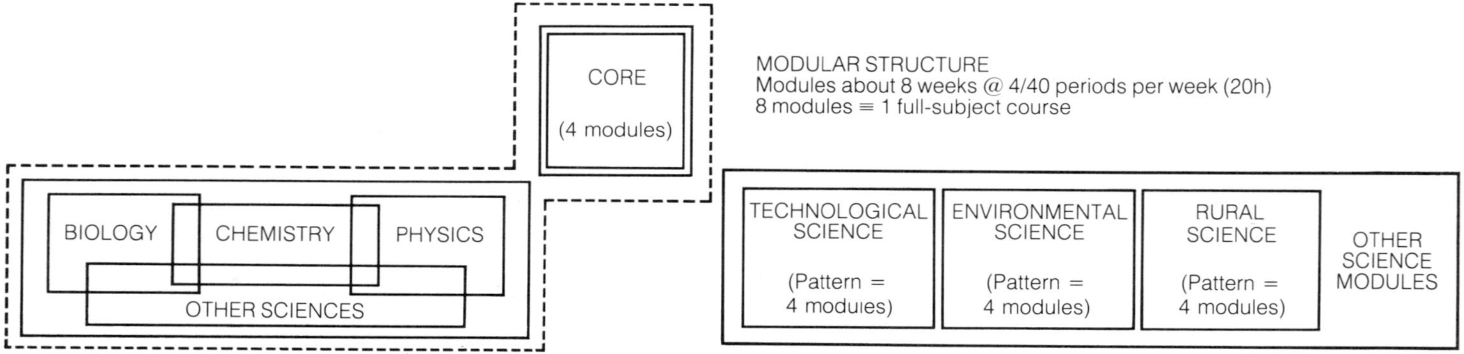


MODULAR STRUCTURE
Modules about 8 weeks @ 4/40 periods per week (20h)
8 modules ≡ 1 full-subject course

DOUBLE CERTIFICATE SCIENCE

(i) Intended to be taken as a whole
(ii) May be taught fully integrated or as separate sciences
(iii) Must include CORE material though it can be integrated rather than taught separately
(iv) Ideally
  (a) room *within* double-subject for, say, 2 option modules from techn. sci., env. sci., rur. sci., etc.
  (b) allow extension to 2½ subjects to provide room for more applied science modules (possibly including a half-subject pattern)

CORE MODULES

Energy
Materials and their uses
Environment

The human system

(Note: content overlap allows consolidation & integration without dictating sequence)

POSSIBLE RANGE OF OPTION MODULES

| | | | |
|---|---|---|---|
| Machines | Earth's resources | Horticulture | Making new stuff |
| Flight | Water | Protected cultivation | Metals |
| Biotechnology | Waste/pollution | Forestry | Living things |
| Structures | Food production | Agriculture* | Communications sci. |
| Electronics | Geology/Earch sci. | (*up to two from range of areas) | Colour |
| | | | Sci. & motor vehicles |
| | | | Sports science |
| | | | Space science |

(Note: Provision for Mode 3 modules also available)

APPLIED SCIENCE COURSES

*Single subject*
CORE + 4 modules (which may, but need not, form a pattern)

*Double subject*
CORE + 12 modules (to include at least two patterns of 4)

[and, ideally,
*One-and-a-half subject*
CORE + 8 modules (to include at least ONE pattern of 4)]

MODEL B **Possible GCSE science structure**

# Resources and further reading – an annotated list

## 1 Relating to the whole chapter

(a) Broad discussions of many of the issues raised in this chapter are to be found in: Hull and Adams (1981) and Ingle and Jennings (1981).

(b) A somewhat stipulative set of definitions of different types of science course is to be found in *GCSE The National Criteria: Science* (1985). These could well become standard terminology.

(i) *integrated* a multi-component area of study where, possibly in the syllabus but certainly in the teaching and in the examination, the inter-relationships between components are stressed.

(ii) *combined* a multi-component area of study where in the syllabus, in the teaching and in the examination the components are, as far as practicable, mutually supportive while retaining much of their separate identities. The components are not necessarily equally represented in the overall syllabus.

(iii) *united* a bi-component area of study where, possibly in the syllabus but certainly in the teaching and in the examination, the inter-relationships between the two components are stressed.

(iv) *associated* a bi-component area of study where in the syllabus, in the teaching and in the examination the two components are, as far as practicable, mutually supportive while retaining much of their separate identities. The components are not necessarily equally represented in the overall syllabus.

(v) *directed* an area of study which, built from a multi-component core as a base, develops one or more particular areas of interest – possibly of an applied, technical or vocational nature. Such syllabuses may be modular in structure with the further possibility of there being (guided) choice of module.

(c) *Science 5–16: A Statement of Policy* (DES, 1985)
This policy statement, published subsequent to the writing of this chapter, contains much that is relevant to it.

## 2 Science in the early secondary years

(a) Though it has become common for schools to devise their own courses, these often draw quite heavily on material from published schemes.

Two recent schemes often used in this way are:
ILEA, *Insight to Science*;
*Science 2000* – formerly *Science for the 70's* by Mee, Boyd and Ritchie (1980)

Confining comment exclusively to matters relevant to this chapter, it should be noted that *Science for the 70's* is very much the stronger on coherence, continuity and progression, both within and between units, though its conceptual demands are also greater. Neither scheme provides much opportunity for more open-ended experimentation except for the extension work for the more able in the Scottish material.

(b) Home-brewed schemes with a predominantly practical (if insufficiently experimental) approach have tended to make the 'complete course' type of textbook inappropriate. A different style of text complementing the practical work and including written materials of a historical, social, economic, technological or environmental nature has emerged. Examples include:
Kellington (1982), *Reading about Science*;
Bateman and Lidstone (1984), *Steps in Science*,

(c) Shayer and Adey (1981 pp. 119–121) – see Sections 4 and 6 below – contains interesting comment on the conceptual level of another widely used resource 'Nuffield Combined Science'.

## 3 Science in Years 4 and 5

(a) No attempt is made here to list the numerous texts and courses relating to separate science provision. It is, however, worth noting two schemes which aim to provide a broad science education within the equivalent of two full subjects:
*Schools Council Integrated Science Project* (*SCISP*) by Hall and Mowl (1973) an interesting development but with high conceptual demands;
*Nuffield Science 13–16* (1979) – a more recent course which is in some respects derivative from SCISP but which adopts a core plus enrichment approach intended to make it suitable to a wider ability range.

(b) So far as a more applied or directed approach to science is concerned, two schemes which have been widely used as the basis of Mode 3 courses for the lower and middle ranges of ability are:
*Science at Work*, edited by Taylor (1979);
*Open Science*, Schools Council (1979).

Much more demanding material of a technological nature is to be found in the Schools Council Modular Technology Scheme, details of which are given in Chapter 7(c).

(c) Materials concerned with social, economic and historical aspects of science and technology, though targetted at 16–18 year olds, are also listed in Chapter 7(c). An ASE (in preparation) project, *Science and Technology in Society* (*SATIS*), is currently preparing similar material which can be used to enrich courses for 14–16 year olds. (An interim report is to be found in *Education in Science*, January 1985).

Enrichment material of a different kind is also being published in the ASE/SCSST (1985) *Experimenting with Industry* series.

(d) *Rural Science – an Applied View of Science*, ASE (1984), extends the technological approach into the biological domain; *Biotechnology and Education*, The Royal Society (1981), argues (pp. 8–16) for relevant modules to be included in other courses. Such modules are, in fact, being developed by several SSCR and TVEI groups throughout the country.

*Rethinking Science?* by ASE (1984), *Environmental Education* by DES and *Environmental Science: A Review* by DES (1981) each contain much that is relevant to this chapter.

## 4 Differentiating science with respect to ability

(a) Shayer and Adey (1981), *Towards a Science of Science Teaching* (especially in Parts 1 and 4), argue that much science teaching is pitched at an inappropriate conceptual level.

(b) *The Children's Learning in Science Project* (*CLISP*) (1984), based at the Centre for Studies in Science and Mathematics Education at the University of Leeds, has produced a series of reports (in full and in summary versions) on children's understandings and misunderstandings in the following concept areas:

| | |
|---|---|
| Energy | Particulate nature of matter |
| Heat | Air and air pressure |
| Conservation of matter | Simple chemical reactions with oxygen |
| Plant nutrition | Light: vision, transmission and reflection |
| Elements, mixtures and compounds | |

Though these studies are obviously of most relevance to the question of how best to teach these topics (the concern of Chapter 3), they are also relevant to the questions of whether we should teach them, to whom, at what stage(s) and in which context(s). The following extract from the summary report on energy clearly illustrates this point:

> It may be that the time has come for an integrated approach to teaching about energy, and that the role of all science teachers in developing students' ideas in this area warrants closer scrutiny. If there could be a co-ordinated approach by all science teachers in the 11 to 16 age range, in which a programme was constructed to take into account the best of both science and everyday ideas and set them in meaningful contexts, it may be that a deeper understanding of the energy concept could be developed in many students by the time they complete their compulsory schooling.

## 5 Continuity in science education 5–18

(a) Ruth Jarman (1984), *Primary Science, Secondary Science: Some Issues at the Interface*, raises important issues in a stimulating manner.

(b) As indicated earlier in this chapter, provision beyond 16 is complex. Articles by Job (1984) and Fairbrother (1984) provide useful information and suggest many further references.

## 6 On 'soft' sciences as opposed to 'hard' sciences

Shayer and Adey (1981) (see Section 4(a) above) argue in chapter 13 the case for the inclusion of more behavioural science in any core science education intended to match the needs and abilities of the majority of young people.

Having compared the conceptual and mathematical demands of different sciences:

(a) *The 'hard' sciences*
- Measurement
- Precision
- Functional relationships (1:1, or 3 or 4 variables at the most with a strict relationship)
- Deductive models tightly related to the data they explain (e.g. kinetic theory; electrons)

(b) *Social sciences and biology*
- Mean values
- Variation
- Correlation relationships
- Interaction between variables
- Questionnaires
- Interviews
- Problem of subjective bias
- Sampling, and generalization from a sample

The first tends to produce models that are atomistic and analytic: the second tends to holistic models.

Shayer and Adey go on to draw what they see to be the curriculum implications:

Traditional school science has drawn heavily from the left-hand list, and very little from the right. Yet, as was pointed out in the discussion of the mathematics connection all the methods in the right-hand list have a valid realisation 'in some recognisable form' accessible to concrete thinking. They are also capable of great sophistication without contradicting the insight obtainable by concrete thinking. Therefore on grounds of cognitive development alone there is a strong case for some new curriculum invention being drawn from the softer side of the spectrum.

There are three other good reasons for choosing activities and content from the 'soft' side.

(a) It offers the opportunity for a connection with mathematics to the benefit of both, and at a lower level than do the 'hard' sciences.
(b) The subject-matter of the social sciences and biology offers an approach to scientific thinking more in accord with the personal interests of most young girls and of those boys who at present choose against studying traditional sciences as soon as they can.
(c) related to (b). The methods of the social sciences relate scientific thinking more obviously to the issues of everyday life than do the hard sciences. To the future citizen this is a more direct reason for their study.

(Shayer and Adey, 1981)

Once again, however, we must beware of polarities. We can both make the 'hard' sciences accessible and relevant (e.g. via an applications focus) and include more than we currently do from the 'soft' sciences. This latter responsibility does not necessarily rest exclusively with science departments, a matter which is discussed further in Chapter 7c.

## Bibliography


APU, 1982, *Science in Schools Age 15*, Report No. 1 (HMSO, London)

ASE, 1984, *Rethinking Science?* (Association for Science Education, Hatfield)

ASE, 1984, *Rural Science – an Applied View of Science* (Association for Science Education, Hatfield)

ASE, in preparation, *Science and Technology in Society(SATIS)*, (Association for Science Education, Hatfield)

ASE/SCSST, 1985, *Experimenting with Industry* (Association for Science Education, Hatfield)

Bateman, R., and Lidstone, P., 1984, *Steps in Science*, 3 vols (Hutchinson, London)

DES and Welsh Office, 1985, *General Certificate of Secondary Education, The National Criteria: Science* (HMSO, London)

DES and Welsh Office, 1985, *Science 5–16: A Statement of Policy* (HMSO, London)

Driver, R., and Bell, B. (Principal Editors), 1984, *Children's Learning in Science Project (CLISP)*, (HMSO, London)

Fairbrother, R. W., 1984, (November) 'Examinations: An update' (pp 41–45), *Education in Science*, ASE

Hall, W., and Mowl, B., 1973, *Schools Council Integrated Science Project (SCISP)* (Longman, Harlow)

Holman, J., 'Science and Technology in Society – A New Initiative' (p. 44, 1985 (January)), *Education in Science*

Hull, R., and Adams, H., 1981, *Decisions in the Science Department* (Schools Council/ASE, London)

ILEA, 1978, *Insight to Science* (Longman, Harlow)

Ingle, R., and Jennings, A., 1981, *Science in Schools: Which Way Now?* (Studies in Education 8, Heinemann Educational Books for the Institute of Education, University of London)

Jarman, R., 1984, *Primary Science, Secondary Science: Some Issues at the Interface* (Secondary Science Curriculum Review, London)

Job, G. C., 1984 (November), 'The Certificate of Prevocational Education (CPVE)' pp 37 & 38, *Education in Science*, ASE

Kellington, S. (ed.), 1982, *Reading about Science*, 5 vols (Heinemann Educational Books, London)

Mee, A. J., Boyd, P., and Ritchie, D., 1980, *Science 2000*, formerly *Science for the 70's* (Heinemann Educational Books, London)

The Royal Society, 1981, *Biotechnology and Education* (The Royal Society, London)
Shayer, M., and Adey, P., 1981, *Towards a Science of Science Teaching* (Heinemann Educational Books, London)
Schofield, B. (Organiser & General Editor), 1979, *Nuffield Science 13–16* (Longman, Harlow)
Schools Council, 1979, *Open Science* (Hart Davis/Hutchinson, London)
John Taylor (Project Organizer), 1979, *Science at Work* (Longman, Harlow)

# 3 How is science taught and learnt?

**Ken Dobson**

- ★ The *developmental* theories of Piaget's work, the *construct* theory and the theory based on an understanding of the *dynamics* of groups should guide science teaching.
- ★ Group size, activities, rationale and motivation, interaction and involvement, and lesson type, should be considered in planning a lesson.
- ★ Writing, listening and talking are *all* part of learning.

This chapter is not so much about teaching as about learning. The primary task of the teacher is not to teach, but to ensure that students learn. For most readers, this will be a statement of the blindingly obvious, but in practice the statement 'I teach, therefore the student learns' is not as logically inevitable as we might hope and suppose. People can learn without teaching, and 'teaching' can certainly take place with no detectable learning to follow it, as we would all, with honesty, recognize. To devote a chapter to methods, styles and techniques of teaching without considering the modes and nature of learning would be to accept unstated assumptions about the way people learn and, perhaps, to fail to expose the mismatch that so easily occurs between what we are trying to achieve and the methods we use to achieve it.

Theories about the way people learn change with time: sometimes the change is so slow that we teachers do not actually notice it, at others it is so quick that we do not actually believe it. In any case, an unquantified but probably large proportion of teachers are so busy teaching (and doing all the other things that the school system expects from them) that they do not follow the research as closely as professional educationalists would like. There is evidence to suggest that, particularly in science teaching, the learning theories underpinning a course or method of teaching are not assimilated by teachers – either because the language in which they are written is not understood or because the theories conflict with day-to-day experience in the classroom (Olsen *et al*, 1980). Conceptual revolutions in teaching/learning science seem to occur at roughly 20-year intervals: the move towards 'active', practical science in the 1940s, 'discovery' methods in the 1960s and, in the 1980s . . . ? Piaget comes and goes, and comes again, Skinnerian programming, without and then with computers, progressive methods, team teaching, open plan schools, individualized learning, the sociological dimensions of learning and the 'hidden curriculum' . . . have left their detritus of worries and worksheets in all our filing cabinets. In practice, we just get on with it, choosing well-tried remedies for recurrent problems, being as capable as our students at accommodating wildly contradictory theories and choosing the one that seems to give the right answer at the time. Behind us, the massive inertia of the examining system chunters quietly away to itself, validating our human output with blind justice. The only justification for all this, of course, would be that it works. Unfortunately the accumulation of evidence suggests, increasingly strongly, that this eclectic, scatter gun approach is failing (ASE, 1979; DES, 1972; DES, 1981a). This is not too surprising, and is not necessarily a *fault on the part of teachers or schools.* We are experiencing a period of very rapid economic, social and industrial change, and almost any system that was successful in the late 1960s would be bound to require modification now. Our problem is to design, create and maintain a system of learning that can respond positively and actively to a state of seemingly continual change.

## Theories of learning

There is a story about a Gurkha soldier left hundreds of miles behind enemy lines as the British retreated from Burma in 1942. After several months he reappeared, emaciated, exhausted, but alive. How had he found his way across miles of trackless jungle, infested with wild animals and enemy soldiers? He had a map, he proudly replied, withdrawing from his pocket a tattered scrap of paper – a map, indeed, torn from an old diary, of the London Underground. We too have our maps of the learning mind, possibly more closely modelling the ground, but nonetheless requiring imaginative interpretation and a judicious mixture of faith and scepticism if they are to be useful. It also helps to have some idea of where we want to go, and where we are before we start.

There are a number of books and articles which ought to be read to gain a respectable and developed understanding of the learning models which are described in the following paragraphs. In order to give particular consideration to the issues that these models raise with regard to teaching, and to relate the issues to the constraints of time, resources and training within which practising teachers work, it is almost inevitable that the descriptions will be over-simplified.

Three landmarks stand out as main features to guide our teaching:

1 the *developmental* theories based upon Piaget's work;
2 the *construct* theory, which supposes that learners play a very active role in building a network of concepts;
3 the theory based on an understanding of the *dynamics* of groups and the ways in which pupils interact with each other and the teacher.

(Little credence is nowadays given to models of learning in which students passively absorb information and ideas from teachers who dole out suitably digestible pap in much the same way as vital fluids are drip-fed into comatose patients.)

### 1 Piaget : the development of the capacity for cognitive learning

Piaget wrote much, and much of what he wrote is difficult, obscure and certainly not written with the prime aim of being useful to practising teachers. It is also capable of being gravely misunderstood.

Briefly, as children get older, their ability to use more abstract ideas increases. Two main stages are recognized, characterized by the child's ability to undertake:

concrete operations; and/or
formal operations.
Concrete operations involve the child thinking through such tasks as:

classifying objects into two groups, e.g. those that float and those that sink;
recognizing simple cause-effect relationships, e.g. if you warm up the solutions the reaction goes faster;
handling directly experienced ideas (single variables) like force – but being confused by compound variables like pressure;
etc.

The ability to carry out formal operations tends to develop later (but see below). Examples of formal thinking include:

using the concept of density to explain why some things float in some liquids but not in others;
using a kinetic particle theory to explain why temperature affects reaction rate;
using the ideas of pressure as force per unit area, and of force being defined in terms of mass and acceleration;
etc. (Referred to in Shayer and Adey, 1981.)

The work of the Geneva psychologists (Piaget, Inhelder *et al.*) has been to describe what samples of children are able to do at different ages, and then from these observations to develop a model of what is going on inside children's heads as they do them. Two stages are not enough to be useful, and have been extended to five:

1 pre-operational;
2(a) early concrete;
2(b) late concrete;
3(a) early formal;
3(b) late formal.

Shayer and Adey (1981) use such a stage model in their readable, stimulating, useful and dangerous book *Towards a Science of Science Teaching*. It is useful because it stimulates us to take a close look at what we teach to a particular group of pupils, and it helps us to analyse whether or not our demands upon them are too heavy. The message is that we must, somehow, match what we teach to what our pupils are able to learn, and do this rationally, not by guesswork or because, traditionally, the syllabus always puts osmosis before digestion or atomic structure before acid–base reactions. The book is dangerous because we may fall into the temptation of using the authors' work as a recipe, thereby limiting what we should perhaps *try* to teach.

The 'taxonomies' in the book provide a do-it-yourself analysis scheme for

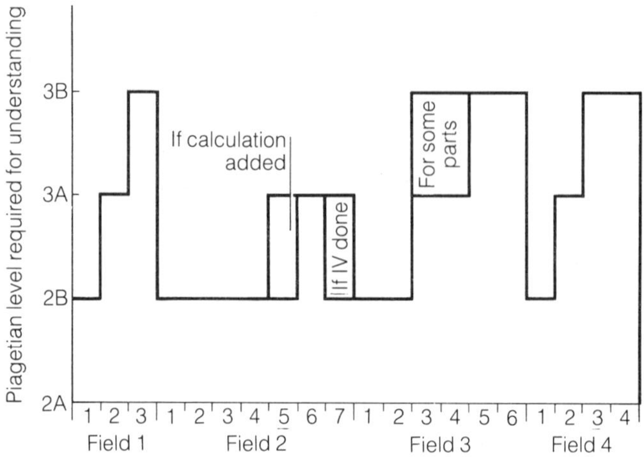


FIG. 3.1 **Level of thinking required by different topics in NSS 'Harnessing Energy'.** (From Shayer and Adey, 1981)

syllabuses in the three main sciences, allowing classification into one of the five stages listed above.

An example of the results of such an analysis is shown in Figure 3.1, which shows the levels of thinking required of students by the Nuffield Secondary Science Theme 'Harnessing Energy'.

The authors' research provides a guide to the concepts that one might expect average students to operate with at various ages, and it also gives the range of expected performance at a particular age. For example, the 'Range of ability in an "average" class' at various ages was found to be as shown in the table below.

**Range of ability in an 'average' class**

| *Stage* | *Age* / *Form* / *Grade* | *11+* / *1* / *6* | *13+* / *3* / *8* | *15+* / *5* / *10* |
|---|---|---|---|---|
| < 2A | | 2 | 0·5 | 0 |
| 2A and 2A/B | | 15 | 7 | 3 |
| 2B and 2B/3A | | 11 | 17 | 17 |
| 3A | | 2 | 4 | 6 |
| 3B | | 0 | 1·5 | 4 |

(From Shayer and Adey, 1981.)

This is where, as teachers, we are well advised to be careful. We must bear in mind the following:

(a) *There is no such thing as an average youngster.* Young people not only develop at different rates but a given individual is also, infuriatingly perhaps, likely to develop in different cognitive directions at different rates. Some students may be thinking quite formally in, say, biology or mathematics, but are stubbornly concrete in physics.

(b) *Our perception (or guess) of the youngster's stage of development could be wrong.* A student may lack confidence, or the 'right' words – or find the whole thing rather boring. We are not, in general, very good at assessing exactly how students think or why they give the wrong answer.

(c) *An individual's performance is variable.* Although capable of formal operations at a given level, an individual may by choice or by default deal with a particular problem in much more concrete terms.

Examples of the descriptive taxonomy that Shayer and Adey (1981) use are as follows:

**Example 1**
Oxidation and reduction

*2A early concrete*
Pure oxygen makes things burn more brightly than air itself.

*2B late concrete*
Carbon can reduce metal-oxides to metal. Oxygen can oxidise a metal. Metals can be placed in a reactivity series by their speed and vigour of burning.

*3A early formal*
Have a model of a chemical reaction, conserving the elements, so can predict that when carbon or a reactive metal reduces an oxide, carbon dioxide or a metal oxide must be produced. From a set of competition reactions can work out a reactivity series, and from a reactivity series can predict which reductions will succeed. Oxidation is increase of oxygen or other reactive non-metal.

*3B late formal*
Can appreciate that there are different theories or models of oxidation/reduction and can critically compare them. Can use model of reaction even where what they *see* is paradoxical e.g. magnesium 'burning' in steam – gas produced *must* be hydrogen. Ready for a valency change or bond-forming account of oxidation.

**Example 2**
Use of models

*1 pre-operational*
Not possible

*2A early concrete*
*Concrete modelling* is the organisation of reality by seriation or classification or 1:1

correspondence. At this level simple comparisons only, and elementary causes — '*this* opposes *that*'. Unstructured notions such as 'pureness'.

*2B late concrete*
Modelling by seriation extends to any linear scale. 'Model' now has dictionary definition of simplified 1:1 correspondence model (skeleton; gearbox, etc.).

*3A early formal*
*Formal modelling* is the indirect interpretation of reality by deductive comparison from a postulated system with its own rules. At this level student usually needs guidance in deducing how a system with several variables may behave. Unless quantitative relationship is simple (as with 'caloric' model of heat transfer, or 'pressure' as $F/A$) deduction is likely to be qualitative only (exchange reactions with metals and oxides). Model is taken as true, not hypothesis, so this level does not allow critical comparison of alternative formal models.

*3B late formal*
Can actively search for an explanatory model, extend one that is given, and compare alternative models for how they account for the same data. Since proportional thinking is readily available (relating two independent variables to each other) can formulate quantitative deductions from the model, and reflect on the relations between the variables.

**Example 3** Respiration, Nutrition and Transport.

**2A early concrete** Food gives energy.
Heart as a pump (from experience of own pulse). Blood flows to parts of body and to lungs delivering and collecting.

**2B late concrete** Respiration provides air (oxygen) so food can be used/broken down to give energy. The heart and lungs are a circulation system to facilitate this. Transport of food in plants: experiment of ringing, cutting phloem vessels, and so simple associative relation between phloem and transport.

**3A early formal** Gas transport in plants. Diffusion appreciated analytically: simultaneous $O_2/CO_2$ movement across membranes in lungs, etc. Efficiency of capillaries in distribution to cells. Pressure as force per unit area, and valve function in terms of pressure differentials. Transpiration pull in terms of evaporation causing water to be pulled up. Functional relationship between capillaries, cells, lymph and diffusion. Osmosis as a process occurring between solutions of different strengths.

**3B late formal** Homeostasis. Plasmolysis and turgidity. Extension of model of semi-permeable membrane to root hair and osmotic unit. The need for transport systems in terms of the ratio of volume to surface area of body. Model of osmosis as differential vapour pressure or 'activity' of solvent.
(From Shayer and Adey, 1981.)

An exercise based on these examples to analyse the demands made by some APU questions is given below (p. 16).

(d) *Changing our minds about things.* Sometimes a more primitive concept (of 'weight', 'heat', 'cold', 'insect') is so powerfully held that a logical refutation of what we feel is right is quite hard to believe, even though we accept and understand the logic. We may quite happily use such advanced ideas for the purpose of passing examinations but base our normal lives and thinking on the models we have developed very early in life. Even highly educated physicists find it hard to 'believe' relativity or wave-particle duality.

The lesson to be learned from Piagetians is, however, a vital one: first be aware of the cognitive demands a course is making of students, then plan the teaching strategy and tactics accordingly. This advice is reinforced by the second main map-makers of learning, the *personal construct* school.

## 2 Constructivist psychology: children create their own maps and theories of the world

The building blocks of cognitive thinking in science – energy, cause-and-effect relations, cells, heat, force, pressure, chemical change, burning, growth etc. lie all around us in our infancy. Incapable as children might be, according to Piagetian theory, to cope with the high level demands a proper understanding and use of these ideas requires, they cannot avoid hearing the words and experiencing the effects that they are meant to describe or explain. They read, watch television, listen to or overhear older children, parents and teachers talking. They need to make sense of their environment, not necessarily to explain it of course, but certainly to use it to their advantage. Children engage their minds very actively in this process, make their own connections between experiences and the words other people are teaching them to use, and they create their own networks of relationships and patterns of thinking. Children are not passive absorbers, but active constructors: this seems to be how the brain itself works (Gregory, 1981, p. 312, describes the idea of 'kinetic intelligence'). Children do not just sit there, waiting until they are old enough to understand electric current 'properly', they get on with it as best they can, constructing an internally consistent system that allows them to deal with torches, bicycle dynamos, transistor radios, computers, televisions – even the circuit boards they find in schools – in what is generally a quite successful manner. They learn to make things work, maybe even to repair them when they go wrong. They develop an *operational* understanding of what is going on – 'When I do this, it does that . . .', and they may not feel the need to *explain* why it does this. If some interfering adult, usually a teacher, asks for an explanation they will make an attempt. They may have thought about it already but, if they have not, being quite imaginative, they may make it up on the spot. If told that their explanations are wrong, that 'volts' do not actually 'go through' the circuit, or that 'amps' do not get used up in the bulb, they will agree but then forget, because such corrections are not necessary to their operational handling of electricity in everyday life. As they get older they may develop a more serious interest in physics and start getting things 'right' – their 'construct system' becomes capable of explaining a wider variety of experience – or they may not. They may instead develop *two* systems of explanation – one for themselves to be used in solving 'real life' problems, the other to be used for 'satisfying the examiners'.

Research arising from the work of the Assessment of Performance Unit (APU) suggests that a large majority of youngsters at age 15 adopt the first of these alternatives, holding firmly to the ideas they first thought of at a much earlier age. It is a sobering thought that even for those students studying the subject, four years of physics teaching is not enough to eradicate some incorrect ideas about very basic topics in electricity, with only about one-third correctly predicting the brightness of bulbs in a series circuit (Gott, 1985, p. 26 et seq.)

Such findings will have come as no great surprise to the researchers who have studied how and what youngsters really think about basic concepts in science (or indeed, I suspect, to many CSE and O-level examiners!). Current research in the UK into these 'alternative frameworks' that students use to make sense of experience is accessible to teachers in the publications of the Children's Learning in Science Project, based at the University of Leeds, and in Rosalind Driver's (1983) book *The Pupil as Scientist*?

Much of the research has been done on youngster's understanding of physics concepts, but confused or downright incorrect ideas about 'animals', 'insects', 'adaptation', 'burning', 'dissolving' are remarkably prevalent and persistent. (See Bell *et al.*, 1984)

An interesting exercise is to ask a class what they actually think is happening in an everyday (or basic laboratory) situation. This is best done (unless your class is very well trained in philosophical discourse) as an off-the-cuff incidental activity, only marginally related to what they perceive as the main point of the lesson. For example:

After a lesson plotting the current–voltage curve for a lamp, ask 'Why does electricity make a lamp filament hot?'

*or*

After almost any lesson in biology, ask 'What animals live in trees (or in the sea)?'

*or*

After a lesson in chemistry, ask 'What do you think goes on when a match is lit?'

The questions opposite were set by the Assessment of Performance Unit as part of their survey of science performance of students at age 15:

Four sealed tubes were set up as shown below using water-living plants and animals. The experiment was left for twelve hours.

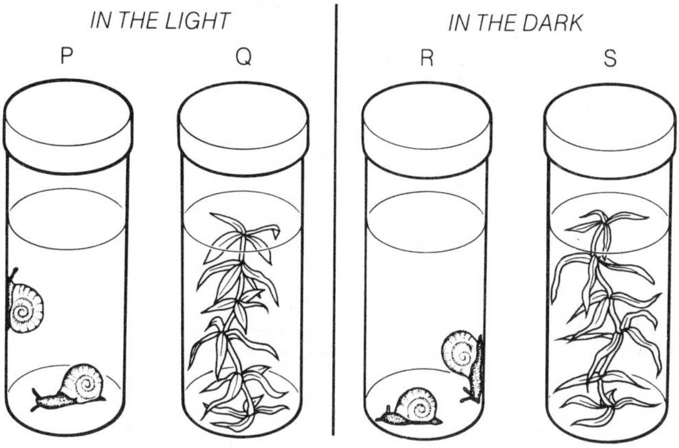


a) At the end of the experiment, in which of the following tubes would you expect there to be the least amount of carbon dioxide in the water?

(Tick one box.)

☐ A Tube P

☐ B Tube Q

☐ C Tube R

☐ D Tube S

☐ E All tubes the same

b) Give reasons for your choice.

. . . . . . . . . . . . . . . . . . . . . . . . . . . . . . . . . . . .

. . . . . . . . . . . . . . . . . . . . . . . . . . . . . . . . . . . .

. . . . . . . . . . . . . . . . . . . . . . . . . . . . . . . . . . . .

. . . . . . . . . . . . . . . . . . . . . . . . . . . . . . . . . . . .

(From APU, 1984, p. 170, Example 8.8 'Sealed Tubes'.)

• Estimate the percentage of correct choices made by:
15 year old students studying biology;
15 year old students not studying biology.

• Which of the wrong answers is likely to be most popular?

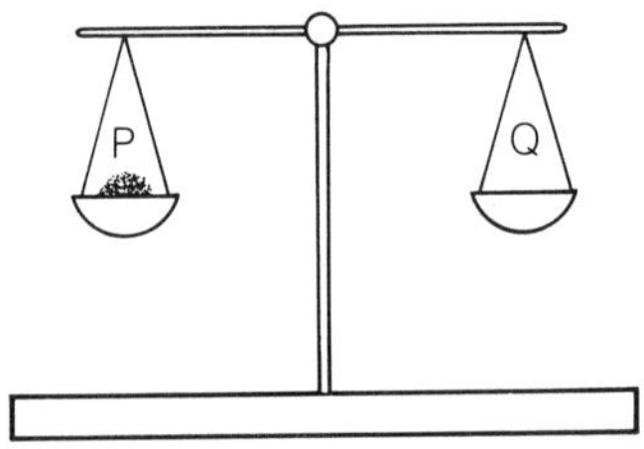


A small amount of iron wool was placed on pan P, and weights were added to pan Q to balance the scales.

The iron wool was then removed and heated in air.

It formed a black powder which was carefully collected and returned to pan P.

What do you expect to happen to pan P?

Explain the reason for your answer.

. . . . . . . . . . . . . . . . . . . . . . . . . . . . . . . . . . . . . . .

. . . . . . . . . . . . . . . . . . . . . . . . . . . . . . . . . . . . . . .

. . . . . . . . . . . . . . . . . . . . . . . . . . . . . . . . . . . . . . .

. . . . . . . . . . . . . . . . . . . . . . . . . . . . . . . . . . . . . . .

. . . . . . . . . . . . . . . . . . . . . . . . . . . . . . . . . . . . . . .

(From APU, 1984, p. 157, Example 8.4 'Iron Wool'.)

• Estimate the percentage of correct choices made by:
15 year old students studying chemistry;
15 year old students not studying chemistry.

• Which of the wrong answers is likely to be most popular?

After many experiments, scientists now think that:
all things are made of small particles
these particles move in all directions
temperature affects the speed they move
they exert forces on each other

Use any of these ideas to help answer the following question:
A football is pumped up hard during the day when it is warm. In the evening when the temperature falls, the football does not feel so hard.
How does this happen? (Assume the football does not leak.)
(From APU, 1984, p. 50, Example 8.3 'Soft Ball'.)

• Estimate the percentage of correct choices made by:
15 year old students studying physics;
15 year old students not studying physics.

• Which of the wrong answers is likely to be most popular?

• The percentages 'getting it right' are given at the end of the chapter. Do the results surprise you? Why were students getting it wrong? What implications does this have for the teaching of these topics? Should teachers:
(a) improve the teaching of the topic?
(b) accept that a substantial number of students of this age cannot grasp the concepts involved and alter syllabuses accordingly?
(c) reduce the emphasis on explanations in science in favour of (i) knowing facts or (ii) solving real problems?
(d) make changes involving some combination of the above?
(e) do nothing about it, because this is the way things are?
It instructive to use the Shayer and Adey taxonomies to analyse the conceptual demands made of students by the APU questions. It is necessary to refer very closely to the book itself, of course.

• Use the descriptions of conceptual levels to determine the *highest* level of demand for each question, if it is to be answered correctly.
Shayer and Adey (1981) state that the following proportions of British 15 year olds are at or above the cognitive levels shown:
3B (late formal): 10%
3A (early formal): 30%
2B (late concrete): 85%
2A (early concrete): 100%
(Approximate percentages, based on *op. cit.*, fig. 2.1, p. 9)

• Does your analysis of the cognitive demands, used with the above figures, correlate at all with the actual proportions of 15 year olds 'getting the right answer'? (See results at end of chapter.)

Research by professional academics, backed up by teachers' insights and experience – made deeper perhaps by the application of some research methods to their own students' learning – allow a more planned and scientific approach to teaching. This is discussed more fully below.

The question for us as teachers is 'What can we do about it?' The constraints seem to be:

(a) Students will only accept 'correct' ideas if they help them to make more sense of what they know;
(b) the students themselves decide whether or not it does make more sense;
(c) students are as strongly influenced by the 'climate of opinion' in their peer group as they are by laboratory experiments or by teachers' explanations, if not more so.

The inferences we might make about teaching style from all this are quite radical, as indeed they might be about what should reasonably be taught to students.

## 3 Learning as a social activity: group dynamics

Human beings are sociable creatures and while students may construct their own working model of the world, the process of construction occurs as a communal activity in the social context of family, gang, teaching group, or Brownie pack etc. The respect or acceptance of the group is a major factor in motivating youngsters' actions as they seek a role to play in whatever group they happen to be in at the time, and they tend to be quite uncomfortable if this role is not clear, or even worse, not accepted or approved. Young people become adept at conforming to a role, and are quite capable of playing different roles in different contexts: the shy second child in a lively family may be the clown of the geography class and the responsible, determined left guard of the netball team. Teachers are usually quite sensitive to the group dynamics of a class, aware of the interactions between students, who the leaders are and who are the followers, or the rivals and rebels. We are becoming more aware of the strong and often dubious pressures to conform to sex roles. It is all this that makes any group of people interesting to observe and work with. However, it is rare to find teaching styles basing themselves on these insights, other than as methods of *control* with the main aim of getting students to conform to a fairly passive learning pattern. It is only comparatively recently that schools have been criticized for emphasizing individual work at the expense of the collaborative working in groups that is the common practice in shops, factories, offices and even in university laboratories. The 'hidden curriculum' of feelings and attitudes, engendered as much as anything by the ways in which groups of pupils – and teachers – are organized, spoken to, listened to, marshalled and administered, is hidden because it is unplanned and generally unrecognized. The basic rules that have to be followed for people to give of their best tend to be lost in the rush to complete tasks – finish the syllabus, get the half-term reports done, produce a 'workable' timetable, make sure that the experiment works. The danger here is again one of mismatch: between the way we do things and the point of doing them at all. We aim, for example, to teach students that science is essentially a process of discovery. We then put so much into the syllabus for students to 'discover' that we end up 'telling' them instead.

The lesson here is that we must base the teaching methods we use on the available knowledge of the social groupings in which pupils work best. Looking ahead to what the young people are going to have to do after they leave school, we should also, as one of the prime aims of teaching, encourage students to organize their own learning. If working collaboratively in groups – designing, problem solving, investigating, preparing reports – is recognized to be not only a good way of learning but also an activity for which it is worth developing skills, then we must consider structuring our classes and activities to ensure that it happens. The implication of this for the content and assessment of school science is discussed in Chapters 2 and 4. The emphasis on the processes of learning as compared with the content of what is to be learned is an important part of some current initiatives in education (CPVE and TVEI, for example), in which students as young as 14 play a part in planning their own courses and in evaluating the course and their own progress (see Chapter 7 Section (e)).

## Purposes of learning

Ultimately, a theory of learning should guide us to ensure better learning for all. However, we also have questions about why people should learn *this* rather than *that*. But the question is a dual one – 'Why should I learn that...?' and 'Why should (the system) want me to learn that?' This is the area of curriculum design in which current orthodoxy, as laid down by the National Criteria, is again that process is at least as important as content and that the outcomes of learning science are more than the recall of factual knowledge or basic laboratory skills. The listed aims of a school science course include:

enabling pupils to become confident citizens in a technological world;
stimulating curiosity, interest and enjoyment in science;
promoting an awareness that the study and practice of science are cooperative ... activities. (DES and Welsh Office, 1985)

Here we are dealing with *attitudes* and *feelings*, which are obligatory and spelt out with some clarity. It remains to be seen whether students who acquire such attitudes are suitably rewarded by assessment schemes.

Looking at this more generally, if teachers are not satisfied that what they are teaching is worthwhile, then they are not likely to do it very well and, similarly, if students are dissatisfied with what they are expected to learn, they will be equally unsuccessful.

## The implications for teaching

The main lesson to be learned from this welter of theory and informed criticism is that *we must know the students*. The first and continual task of the teacher is to listen to what the students say and observe what they do. Only then can we design our teaching tactics to ensure and enhance learning. Thus a teaching style which consists mainly of the teacher talking to classes of (officially) silent students is likely to be unsuccessful, if only because the teacher is working so hard at *presenting* the material and *controlling* the class that too little attention can be given to what the students are learning and how they are thinking. Of course, there are occasions when a lecture-demonstration is by far the best way to teach a particular aspect of a topic – for example, a particularly dangerous or spectacular experiment where a great deal of practical skill is required, or in a summarizing or theme-setting lesson where great pedagogical skill is required. The central message is that teachers must develop the capacity to deploy a variety of teaching methods and the expertise to choose the appropriate method for the task in hand. None of the methods described are new. Some have been used too little and others too much, largely because the purpose of most lessons has dictated one main style of teaching. This purpose has been the dissemination of fact, and the chosen methods, possibly the most appropriate, have been teacher-dominated strategies such as the lecture-demonstration or the closely-controlled practical. Small-group discussions, team projects, investigative or exploratory activities, however potentially rewarding for students and teacher in terms of enjoyment and an acquisition of a genuine understanding of the principles of scientific methods, have apparently not been rewarded by the examination system. Such methods have been reserved for eccentric teachers and perhaps for particularly bright students on the one hand, or for 'non-examinable' students on the other. With necessary realism teachers choose the teaching strategies that produce the best results for the bulk of the students, and in this sense the 'results' that count are examination results.

## The problems of teaching science

These are of two kinds. The first kind is important, recurrent and endemic: it is to do with class control and organization, what to do with problem students, how to organize equipment, set and mark homework and tests, how to introduce new concepts and ensure that old ones have not been forgotten. These problems, like the poor and the weather, are always with us. The second kind resembles major changes of climate: those which occur, or are newly recognized having been there all the time as a result of continuous change in the expectations of students and of society at large. It is to be hoped that the following analysis will be of help in solving both kinds of problem. The climatic concerns (in 1985) about science teaching, although not entirely restricted to science, may be summarized as follows:

1 Examination syllabuses are overloaded in content, rely too much on learning by rote and undervalue the skills and processes of science.
2 Science courses (and lessons) are perceived by students as not closely relevant to their lives.
3 Too few students study a balanced science course.
4 Far fewer girls than boys study physical science.
5 Science is 'too hard', compared with other examination subjects at 16+.
6 Learning is discouraged by an assessment (examination) system that highlights failure rather than success.

These criticisms have been made over a number of years and are to be found set out in detail in ASE (1979), DES (1982) and DES (1981a). As classroom teachers we may not be responsible for the defects of the system, but we are certainly part of it, and we should be fully capable of playing a part in any solutions. Indeed, when there is such pressure for change it is particularly important that practitioners should be fully involved in producing and monitoring suggested improvements. The implications are clear. Each school must have a definite machinery for consultation and for the proper analysis of problems, as they affect both the school as a whole and individual departments within it. There must also be adequate and well co-ordinated systems for making major changes which are both acceptable and practical. If the DES (1985) policy statement *Science 5–16: A Statement of Policy*, promotes the practical consequences it envisages – 'science for all', an increase in the process and skill components of the science curriculum, a decrease in content, increased in-school assessment including hitherto non-assessed activities – we shall experience very different classroom weather from that which most of us enjoy or contend with at present.

To illustrate this point, a fairly typical lesson plan at present might be:

*Aim*: to show that acceleration is proportional to applied force.
*Equipment*: trolleys, ticker-timers etc., trolley boards, elastic 'pulls'.
*Timing of activities*:
0–10 min: Teacher – setting and discussing the problem, demonstrating how to use equipment, emphasizing need for constant pulls and sloping the board to 'compensate for friction'.
10–50 min: Students – carrying out experiment, with help from teacher, obtaining tape charts, cutting them into 'ten-ticks' etc.
50–55 min: Clearing up.
55–65 min: Discussion of results, leading to 'acceleration is proportional to force'.
*Homework*: Write-up of experiment, completing any calculations and stating clearly what the experiment showed.

A more 'student-determined' lesson in the 'new' mode might run as follows:

*Aim*: to introduce the concepts of speed, mass, force, acceleration and *use them* to give opportunities for the processes of *data search* and *designing experiments, small-group discussion, planning and making a report for other pupils.*

*Equipment*: car magazines with data giving maximum speed, acceleration, engine size etc. for a variety of models and/or a computer data base of similar information; access to trolleys, ticker-timers, elastic bands, model cars, a bicycle, poster paper, pens etc.; 'fact sheets' on how to use ticker-timer, computer data base program etc.

*Timing of Activities*:

0–10 min : Teacher – setting and discussing the problem 'What decides how fast a car can go?'; informing students what equipment and data is available; organizing or accepting working groups and agreeing tasks; emphasizing importance of 'report back' session; agreeing or deciding how much time is available for tasks (e.g. one or more lessons).

10–60 min: students – group work on self-selected tasks relevant to lesson aim, helped by teacher when requested; teacher – makes assessment (according to agreed criteria – see the chapter on 'Assessment') of students' performance in, say, 'working as a member of a group', 'ability to use a computer data base program'; teacher – makes decision whether or not a short 'progress report' by groups is needed, perhaps to ensure that tasks do not overlap too strongly. Otherwise . . .

60–65 min: Clearing up.

*Homework*: Each student to make brief notes for his/her own use of what has been done so far, line of attack for next lesson, any special tasks group shares among its members.

It is fairly obvious that the second lesson will have much less predictable activities and outcomes than the first. The requirements of the teacher in terms of assessment are also different, for in the second case assessment is done as the lesson is taking place, rather than in the comparative calm of the prep room over a pile of books. There are implications too for the availability of equipment – in the second lesson it may not be easy to predict what a given group of students might require. Such uncertainty implies the need for a system which allows swift access to a wide range of equipment, thereby preventing student frustration and a loss of time. In the cognitive sense, students begin each of these lessons with much the same problem, but in the more open-ended style they will tend to 'spread', as one group goes for 'friction and drag' and another for 'engine size and weight of car'. In the first type of lesson, the cognitive *end-point* is both tightly defined and under the control of the teacher. The experimental skills expected from students in this lesson are also clearly identified and it is relatively easy to assess students' competence by the results.

## Menus of learning

Some of the kinds of activity, class organization and student interactions that we might consider using are listed in Tables 3.1 to 3.4.

TABLE 3.1 **Groupings**

1 Whole class as a social group: e.g. lecture/demonstration, class discussion, question and answer session, brainstorming.
2. Whole class as a collection of individuals or pairs: e.g. 'class work', undifferentiated worksheet, test, reading from same textbook, standard practicals in pairs etc.
3 Group work: e.g. a 'circus' of experiments or other activities, planning and carrying out group projects or investigations, small group discussion etc.
4 Individualized learning: e.g. self-chosen tasks, individualized worksheets, complex learning programmes.

TABLE 3.2 **Activities**

1 Listening.
2 Answering teacher's questions.
3 Controlled writing (e.g. answering questions, describing experiments).
4 Practical (lab) work, following instructions (with strong guidance).
5 Practical (lab) work, following instructions (with looser guidance, plan given without detailed step-by-step instructions).
6 Designing experiments – for a given end.
7 Designing experiments – for pupil-determined ends.
8 Investigating/exploring (i) practical (ii) theoretical (involving a complex of activities and skills from the ones listed).
9 Looking things up ('data search' – books, magazines etc.), question-and-answer sessions with teachers or others, using computer data bases.
10 Small group discussion.
11 Reporting back – as part of a group (implies the preparation for this e.g. posters, ohp transparencies, notes etc.).
12 Writing individual reports.
13 Reading – for pleasure, for background, to follow an argument or for the development of an idea.
14 Computer assisted learning.
15 Calculating, computing.
16 Quizzes, competitions, crosswords.
17 Students teaching students.
18 Formalized debates.
19 Taking part in learning games, in role play, in simulations.

TABLE 3.3 **Rationale and motivation**

20 Teacher-determined
21 Student-determined
22 Task-determined
23 Socially determined

TABLE 3.4 **Interaction and involvement**

1 Student–student
2 Student–teacher
3 Student–environment (e.g. equipment, books, computers, TV, radio)
4 Student–AOTT ('adult other than teacher'!)

TABLE 3.5 **Lesson types**

1 The standard lesson
2 A circus of activities
3 The lecture/demonstration
4 Investigating/exploring/problem solving
5 Reporting-back sessions
6 Individualized/small group learning
7 The team-taught lesson

*Any given lesson might consist of a mixture of these

## Using the menu

Highly trained, professional teachers, working in a well equipped school and department, will have the means and skill to deploy any and all of the listed techniques and groupings as best suited to the students, the material to be taught and the existing circumstances. Most of us, no doubt, fall short of this ideal standard, but an important task of a head of department, with the help of the LEA's in-service training programme, would be to extend the range of expertise of the members of a school science department.

Some of the menu items are standard fare, others more 'nouvelle cuisine' and need elaboration.

### Tables 3.3 and 3.4

There is evidence that teachers talk rather a lot in lessons, that the bulk of 'official' communications are between teacher and student and that these exchanges are unbalanced, so that teachers ask long questions and receive short answers, or are asked short questions and give lengthy answers. If students are to become *independent learners*, then it is wise to foster the idea that teachers are not the only available source of knowledge or motivation. Students might be encouraged to learn from other pupils who already know something, or who can act as a sounding board for ideas, or experience circumstances where the prime motivation for taking part in a learning activity is the desire to complete a task for its own sake (e.g. learning how to wire a plug or setting up a balanced aquarium), rather than to gain the approval of the teacher. Tables 3.3 and 3.4 go together because motivation and involvement are so closely linked.

Looking at students working in the classrom or laboratory, we might ask ourselves *why* they are working. Would they stop learning if the teacher stopped

Concentrate upon one group of three or four students and observe how much they rely for learning on the agencies listed.

If the results of such a survey show a heavy dependence on just one or two sources of motivation, information or approval, for example, then the range and variety of activities and groupings should be reconsidered.

There is indeed a wealth of choice facing teachers, and it would be an instructive – and possibly a chastening task to pause here and summarize the last ten lessons you gave to a particular class, using the above tables to list the variety of groupings and activities used.

**Self-evaluation**
Analyse the lessons you have given to a particular class during the past month. Award yourself points as follows:
Table 3.1 For each type of grouping used – 2 points
Table 3.2 For each kind of activity used – 1 point
Add up your total score. The maximum is 27. If your score is:
less than 8, check the back row – a few may not simply be asleep but have died of boredom;
8 to 14, most pupils would have been awake most of the time;
14 to 20, very interesting! Check that the technicians are not applying for jobs elsewhere;
more than 20, pupils may need doses of glucose or some other kind of stimulant if they are to cope with the next lesson.

'pushing' or rewarding their efforts? Has the individual student been able to choose what is to be learned, or how to set about it? Does a given student join in the work as a result of group pressure, of needing to be a member of a team? Has the subject itself presented a problem or opportunity that catches the imagination? It may be easier to answer these questions after analysing activities using Table 3.4.

Of course, there is a sensible balance of activities and groupings somewhere between the utterly boring and predictable, and a frantic hyperactivity that is as likely to unsettle pupils as to stimulate them to participatory learning.

## Table 3.5: lesson types

**1** *The standard lesson* may not be as common as it once was, but is still likely to form the bulk of a student's diet in a science course. It will consist, in classical style, of a beginning, a middle and an end. Here is an example, discussed more fully in Dobson (1979).

| | *Activity* | *Time (min)* | *Pupil concentration* |
|---|---|---|---|
| 1 | Arrival and settling in | 5 | low |
| 2 | Teacher introduces lesson | 5 to 10 | initially high |
| 3 | Collecting apparatus | 2 to 5 | low |
| 4 | Setting-up apparatus, doing experiment, ancillary reading and writing | 15 to 40 | variable; pupils are able to pace themselves, teacher works with small groups |
| 5 | Clearing up apparatus | 5 | low |
| 6(a) | Class discussion | 5 to 10 | high |
| 6(b) | (Pupils return to 'writing places' if collected together for the discussion) | 2 | low |
| 7 | Summary of discussion or homework questions written down | 5 to 10 | high |

The 'meat' of the lesson is what occurs in activity number 4, and it is here that variations of lesson-type, appropriate to the topic and the class-grouping will occur. Unless the experimental work is completely open-ended there will have to be a summary of the procedure available for reference during the lesson on the blackboard (it may be written as the apparatus is collected), on worksheets or an overhead projector.

(Dobson, 1979, p. 22)

Its advantages are that all students are doing much the same thing at the same time so that they encounter common problems and the teacher can more easily help overcome them. Content and activities if well matched to the abilities of the class can create the feeling of progress and success. The timing of the various activities is important, and less able students are likely to need a greater variety of activities, each lasting for a shorter period of time. The teacher has the responsibility of ensuring that the lesson content has been assimilated by all the students (within reason!), and the summary at the end, perhaps produced by question-and-answer, is meant to ensure this.

**2** *A circus of activities* involves setting up a variety of experiments or activities, often around a common theme (energy changes, observing animal behaviour, making observations of a display of chemicals etc.), and students are expected to move from one 'station' to the next. Such an approach needs careful planning and is usually controlled by using worksheets or workcards. (See many examples in the Nuffield Secondary Science scheme.) Circuses make for active lessons, but can be hard on teachers and technicians if too many things break down at the same time!

**3** *The lecture/demonstration* is more straightforwardly didactic and is not necessarily the worse for that. It can be the science teacher's version of telling a story and, like any good story, needs a good beginning, a satisfying if not a surprising end, and in between a clear story line full of incident, humour and excitement matched to the age and experience of the audience. It is hard to do this well (eight times a day!) and needs real and regular practice. Some teachers are naturally more adept at this than others, but all should have a few such lessons in their repertoire. From time to time we can fall back on the professionals and use film, video or an outside lecturer. Such lessons can be splendidly stimulating (or, paradoxically, relaxing: 'Don't make us do any work today, sir' – 'Why don't you just teach us something, Miss?'). Lecture demonstration lessons, well prepared and perhaps delivered by the team might figure at the beginning or end of a team-teaching scheme.

**4** A lesson based on *investigating, exploring or problem solving* is obviously open-ended and may be unpredictable in terms of the time and materials required and the final outcomes of the activity. Problem solving may be more manageable to begin with, since all students can be given the same task to perform using the same materials (as in the various kinds of 'egg race' – see *Ideas for Egg Races*, 1983). Students have a choice of methods, but not of task. However, once the novelty has worn off, only the dedicated puzzle-book buyers will be captivated. More natural problems are likely to occur in open-ended investigations or explorations on topics, or aspects of a topic, chosen by the students themselves. The starting point may be a brief question – 'What decides how fast a car can go?', 'What is a will-of-the-wisp?', 'How do you make strong concrete?', 'Why are some people better at sports than others?' and so on. Such investigations may be theoretical (looking things up, working things out), experimental, or a mixture of both. They may be completed in a lesson or take one or two weeks. They also bring problems for the teacher – of management, of equipment and safety, of assessment, to name but a few. It seems likely that such activities will feature more strongly in future science courses than they do at present.

**5** *Reporting back* to other students is seen as a valuable activity not only because it reinforces and internalizes learning but also because it develops skills of organization and language that have tended to be neglected in traditional science schemes. It will naturally follow an investigation sequence in which different groups consider different aspects of a problem or topic and then present their findings to the rest of the class. This can be done with the presenting group 'out in front' sharing the task of explaining, describing and demonstrating, so giving further opportunities for planning and design and encouraging the collaborative skills required for effective teamwork. The rest of the class listens, takes notes and is expected to ask questions. Being a presenter is quite a strain for some students, while others need the imposition of strict time limits. Time indeed may be a problem in this activity, as a large class may need to spend more time in reporting back than was spent on the original investigation.

A less exposing (for shy students) and quicker method is the 'poster session', in which each group of students sets up a stand (with posters, notebooks, graphs, a working experiment) and takes it in turns to man it. Half the group stays at the display to explain it, the other half, notebooks in hand, act as a perambulating audience. They exchange roles half way through the lesson.

**6** *Individualized or small group learning*, and

**7** *Team teaching* often go together, but of course need not. Team teaching may be used to solve some of the problems associated with teaching an integrated science course, in that different teachers can develop expertise at teaching different topics in the course, thereby saving preparation time and effort. Coordination of the team is needed to ensure that all students cover the required topics and that interchanges between classes and teachers take place smoothly. In an individualized learning programme the teachers may rarely teach a class as a whole and act instead as consultants, stimulators, evaluators and providers of suitable resources within their speciality. Open plan school design assumes that this is the main mode of learning. Programmed learning using teaching-machines or programmed-texts are not often seen nowadays, but computer-assisted or computer-controlled learning may yet add richly to the future student diet. Information about computer-assisted learning may be obtained from the Computers in the Curriculum Project (Chelsea College, University of London, 552 Kings Road, London SW10).

What rules should we apply in making a selection from such a rich menu? Obviously, whatever is chosen has to be digestible, by both teacher and student, and some tastes take time, and palate training, to be acquired. Without pushing this analogy too far it might be generally agreed that a continuous diet of just the one main dish is not only monotonous but unlikely to be nourishing.

Groupings, activities, interactions and motivations combine to form the *texture* of learning. Variation may be introduced merely to avoid boredom (of teacher as well as student), but that is not the only reason. As is pointed out in Chapter 4, broad syllabus aims are ultimately translated, more or less reliably, into the hard concrete of examination questions. But just as syllabus content is changing, broadening the term to include the skills, processes and attitudes listed, so are the means of assessment. Examination questions, of the kind with which we are still so familiar, perhaps the ideal vehicle for testing the acquisition of factual knowledge, fare less well when called upon to test the higher (Bloomian) attributes of application, analysis and synthesis. That they have been called upon to do so for so many years is not because it was considered that they are good at doing so but because they seemed the only means available. The effect of this upon teaching – and learning – science has been to emphasize the acquisition and more or less automatic regurgitation of fact rather than the skills associated with their acquisition or use. The move toward the recognition in assesment procedure of different competencies frees (or compels) the teacher and learner to consider them more deeply. Thus the main point of a particular lesson or group of lessons about 'machines' may not be the acquisition of facts, directed towards questions such as:

> Draw a diagram of a spanner and mark on it the positions of *load*, *effort*, *fulcrum*.

Instead, the spanner – among other machines – may be an optional item in a lesson the main point of which is *using machines as a vehicle* for a problem-solving exercise. Then the assessment would be of a student's skills in problem solving, or in working effectively as part of a group, or designing an experiment, or making an effective contribution to a reporting-back session. Clearly, a lecture demonstration by the teacher on 'The theory of machines', however valuable intrinsically, would not be the appropriate vehicle for achieving the objectives of the lesson.

Thus, planning lessons requires a clear analysis of its objectives. Not that it has not always done so, but now the objectives are likely to be more complex. One scheme of analysis (used in developing learning modules in *Suffolk Science*, details from Science Adviser, County Hall, Grimwade Street, Ipswich) is as shown in Table 3.6.

TABLE 3.6 **A scheme of analysis for a learning unit**

| | |
|---|---|
| Topic | age group |
| Length (double-periods) | |
| Knowledge/content | |
| To be known '*about*': | |
| To be *understood*: | |
| Know how to: | |
| The significant skills/processes involved | |

(From *Suffolk Science Scheme*.)

Examination syllabuses, however, are still likely to be produced without too much detail as to where exactly skills and processes fit into the knowledge-base used to define the subject. Teachers will still need to use their experience and professional expertise to analyse the *content* listed in the syllabus to determine where *skills* and *processes* might be most appropriately developed. A recent syllabus (Physics (Nuffield), Midland Examining Group, 1986 Syllabus for Joint GCE O level/CSE Examination) lists its assessment objectives under four main headings:

knowledge
understanding
application of knowledge
exercising of judgement

As this syllabus is based upon a well known course with detailed teachers' guides and students' texts it may be comparatively easy for teachers to follow it in the way most likely to maximize examination success for their students. In an ideal syllabus, of course, examination success is a genuine measure of the students' achievement of the clearly stated objectives of the course, and these in turn are genuine operational statements based upon the declared aims of the course. But in this syllabus three of the aims stated are:

1 to stimulate and sustain an interest in and enjoyment of physics and its applications;
2 to foster relevant communication skills, and the ability to work with other people;
3 to foster independent thought both on physical principles and, through discussion, on the construction of appropriate models and theories.

Nowhere in the lists of assessment objectives, or in the detailed content-syllabus, is it prescribed where the attitudes of enjoyment and interests, or the skills of discussion, say, are best developed. And why should it, one might ask? Are not such analyses within the professional competence of the teacher? There are traps for the unwary, of course. If the assessment objectives do not include the assessment of such attitudes and skills, it might be a disservice to students to spend too much time on them. While it might be argued that interest and enjoyment are conducive to learning, it might turn out that a kind of miserable accuracy is ultimately better rewarded in examinations than a joyful independence of thought.

As an exercise, take the natural 'learning units' of a syllabus and analyse them in accordance with the objectives, using a pro forma as in Table 3.6 above.

It is at this stage, taking into account also the *actual* assessment objectives as realized in examination questions, that a decision might be made as to whether the syllabus does in fact:

1 live up to its declared aims and objectives;
2 serve the needs of the pupils for which it is intended.

This leads us into the interesting but controversial paths of curriculum development.

## Planning for successful learning

As that old military theorist von Clausewitz might well have said, strategic errors only become obvious as a result of tactical defeats. To put it another way, when the generals make mistakes it's the poor infantry that get shot up. 'Preparing a lesson' is the last stage in the planning process and, however well it is done, if the previous steps are seriously at fault, then the lesson is unlikely to go well. The chart overleaf indicates the main planning steps that lead to at least the probability of success.

A teacher will in general have more than one role to play in the school system, as tutor or deputy headteacher, as a member of a working party at school, LEA or even at national level. As a teacher, however, he or she has the key part to play. All the rest of the system is there to ensure that the teacher is effective at the point of contact with students. In so far as the teaching is felt to be failing – for example with the more disgruntled end of the fifth year in the last two periods on a Friday – there is an almost universal agreement that it is the teachers and/or the students who are at fault. While this is indeed sometimes the case, in general it is not. The likelihood is that they are merely the casualties of the tactical defeats that stem from defective strategy or some other breakdown along the line. The gifted teacher may cope and, indeed, snatch an exhilarating victory from the very jaws of defeat. But this is, ultimately, to rely on amateurism, a mode of operation that relies historically on luck, courage or grim determination, instead of on the professional qualities of adequate training, full preparation and the conscious deployment of appropriate skills.

Tables 3.1 to 3.5 gave the menu of tactics we have at our disposal. Assuming, if we dare, that the prior planning of resources, aims, syllabuses and objectives has been done effectively, we are now in a position to select and deploy them. In a well organized department, schemes of work will have been prepared which will already have indicated the most likely choices for us to use. Nevertheless, the ultimate decision as to whether this or that technique will actually work with form 3C this particular afternoon is up to the teacher. It is worth noting too that success is relative. Nothing will ever go precisely according to plan, and not all our objectives will be achieved on any one occasion. The important thing is to *know*, hence the importance of some kind of assessment (feedback) system. Again, a well planned course will have such opportunities for feedback fitted in as an integral part of the learning process.

The planning chain

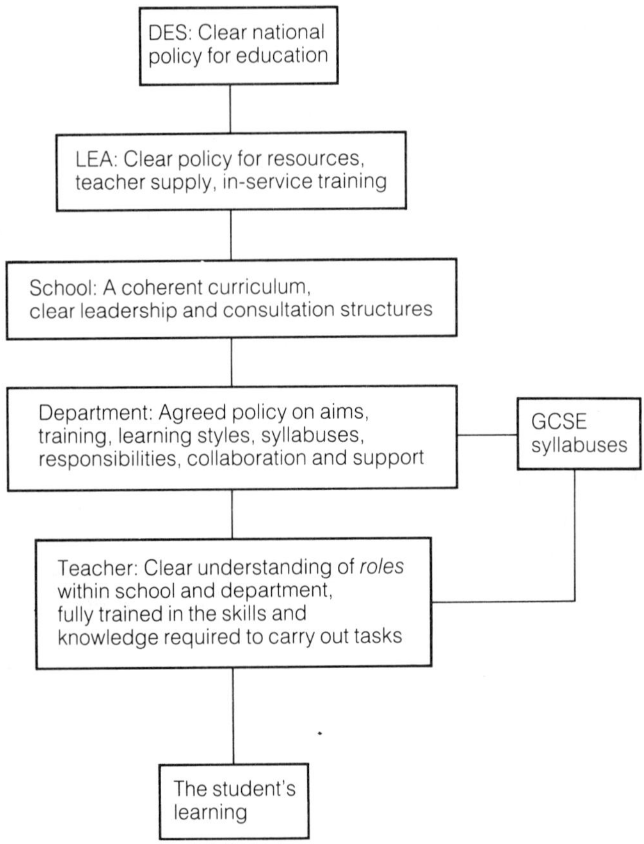

Plan to achieve the following learning objectives culled from current syllabuses. They should fit into a lesson of about 70 minutes' duration.

Topics for a lesson (from Chapter 1)

1 Strength of structures – girders, triangular frameworks.
2 Production of sound, vibration of strings (guitars etc.). Resonance.
3 The Earth's crust as the source of almost all chemicals.
4 Electrolysis explained operationally, as a process using electricity as a source of energy to bring about formation of new substances, without using the concept of the ion.
5 Living organisms can only survive in limited climatic conditions, especially temperature.
6 Circulation: simple properties of blood.

(Or, of course, you could more usefully design a lesson for a syllabus item that you intend to use in your own school.)

Your planning solution should give:

1 clear statements of objectives for the lesson, having decided the age and general ability level of the group;
2 a method for knowing that the objectives were in fact achieved (to be assessed in the lesson if possible);
3 the sequence of activities, timed as accurately as possible;
4 the relevant content (knowledge) assumed;
5 the content (knowledge) to be covered during the lesson;
6 the skills required by students during the lesson;
7 the skills to be acquired by students during the lesson;
8 the significant processes involved;
9 the significant student interactions you wish to occur;
10 the kind of report (oral or in writing) the students are expected to produce;
11 the equipment needed;
12 a brief synopsis of what you would say to start the lesson;
13 a brief synopsis of how you would expect to summarize the lesson for the students at the end;
14 a clear statement of the assessment objectives of the lesson, if different from (1) and (2) above;
15 suitable follow-up work (e.g. homework).

You will have to decide whether one lesson is enough to cover the science involved.

A suitable format for this kind of exericise is given in Table 3.7; clearly, to make such an analysis for every lesson is a time-consuming task, best done as a collaborative exercise by a departmental team. Again, experienced teachers will not need to make a laborious analysis of each and every lesson. Once this has been done as an exercise for one or two, the questions may be used as a check-list or, perhaps more usefully, as an aid to the planning of a whole course of work. Here the aim will be to ensure that a rich enough variety of skills and processes are involved, in an appropriately balanced pattern.

TABLE 3.7 **Planning a lesson**

Topic/unit.................. Age.....

Group..................

Objectives

Knowledge Skills/processes

Relevant previous knowledge/skills assumed

Knowledge/skills/processes to be assessed Mode of assessment

Timing

Equipment/aids

Notes

## Towards a coherent curriculum

Planning a science course for students without reference to what they may be doing in other parts of the curriculum may be unwise, counterproductive or, in some schools, simply impossible. There is a strong trend towards *coherence* in the curriculum, by which is meant that the total experience of the students is to be co-ordinated, as day by day and 'subject' by 'subject' they make their way

TABLE 3.8 **Tracking exercises**

The school's
statement of entitlement

↓

Aims and objectives
(i) eight areas of experience
(ii) skills
attitudes
concepts
knowledge

↓

Selection of content
taking into account the
range of ability

↓

Methodology
taking into account the
range of abiity

↓

Assessment and evaluation

assessment of pupils
evaluation of the
courses by
(i) teachers (ii) pupils

↓

Subsequent action

↓

Realisation of entitlement

'Subsequent action' may include one or more of the following:

(i) modification of aims and objectives;
(ii) modification of content selected;
(iii) changes in methodology.

If the outcome of assessment and evaluation is wholly positive the decision would be that no subsequent action is needed and the entitlement is realised.

---

*Attitudes*: To promote self reliance; safety consciousness; open mindedness; curiosity; perseverance; cooperation.
*Concepts*: states of matter, change of state, combustion.
*Knowledge*: (selection of content) smokeless fuels

*Methodology*: *Lesson 1* – Objectives 2, 5, 8, 9, 12
Pupils read a passage, which included diagrams, about burning coal without smoke. They were asked to work in pairs and to construct ten questions which they thought would test another group's comprehension of the passage. In introducing the exercise the teacher warned pupils to check that the questions they asked did indeed require the answer which they sought. After producing the ten questions one group exchanged questions with another and then tried to answer the other group's questions. As an additional incentive a competitive element was introduced as follows:

1 point for answering a question correctly.
1 point for spotting a faulty question.
1 point for correctly rewriting the faulty question.

Agreement had to be reached between groups before the allocation of a point.

*Assessment/evaluation*
*Teacher/observer comments* – The exercise succeeded in getting pupils to think more carefully about the way they structured questions. They extracted a lot of information from the passage often splitting questions into several parts in order to make a greater challenge to the opposing group. The activity created greater pupil involvement than in the previous year when a set of questions provided by the teacher had been tackled with less interest and enjoyment and had not demanded the same scrutiny of the passage. Very heated discussions took place between some groups when discussing the value of each others questions. In some cases the teacher had to step in to act as the final arbiter. All of the children were involved for most of the time. Pupils produced questions which reflected their level of ability.

*Pupil comments* – 'Liked this better sir because we made questions which we would understand, yours are too difficult.'
'It was a good game sir.'
'Johnny did all the work and would not listen to me.'
'It made me think more carefully about what I write.'
'Alan is trying to ask questions which cannot be answered from the sheet.'

*Conclusion* – An enjoyable exercise for both staff and pupils. For a mixed ability group the exercise was extremely valuable since each pupil used his "own" language to great effect. The exercise made pupils question themselves and each other and made them more aware of the effective use of language. Vigorous discussion took place and pupils criticised each other. The desire to complete the activity ensured that some level of cooperation was established.

(From DES, 1983 pp. 45 and 48.)

through the educational system. The inverted commas draw our attention to the possibility that the traditional subjects are themselves changing and that the boundaries between them are becoming less obvious. (See Chapter 7(e).) In response to the DES (1981b) circular '6/81', a number of education authorities are requiring schools to restructure their curriculum into eight 'areas of experience'. One of these is the 'scientific', but it is made clear that scientific experiences do occur outside the territory of the science department, just as aesthetic and linguistic experiences, for example, occur within it. An account of 'planning across the curriculum' is given in *Curriculum 11–16: Towards a Statement of Entitlement* (DES, 1983). A group of schools and local education authorities collaborated with the inspectorate on the exercise, which had as its aim the improvement of a student's experience across the whole curriculum, with each subject area playing a co-ordinated part. Each school agreed on its own 'statement of entitlement' – a description of what benefits students are expected to gain from their education at school – and then set up a 'tracking exercise' to check that these benefits did indeed accrue. Table 3.8 illustrates the tracking exercise, with examples of how this operated at department level.

Similarly, in response to the Hargreaves Report on London Schools (ILEA 1984), teachers and school departments are involved in planning courses which permit intersubject learning and assessment. The rationale for this is not argued here. Interested readers are advised to read the report itself. The following quotations from a discussion paper (Hargreaves, ILEA, 1984) indicate the nature of the planning required:

Another way in which units have considerable potential for curriculum development and change is through cross-curricular or multi-disciplinary units especially in areas such as personal and social education which at present are too often seen as peripheral. Such developments are often weakly represented in public examinations; the creation of units and credits of this type permits a better method of recording achievement in a way which might be especially valued by employers and FE colleges.

...Most important of all, units and credits maintain and perhaps increase teacher involvement in course design and assessment. When the unit and credit scheme has been developed as part of the implementation of ISS (Improving Secondary Schools), the outcomes may be used for a creative dialogue with the examination boards.

A unit is defined as follows:

A unit is likely to be a discrete and coherent programme of work which has clearly stated objectives either in terms of learning goals, or of experiences to be undertaken. The unit will take place over an agreed length of time and may be implemented in a number of ways.

(a) Within the classroom a unit will:
  (i) clearly set out the knowledge and skills to be acquired and the context within which the pupils will acquire them;
  (ii) involve the pupils in self assessment and diagnosis for future negotiation;
  (iii) be part of an understandable structure;
  (iv) explain how achievement is to be recognised and assessed.

(b) For the teacher the unit should:
  (i) provide a coherent framework to help pupils achieve more;
  (ii) give opportunities for the development of a variety of teaching modes.

Units may be free-standing or related in a system.
(From Hargreaves, ILEA, 1984.)

Such approaches to the planning of lessons emphasize what seems to be an increasingly strong element in teaching: the continuous assessment of learning, not only for diagnostic purposes but also as part of a formal examination scheme. Staged assessments (see Chapter 4) leading to a profile and/or aggregated to give a final summative grade are likely to feature in many courses in the near future. Few teachers (other than those who have taught SCISP or have been involved in the Scottish initiatives) have much experience in this area. The educational advantages are well stated (see Hargreaves, ILEA, 1984) and are discussed in Chapter 4: any practical difficulties following such a major change in assessment procedures centred on the classroom have still to be experienced.

If we refer back to the planning chain (p. 47), we can see that the higher elements in it are beginning to exert their influence more explicitly and perhaps more strongly than they did before. It is to be hoped that an equally strong influence works up the chain, giving usefully corrective feedback from pupil to teacher and teacher to hierarchy. The theory, at least, suggests that it might: it seems to be generally recognized in newer curriculum initiatives that accountability in education is not only to the ratepayers, but also to the students. Such 'tracking exercises' can only be to the good if the result is an increased awareness by teachers of the real changes in students that result from attending schools. Such thoughts lead us to consider now some aspects of teaching which were, until fairly recently, ignored or taken for granted.

## The hidden curriculum of science

The 'hidden' curriculum is the part of our teaching that we tend to take for granted: the language we use and expect; the unconscious attitudes we have, both to our students and to the subject itself; the assumptions we make about what students can and cannot do, or should and should not do. It is impossible in a single chapter to do more than attempt to raise awareness about these issues. One aspect, that of language, will be looked at in some detail, not only because of its intrinsic importance but also because it may serve as the key to a better understanding of other 'hidden' aspects.

The point to be made is that by a combination of teaching and language styles it may be possible to understand, and so make explicit, the problems caused by unconscious assumptions about students. These problems are:

the differing attitudes of girls and boys to science;
racism;
the switched-off teenager (class, family, background?).

Formidable problems indeed! Certainly, they are not likely to be amenable to any *single* change in, say, the teaching of science – or of anything else for that matter. Nevertheless, without an understanding of a problem there can be no solution to it. As the professionals in closest contact with young people, teachers have the responsibility and the opportunity to learn as much as they can about their students, and the key medium of understanding and influence is that of language. (See also Belbin *et al.*, 1981.)

## Writing, listening, talking

### Writing

Young people in school spend an amazing amount of time *writing*. A recent HMI (1979) survey found that some O-level candidates wrote the equivalent of a Dickens novel in the last year of the course, mostly in the form of 'notes' or fairly automatic regurgitation of facts in essays. Many students – and particularly the most able – are convinced by the age of 15 that 'work' in school equals 'writing'. The most exhaustive investigation of writing in schools (Britton *et al.*, 1975) defined three main functions of writing:

1 *the transactional* – the language of getting things done, of giving information, of persuading, of giving advice, of constructing theories;
2 *the expressive* – of our feelings, moods, personality, with an implication of shared experience and attitudes;
3 *the poetic* – using language as an art medium, in which the use of language is as important and satisfying as the ideas expressed.

Coupled with this kind of categorization was the writer's feeling of a sense of audience – whom is the writing for, what is the writing expected to achieve? The range of audience was:

Self – writing from one's own point of view without considering the intelligibility to others, a written form of 'speech for oneself', e.g. brief notes of a lesson or for an essay, diary entries;

Teacher – (a) as a 'trusted adult' who is interested in what one thinks – a feeling more common among younger children than secondary students; (b) as a 'teacher', a person interested in finding out what one knows as part of a dialogue helping further learning; (c) as an 'examiner' who is interested only in assessing or evaluating the piece of writing;

Other students – (a) as a peer group; (b) as from an 'expert' to known 'laymen' (e.g. an expert fisherman or horsewoman writing for a class magazine); (c) as a group member to his working group.

The analysis of a large number of students' scripts in a wide range of school subjects showed that most writing (87.5 per cent) was to the 'teacher as audience', with the 'teacher as examiner' proportion increasing with age of students. Transactional writing comprised 63 per cent of the sample. In science, an average of 87 per cent of the writing was to the 'teacher as examiner' (ranging from 77 per cent of 11 year olds' writing to 97 per cent of 16 year olds' efforts), with 92 per cent of all writing in the transactional mode. By comparison, only 18 per cent of written work in English and 69 per cent in history was 'student to examiner'.

There was no 'expressive' or 'poetical' writing in science, the missing few per cent due to difficulties of classification, it would seem.

What does this matter, one might ask at this point? Language is, however, the main mode of human interaction, people use it to talk and to think with, as well as write. There is a sense in which the learning of physics, for example, may be thought of as gaining deeper and richer versions of the meaning of *mass*, *force*, *electron* etc. The ability and readiness to speculate, make hypotheses, suggest solutions to problems is as much dependent upon language as upon the underlying concepts and experiences which create the need for such thinking. The transactional mode is essentially an authoritative one, in which answers are presumed known and speculation difficult if not impossible. In writing to 'examiners' one is playing safe, frightened of making errors, suppressing originality, hiding enjoyment and pleasure, wonder and anger. If the language, and the acceptable modes of using it, associated with science in schools is too limited then the full potential of the learner is untapped. The image of science will be seen as hard and inhuman, with consequences that are only too obvious. (See also Marland 1977)

> Check through a fourth year student's exercise book in science. Count the separate pieces of written work then read each one to see how many contain *any* sign of (a) humour (intentional, that is) (b) pleasure, (c) concern, or (d) personal feeling. Express the result as a percentage. Then think about it.

This is not to say that we must now go to the opposite extreme and expect all our homework to be done in blank verse. The ability to describe an event or an experiment fully and clearly is an important part of science, as is the writing of a clear and logical explanation of a complex phenomenon. But these represent the higher levels of competence, and are the sign of a mature writer (Britton *et al.*, 1975, p. 83). In valuing these goals we must take care that:

1 we do not devalue other modes of writing, such as the expressive;
2 insist on 'hard', transactional writing too soon, where it becomes an imposed, meaningless style rather than a freely chosen 'best method'.

Interesting results were produced when the same question was set to students by both the English and the science researchers of the APU, a question which asked students to describe a large, colourful butterfly specimen. In the English context the responses were not only much longer than with the 'scientific' responses, with definite expressions of feeling, but the actual quantity of careful, accurate observations was greater.

Anyone who has, as a 16 + examiner, marked 600 answers to a question like, 'Describe an experiment to determine the specific thermal capacity of copper', will be well aware of what 'transactional writing to teacher as examiner' means (and other readers will no doubt be able to imagine it); it may not be so easy to recall examples of more expressive writing. The more able students get trained out of it in science at an early age, and so teachers tend to link it with less able students who are, in any case, 'failing to answer the question set'. Here is an example in which, with typical human perversity, a girl mixes her modes:

Jill and me got a bowl with a ½ litre of water and put an egg in it and it sunk to the bottom. Then we got another bowl of water and put six spoons of salt in and when we put the egg in it floated. Then we put three spoons salt in the first bowl but the egg wouldn't float. So the egg only floats in the water with most salt in. I think it must be like the Dead Sea. Mrs Norris gave me and Jill an egg each for our tea. (Girl aged 11)

(From Burgess *et al.*, 1973, p. 74.)

Making young people write has a variety of objectives, some purely instrumental (the teacher can have a rest or set up an experiment, the students are fairly quiet and they do not move about too much). There is, of course, a value in writing for its own sake, but we should consider more carefully whether the time and effort spent on this activity by students would not be better spent doing something else – such as *preparing for writing* perhaps. The quality of writing is improved by thinking about it before starting, and by considering audience and message more carefully. This can be induced by changing the social conditions in which writing is done, away from the traditional scholar-in-his-study role of the homework-writer to one of the author/calligrapher/word-processor/editor; roles that are possible when the task is a group task, such as reporting back to other groups in a class after performing an investigation or exploration of some kind. The writing is then part of a presentation, a poster perhaps with graphics or experimental results supplied by other students in the group. The writing has been discussed in advance, perhaps checked by another group member for accuracy and felicity, and is aimed at a known, critical but not too forbidding audience. It has a job to do. As a learning activity a page of this kind of writing is likely to be worth a chapter of isolated drudgery.

> Divide the class into teams of four to six students. Choose a syllabus topic with a reasonably open-ended activity, preferably involving a choice of equipment or even the possibility of achieving a result by using reference books alone. (For example: what decides the period of swing of a pendulum; do girls have slower reaction-times than boys; are all acids equally strong?)
>
> Tell the students that they have to report back their results to the rest of the class by means of a 'poster session'. Allow time for the posters to be produced (longer than you think – they will want to do a good job) and observe:
>
> 1 who does the writing, and who decides this,
> 2 the reactions of other students reading it.
>
> (The organization is as follows: two people from each group take it in turns to act as 'exhibitors', staying at their display and answering questions while the rest of the team wander about making notes – 'two main points about each of the other groups' work'.)

## Listening and talking

If you have tried the exercise above you will be aware that a great deal of talking went on, some of it purposeful, some purely social. If the class was large, young and boisterous, and the room resonant, the lesson would have been 'noisy'. How many decibels are acceptable is a function of the teacher's sensitivities and the room acoustics, in almost equal measure perhaps. A well designed acoustic, students facing inward and working in small groups help to counteract the unwanted positive feedback of sound that makes it difficult for comfortable talk to happen. The value of students talking purposefully is difficult to assess, but the expected advantages include:

opportunities to try out new ideas in a non-threatening situation;
talking through and internalizing new concepts;
sharing new ideas;
gaining an awareness of the variety of 'alternative frameworks' that may exist;
preparing for writing or for a more formal discussion or report-back;
social benefits from working collaboratively and listening to others.

The Bullock Report (1985, p. 189; 12.5) stated:

When we consider the working day in a secondary school the neglect of pupil talk as a valuable means of learning stands out sharply. To bring about a change will take time and persistence. Where pupil talk has been accorded little status in teaching methods, it is not surprising that when the opportunity does occur it tends to be filled by pointless chatter.

The sequence of exploratory talk (often 'expressive') – discussion – formal discourse (e.g. writing) needs to be as clearly built-in to a lesson sequence as the conceptual and science-skills developments we are more accustomed to planning for. However, it is wrong to suppose that talking can be taught in a special 'talking lesson', where the only aim seems to be to improve students' talk. If we are to encourage purposeful – and skilful – talking then it must be seen by students to occur naturally as part of the process of 'learning science' and as a useful way of doing so. (After all, they are there to learn science – they already 'know how to talk'.)

Talking about experiments is a worthwhile activity, but is only one of many that could occur. These range from the informal to the highly structured:

1 planning an experiment or investigation with the rule that no one is to write or use equipment for 10 minutes;
2 preparing for a report-back session;
3 reporting back as a team, with aids and demonstrations;
4 taking part in a debate;
5 taking part in a simulation exercise (with or without role play);
6 almost any extended team task, group investigation, 'egg race' etc;

Unlike that Molière character who was amazed to learn that he had been talking in prose all his life, it should not come as a surprise to the teacher that a well motivated class, working in groups or pairs on a standard class experiment, will be discussing and talking purposefully for most of the time.

(i) So, with considerable self-denial, walk around during such a lesson and *listen to what is being said*, saying nothing whatever yourself. It may be necessary to develop the skill of looking at one group at work while actually listening to the one behind you, or on the other side of the bench. Sample each group for a minute or so and classify under the headings: (a) pointless chatter; (b) purposeful talk about the task in hand; (c) unclassified (e.g. they have worked out what you are up to and are putting on an act).

At the risk of some strain to what hitherto might have been a set of friendly relationships, arrange to overhear colleagues' lessons and check on the amount of time for which they actually talk during the lesson. This may be done by a sampling technique, noting down the speech activity every two minutes (or five minutes) during the lesson. A cassette recorder could be an aid here: record the lesson and play back the recording on fast forward, stopping at equal, short intervals as shown by the indicator for sampling the activity.

### Listening: a very difficult activity

'The difficulty of listening is commonly underestimated . . . Human attention is limited, and the longer people are required to listen, the less effectively they do it.' (Bullock, 1985, 10.19 p. 150). 'There is research evidence to suggest that on average the teacher talks for three quarters of the time in the usual teacher-class situation.' 'Some recent research in a number of American junior high schools showed that the teacher asked a new question every 12 seconds.' (10.4 p. 142)

The point here is not that teachers should not talk to students, but that they should be aware of the balance of activities within a lesson. The evidence that people learn better by interacting with the material to be learned is overwhelming, and opportunities for this must occur, and at frequent intervals. Listening is not interactive enough except under the most highly motivating circumstances, and even the use of the question-and-answer technique to involve students may not be as efficient as we think in a class situation. It is always difficult to ensure that the majority of students are playing a full part in such lessons: many will just sit there and hope that they are not going to be questioned – and if they are, conduct themselves thereafter on the assumption that lightning rarely strikes twice in the same place.

The message is that teachers (possibly) have certain assumptions they hold in common with other teachers, but that these are not necessarily held by their students. It is only by careful observation, giving students the opportunity to talk (and write) more naturally and expressively – and *listening* to what they say – that the common ground will exist for true negotiation of learning to occur.

## Primary science

Many of the new styles of teaching discussed in this chapter will be far from new to the primary science teacher. A coherent curriculum, a child-centred teaching approach, an emphasis on skills rather than content, the use of assessment as a diagnostic rather than a classificatory tool, children working in small groups – all these are more likely to be found in a primary than in a secondary school. This book is about the teaching of science to the 11–16 age group, so little has been said about the special joys and problems of the primary school science teacher. Most children change schools at 11, but a significant minority do so at 12, 13 or 14, in middle school/upper school systems. At any age, such changes can be unsettling, and science teachers need to be aware of the problems that children might encounter in adapting to the new environment.

Ruth Jarman (1984) has written lucidly and entertainingly about the primary–secondary interface, and all teachers should read her short monograph. Liaison between the secondary school and its feeder primary or middle schools is vital, and it should take place on a regular, timetabled basis – say once a term. The aim is continuity of experience for the student, content should not overlap and styles should not be traumatically different. To quote Ruth Jarman (1984, p. 8):

I would sound two notes of caution. Care must be taken that such an attempt at creating continuity is not based on mutual misconception of what actually is happening in local schools. The assumption that all primary school children work on individually selected projects in unstreamed classes during intoxicatingly integrated days is pure fantasy. There will always be a responsibility for secondary science departments to find out how science operates in contributory schools in their neighbourhood. Secondly, receiving schools would be unwise to attempt to eliminate change altogether. A degree of change is desirable and indeed may offer a powerful stimulus to pupils. Thus I would certainly not recommend that science be taught in classrooms rather than a laboratory merely in the interest of paralleling the primary experience. Nor would I wish to see pupils cushioned to the extent that their undoubtedly high expectations of secondary science are gravely disappointed.

I contend, however, that the Quest of the Holy Grail of Continuity is not terminated when we ensure an absence of duplication or even when we ensure effective articulation of science curriculum and pedagogy across the primary/secondary divide. I would argue that curriculum continuity must also involve some sort of rational progression in learning from infancy through childhood and adolescence into adult life. Such continuity implies that pupils are encouraged and given adequate opportunity to progressively develop, consolidate and extend a range of science skills and ideas throughout their period of compulsory schooling. In this context primary science is seen as contributory, laying a foundation of attitudes, skills and ideas that help children to begin to wonder ... to begin to resolve that wonder, and so to begin to understand something of the world in which they live. I do not see the role of science in the primary school as merely one of nurturing interest – the cartoon before the feature film. If this were the only function secondary schools would be at perfect liberty to ignore it. Good primary science practice offers much more than this and secondary schools must learn, with some humility, first how to build on these early experiences and then how to extend them with work that is progressively more demanding. If teachers fail to do this then the quality of the educational experience in some primary schools is such that many pupils may actually suffer a regression on entry into the secondary sector.

Middle schools present different problems and opportunities from primary schools. The upper school has far less time than the 11–18 school has to initiate its entry group into its styles and expectations. The intake group will tend to be larger, and all too soon the GCSE examinations are seen to be looming up. Thus the efficiency of the induction process has to be correspondingly greater if valuable time is not to be lost and students mismatched to further courses in an option system. Thus the need for close liaison and the matching of styles and content is even more imperative. Useful models of primary and middle school aims and methods, which could form the basis for agreement, are to be found in the Leeds Middle School Science scheme (1980) and the booklet *Primary School Science Skills* (School Natural Science Society, 1984).

## What pupils can actually do – results to questions on pages 14–16 (APU, 1984)

### Sealed tubes

At age 15, 37 per cent of all students chose Tube Q, compared with only 25 per cent getting it right at age 13. Forty-six per cent of 15 year old biologists were getting the right answer, compared with 30 per cent of non-biologists. The most popular wrong answer (remarkably stable at 26 per cent for all 15 year olds, biologists or not, and 23 per cent of all students at age 13) was Tube S.

### Iron wool

Forty-two per cent of students studying chemistry were able to reason that because oxygen combined with iron the mass/weight would increase, compared with only 4 per cent of non-chemists. The most popular wrong answer from chemists – that 'stuff was driven off' or 'burnt away' – was chosen by a similar proportion of non-chemists (about one-fifth), but one-quarter of non-chemists were happy in the belief that ash (or powder) is lighter than iron.

### Soft ball

A full answer to this question is quite typical of the kind of reasoning expected in much of the physics taught at this level, a chain of reasoning: fall in temperature – decrease in speed of particles – lower rate of bombardment – lower pressure – therefore football feels softer.

Twenty-one per cent of physics students used all these ideas in their answer, compared with 5 per cent of non-physicists. A further 25 per cent of physicists used the first two steps in the argument but failed to relate this to a change of pressure on the wall of the football. In spite of the wording of the question, one-quarter of the physicists and two-thirds of non-physicists did not refer to particles at all. Twenty-nine per cent of physicists showed more or less serious misunderstanding of basic ideas in kinetic theory. Overall, 'it appears that less than a third of 15-year-old pupils were able to use simple ideas about the particulate theory' . . . 'with less than 10% giving a complete response to the questions' (APU, 1984, p. 154).

## Further reading

A copious list of titles about teaching science is to be found in Lillis and West (1984). This list is meant to be brief and relevant enough for the works cited *to be read by busy teachers*! It is divided up into the different models of learning.

### 1 Piagetian

Shayer, M., and Adey, P., 1981, *Towards a Science of Science Teaching* (Heinemann, London). A discussion of the *difficulty level* of some popular science courses, with do-it-yourself guides for checking levels of difficulty.

### 2 Constructivist

*Children's Learning in Science Project* (*CLISP*), Summary Reports:

Brook, A., and Driver, R., 1984, *Aspects of Secondary Students' Understanding of Energy*

Brook, A., Briggs, H., and Bell, B., 1983, *Secondary Students' Ideas about Particles*

*Driver, R., 1983, The Pupil as Scientist?* (Open University Press, Milton Keynes).

Osborne, R. and Freyberg, P., 1985, *Learning in Science* (Heinemann Educational Books, London).

### 3 Sociological

Important as this model is, there are no books dealing straightforwardly with it in the context of teaching science. Insights may be gained from Eggleston, J. F., Galton, M. J., and Jones, M. E., 1976, *Processes and Products of Science Teaching* (Macmillan, Basingstoke); Young, M. F. D., 1977, 'School science: innovation or alienation?', In *School Experience*, edited by P. Woods and M. Hammersley (Croom Helm).

And picking your way carefully between the blocks of jargon: Young, F. D. (ed.), 1971, *Knowledge and Control* (Collier-Macmillan, Basingstoke).

### 4 Language and communication

This overlaps with the sociological aspects, since speech is the main mode of interaction between and among students and teachers. Our tendency to confuse students with long words and a special 'academic' syntax is well criticized in Prestt, B., 1980, *Language in Science* (ASE)

Wider issues are discussed in the short and very readable book: Barnes, D., 1976, *From Communication to Curriculum* (Penguin, Harmondsworth).

## Bibliography

APU, 1984, *Science in Schools Age 15*, Report No. 2 (HMSO, London)

ASE, 1979, *Alternatives for Science Education* (Association for Science Education)

Belbin, Downs, and Perry, 1981, *How Do I Learn*?, Further Education Curriculum Review and Development Unit (Longman Group, Harlow)

Bell, B., Watts, M., and Ellington, K., (eds.), 1984, *Learning, Doing and Understanding*, Proceedings of an SSCR conference (Secondary Science Curriculum Review, London)

Britton, J., *et al.*, 1975, *The Development of Writing Abilities (11–18)* (Secondary Science Curriculum Review, London)

Burgess, C., *et al.*, 1973, *Understanding Children Writing* (Penguin, Harmondsworth)

DES, 1975, *A Language for Life* (The Bullock Report), (HMSO, London)

DES, 1983, *Curriculum 11–16: Towards a Statement of Entitlement* (HMSO, London)

DES, 1981a, *Girls and Science* (HMSO, London)

DES, 1981b, *The School Curriculum: A Consultative Document* (HMSO, London)

DES and Welsh Office, 1985, *General Certificate of Secondary Education, The National Criteria: Science* (HMSO, London)

DES and Welsh Office, 1982, *Science Education in Schools – A Consultative Document* (HMSO, London)

DES and Welsh Office, 1985, *Science 5–16: A Statement of Policy* (HMSO, London)

Dobson, K. I., 1979, *This is science: Teachers' Guide* (Macmillan, Basingstoke)

Driver, R., 1983, *The Pupil as Scientist*? (Open University Press, Milton Keynes)

Driver, R., *et al.* (Editors), 1985, *Children's Ideas in Science* (Open University Press)

Gott, R., 1985, *APU Topic Report No. 1: Electricity Age 15* (HMSO, London)

Gregory, R. L., 1981, Mind in Science (Penguin, Harmondsworth)

Hargreaves, D., 1984, *Units and Unit Credits*, an internal discussion paper from the Chief Inspector (Inner London Education Authority, London)

HMI, 1979, *Aspects of Secondary Education in England* (HMSO, London)

ILEA, 1984, Improving Secondary Schools (Inner London Education Authority, London)

Jarman, R., 1984, *Primary Science, Secondary Science: Some Issues at the Interface* (Secondary Science Curriculum Review, London)

Leeds Middle School Science Scheme, 1980, *Core Intentions for Science in the Middle Years* (Department of Education, Leeds City Council)

Marland, M., 1977, *Language across the Curriculum* (Heinemann Educational Books, London)

Olsen, J. K. *et al*, 1980, *Innovation in the Science Curriculum* (Croom Helm, Beckenham)

Osborne, R., and Freberg, P., 1985, *Learning in Science* (Heinemann Educational Books, London)

Shayer, M., and Adey, P., 1981, *Towards a Science of Science Teaching* (Heinemann Educational Books, London)

School Natural Science Society, 1984, *Primary School Science Skills* (School Natural Science Society, Faversham)

# 4 How is science teaching evaluated, assessed and examined?

**Bob Fairbrother**

---

★ Assessment provides feedback for decision making.
★ The purposes of assessment must be clear. Whether the teaching objective has been realized, what the student can and cannot do and how one student compares with another can all be assessed.
★ Feedback to students can influence how the student works and helps in selecting subject and exam options. Careful consideration should be given to what the 'score' means.
★ The feedback from students' assessment to teachers should influence their teaching.
★ Assessment provides feedback for other teachers in the school, parents, employers and institutions of further and higher education.

---

## Introduction

Assessment can cover several broad areas:

students
teachers
teaching methods
materials
schools, LEAs etc.

This chapter is concerned mainly with the assessment of students. However, no area can be divorced entirely from the others and we must accept that information about students is also information about many other things. As teachers we are pleased to share students' successes, but we must also be prepared to share their failures. A students' success or failure is rarely his or hers alone, and one of the major concerns of education is to identify the causes of success in order to strengthen them, and the causes of failure in order to eliminate them. Assessment is not an end in itself; much of its value lies in the feedback it should provide so that the education process may be improved.

The major theme of this chapter is providing feedback for decision making, i.e. for a purpose. It starts by clarifying various concepts and terminology, and suggests doing some quick self-appraisal in order to get a clearer understanding of present practices. It then goes on to deal with feedback to three main groups of people:

students
teachers
others, viz. parents, employers, admissions tutors

These are not natural divisions because much that is said of one group can apply to another, but they provide one way of dividing up a complex topic.

The chapter does not attempt to justify assessment. It takes the view that assessment is a fact of school life and, if properly used, can be beneficial. Teachers continually make assessments, sometimes without realizing it! All teachers appreciate that some form of assessment is necessary for the effective performance of their job, although disagreements can arise over the details of *what* should be assessed, *how* it should be assessed and *why* it should be assessed. One of the commonest causes of disagreement is the vexed question of equality and divisiveness. The position taken by most teachers is that of giving students equal opportunity and consideration while recognizing differences in ability. As Professor Dahrendorf said in his 1974 Reith lectures:

I have always assumed that equality provides the floor of the mansion in which liberty flourishes; it is condition, not purpose. Equal opportunities are opportunities for unequal choices... All men are equal in rank and right as human beings and as citizens, but they differ in their abilities and aspirations. To deny such differences is to deny life-chances, thus liberty.

## Some terminology and concepts

### Purposes, aims and objectives

The purposes of assessment are not the same as the aims of education, although they are closely connected. The purposes of assessment are concerned with what we do with the results of assessment or with what effect the assessment is intended to have. They involve such things as monitoring progress, making selections and motivating students. A good summary of purposes is provided by the Scottish Council for Research in Education (1977):

1 to enhance pupil's self-knowledge;
2 to provide users with useful information;
3 to orient teachers towards a guidance model;
4 to support the school in its programme of total education.

Basically they are concerned with using information to make decisions, and the purposes must be clear before assessment is undertaken. (See next box.)

The aims of education, and hence of teaching and learning, are concerned with the kinds of people we wish our students to become and the use we wish them to make of the subjects we teach them. The aims for GCSE science are given in Chapter 1 and include such things as:

1 to provide the opportunity for students through practical studies in science to obtain sufficient understanding and knowledge to become well informed and hence confident citizens in a technological world;
2 to develop abilities and skills that
   (a) are appropriate to the study and practice of science;
   (b) are useful for everyday life and encourage safe practice;

> In order to review your own purposes, make a list of all the occasions when some kind of assessment is done in your school (homework marking, class tests, departmental examinations, 'mock' 16+ examinations etc.). For each occasion note down the purpose(s) of the assessment and the use which you make of the results. Compare your list with that of your colleagues, not only from within your own department but from others also and, if possible, with that of the Head and Deputy Head(s) of the school. The results could form the basis of a valuable departmental meeting, and even of a full staff meeting.

3 to stimulate curiosity about science, enquiry into science, interest in science, enjoyment in science;
4 to promote an awareness that the study and practice of science are co-operative and cumulative activities and are subject to social, economic, technological, ethical and cultural influences and limitations.

The achievement of aims cannot normally be assessed because the aims are too general and distant, concerning themselves with hopes and aspirations rather than with more immediate objectives.

Objectives are the stepping stones to the achievement of aims. They are more specific, more directly achievable and more open to assessment than are aims. The assessment objectives suggested for GCSE science and given in Chapter 1 are typical of an increasing number of such objectives, e.g.

1 Candidates will be expected to show that they have knowledge and understanding of
 (a) scientific phenomena, facts, laws, definitions, concepts, theories;
 (b) scientific vocabulary, terminology, conventions; etc.
2 Candidates will be expected to show that they have the ability
 (a) to observe, measure and record accurately and systematically;
 (b) to follow instructions accurately for the safe conduct of experiments;
 (c) to draw conclusions from, and evaluate critically, experimental observations and other data; etc.

> The examination boards and schools offering Mode 3 examinations will have to work to these kinds of objective when composing their assessment schemes. Try to anticipate the kinds of assessment they might use. Choose one or two of these objectives, preferably from group 2, and give details of the tasks (an exam question, a practical problem etc.) you would ask the students to do to find out if they have achieved them.

While the above objectives are more specific than the aims stated earlier, they are still not stated in *operational* or *behavioural* terms. They do not say precisely what it is that the students must do. For example, we do not know exactly what we expect a student to do when he 'shows an understanding of scientific phenomena' or 'interprets data'. As stated, these objectives are open to different interpretations by different people, and hence there will be some unreliability in their assessment. The search for unambiguity and reliability will be discussed further in the section on processes and criteria.

For each lesson, and certainly for a series of closely connected lessons, we should be clear about the major objectives we wish to achieve – *and we should tell the students what they are.*

If you do not do so already, try the following:

1 Choose a single lesson or a small number of closely linked lessons which you are going to teach in the very near future.
2 Decide upon the two or three most important objectives which you want the students to achieve as a result of teaching the lesson(s).
3 Tell the students what the objectives are.
4 At the end of the lesson(s) try to find out if the students have achieved the objectives.
5 What will you do if all/some/none of the students achieve the objectives?

One can teach in order to achieve objectives, and the extent of the achievement can be assessed. While we are concerned ultimately with the achievement of aims, we can really assess only the achievement of objectives. For this reason, professional experience and expertise are needed to decide upon those objectives

Try linking objectives to aims as shown on the next page. Decide which aim(s) (from your own list or from the one given above) is(are) most likely to be achieved as a result of achieving the objectives you chose in the lesson or series of lessons above.

Try grouping the assessment objectives into clusters which could form the basis of a content/process assessment grid (see the section on content validity on pages 121–122) which can be used to design an assessment scheme. One cluster might be concerned with communicating, another with investigating, and so on.

which are most likely to bring success in the achievement of aims. The GCSE National Criteria for Science (DES, 1985a ) suggest the following relationship between its aims and its objectives:

| *Aims* | *Objectives* |
|---|---|
| 2.1, 3.1 | 2.1, 2.2, 2.6, 2.8, 2.15 |
| 1.2, 2.1, 3.1 | 1.3, 1.4, 2.1, 2.2, 2.7, 2.8, 2.9, 2.10, 2.15 |
| 1.1, 1.3 | 1.1, 1.4, 2.4 |
| 1.2, 1.3, 2.1 | 2.4, 2.5, 2.6, 2.7, 2.13, 2.14, 2.15 |
| 1.3, 4.1, 4.2 | 1.2, 2.3, 2.11 |
| 1.1, 1.2, 1.3, 2.2 | 2.11, 2.12, 2.13, 2.14, 2.15 |
| 3.1, 3.2, 4.1, 4.2 | |

## *Summary*

| *Aims* | *Objectives* |
|---|---|
| What we want students to do in the future | What we want students to do now |

*Purposes*
What assessment is for, i.e. the use to which the results will be put. Assessing the achievement of aims and objectives gives information which can be used for various purposes.

---

## Formative assessment and summative assessment

Formative assessment is an integral part of teaching. It is on-going and diagnostic; that is, it is concerned as much, if not more, with what students *cannot* do as with what students *can* do. An essential aspect of formative, diagnostic assessment is the feedback which is necessary to improve the performance of students, i.e. to produce changes.

Formative assessment is private and parochial. It concerns the students and their teacher, and not outsiders such as employers and admissions tutors. The only exception to this is if the assessment contributes to an on-going appraisal across the school of the achievement and behaviour of students. In this case assessments made in different areas of activity are pooled in some way to give a composite picture of performance, usually in the form of a profile (see pages 171–177). Under such circumstances it is particularly important that everyone concerned is clear about the purposes of the assessment. A common policy throughout the school is needed; certainly it should be common among all the teachers in the same department.

Summative assessment comes at the end of teaching (at the end of a topic, a term, a year, or of schooling), and hence there is little or no opportunity to provide feedback. It is concerned with achievement and tends to be much more public than is formative assessment. There is a strong sense of sitting in judgement, of labelling and of using the results to make choices.

The interrelation of formative assessment and summative assessment is complex and confusing. Most of teaching should involve formative assessment, with students and teachers accepting it as an integral and helpful part of the teaching/learning process. However, it is strongly affected both in its techniques and interpretation by summative assessment, influenced particularly by the powerful 16+ examinations. The result is that most people, and students in particular, view any kind of assessment as a threat.

> For each of the occasions when assessment is done in your school:
>
> what information do you get?
> what information is given to the students?
> what information is given to anyone else?
> what does everybody do with the information?
> is the assessment formative or summative?

## Criteria and norms

Criterion-referenced decisions are based on what students can do; they make reference to the subject matter being taught. Norm-referenced decisions are based on comparisons between students and make no mention of what the students can do. A statement such as, 'Can read a thermometer' is criterion-referenced, whereas 'Is in the top 10 per cent' is norm-referenced. In order to make norm-referenced decisions it is necessary to distinguish between students. Finding out that all students, or that no students, can do something is useful criterion-referenced information but useless norm-referenced information.

The GCE and CSE examinations are based upon the not unreasonable premise that with a large entry of candidates to an examination there will be a spread of ability. These examinations are further required to discriminate between candidates for the purpose of awarding a range of grades. This means that any questions which all candidates can answer (having a facility value of 1) or which no candidates can answer (having a facility value of 0) are unsuitable and, particularly with multiple-choice questions, are rejected as a result of pre-testing.

This contrasts with a strictly criterion-referenced approach in which you would first decide what you wanted your students to do, and you would then compose a 'question' (some kind of task) in order to find out whether they could do it. If they could all do it, you would, or should, be very pleased since it would indicate they they had achieved the criterion which you had set. However, if all the students succeed, it is natural to think that you have not been making the

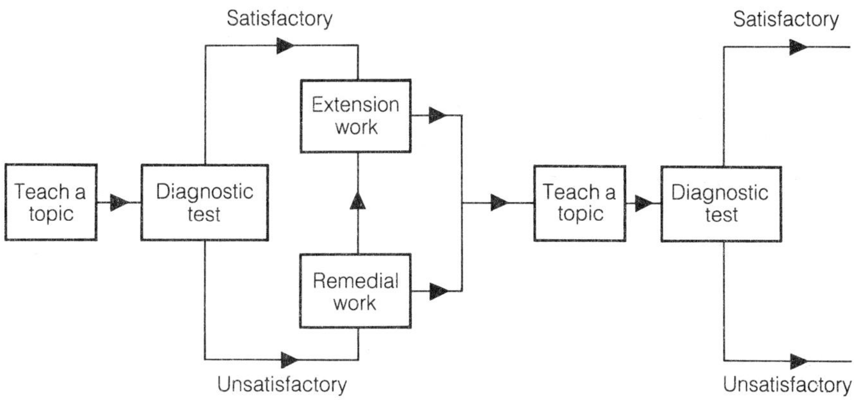


FIG. 4.1

most of their ability and that you should have set a harder criterion. There is no satisfactory solution to this problem because it is largely an attitude of mind. If you have chosen the criteria properly because their achievement is necessary for a particular purpose, e.g. to go on to the next stage of teaching, then success is a matter for celebration and not concern. If your purpose is to encourage students to perform to their maximum potential, then this is close to being a norm-referenced purpose, and not a criterion-referenced one. One possible solution to the problem is to set a series of increasingly demanding criteria for a series of related purposes. The least demanding criterion is the one which everyone is required to achieve, and the others represent extension work. The teaching pattern is then something like that shown in Figure 4.1 above.

This is a convergent model which attempts to keep the students together as much as possible. Many teachers need this kind of pattern in order to be able to keep track of the progress of students and to retain a hold on their sanity! However, the requirement of the GCSE to have differentiated assessment (see pages 131–132) favours a divergent model with alternative components in the scheme of assessment to cater for a wide range of ability.

Teaching is largely criterion-referenced since we want all our students to succeed. The aims of question analysis which are adopted by the examination boards are thus not those which normally apply to school examinations. This is because it would lead to a situation in which we would reject questions with a high facility value, i.e. we would tend not to ask those questions which most of our students can answer.

## Processes, criteria and skills

Processes, such as selecting, recalling and hypothesizing, are what scientists (and others) are concerned with. Ability in a process is developmental, i.e. a student is positioned somewhere in the continuum of increasing competence in the process as shown in Figure 4.2.

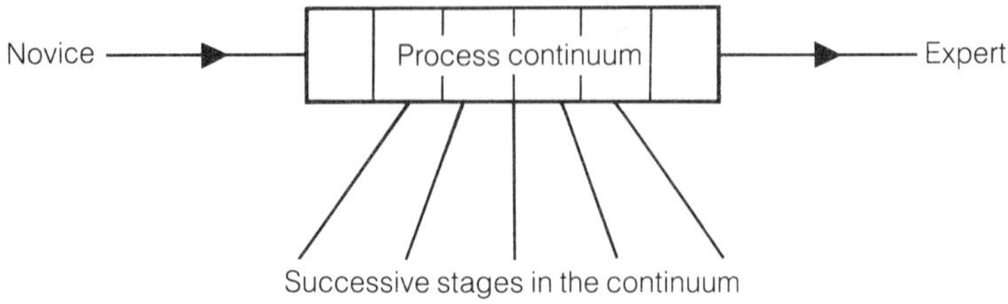


FIG. 4.2

A criterion is a characteristic by which the performance of a process at a particular level of competence is judged, and the level of competence should be chosen for a purpose. A statement such as 'On at least three occasions out of five the student can take the steady reading, accurate to $\pm 0.5^{\circ}$C, of a mercury-in-glass thermometer calibrated from $-5^{\circ}$C to $110^{\circ}$C in one-degree steps' is a statement about a student's position in the continuum concerned with the process of measuring. The statement becomes a criterion if the student needs to achieve it in order to be awarded a particular grade. The criterion for *mastery* also needs to be related to a purpose since there are different levels of mastery depending upon what the student is required to do. Mastery of cooking in order to look after one's self is at a different level of competence compared with mastery for the purpose of preparing a formal banquet. Mastery in an absolute sense, devoid from purpose, has no meaning.

The level of competence in science required of a research scientist is greater than that required of a school laboratory technician. The criterion for the researcher is probably possession of a first-class honours degree; for the technician it might be possession of a BTEC certificate. In each case the process involved is that of doing science, although the precise nature of what is involved is very vague and is certainly not the same for each occupation.

Similar considerations apply when attempting to use criteria to determine which grades students should get from an examination. A Grade C demands more than a Grade D either in terms of the level of competence or in terms of the number of criteria or both.

The Secondary Science Curriculum Review (1984) identifies *skills* as being separate from *processes*. A skill is seen as 'a specific activity which a student can be trained to do'; a process is seen as 'a rational activity involving the application of a range of skills'. They propose the following as the 'minimum entitlement' for all young people studying science in our schools:

*Skills*

| | |
|---|---|
| Listening | Nonverbal communication |
| Talking | Observing |
| Writing | Searching |
| Drawing | Measuring |
| Reading | Manipulating |

| | |
|---|---|
| Numeracy | Graphicacy |
| Estimating | Recording |
| Small group skills | |

*Processes*

Communicating and discussing, which include

thinking
questioning
seeking help
negotiating

Processing of information, which includes

selecting
using relationships
controlling interacting variables
designing
drawing conclusions

Problem solving, experimentation and decision-making, which include

predicting
inferring
formulating hypotheses
interpreting
modelling
evaluating
assessing
classifying
managing time

Whether or not it is helpful or confusing to try to distinguish between processes and skills is a matter for personal preference. The point is that neither the skills nor the processes are given with sufficient precision to be unambiguous; and for none of them is a criterion given which indicates the level of competence which it is thought students should reach. In order to increase the precision with which a criterion is stated, and hence to increase the reliability of its assessment, it needs to be more specific than simply saying 'Can do science'. A more precise statement is, 'Can solve numerical problems', but it is still not precise enough to be an unambiguous criterion, and in addition it is now only a part of what is involved in doing science. 'Can solve numerical problems in which the principles involved and the method of solution are given' is even more precise, but we still do not know the content area involved nor whether a student is required to solve all problems presented or whether an 80 per cent success rate is sufficient to meet the criterion.

The statement above about being able to use a thermometer is much more specific and is capable of being assessed with reasonable reliability. It can be seen, however, that the search for unambiguous criteria has several unfortunate effects:

1 an increase in specificity and hence in triviality as we try to make clear exactly what it is that students are required to do;
2 a proliferation of criteria in order properly to define a subject or a topic;
3 a disintegration of the subject when we try to assess the separate achievement of each criterion.

Specific criteria fit better into formative assessment than into summative assessment. Formative assessment involves an analysis of teaching and learning which leads to a step-by-step approach in which specific criteria can more easily be identified and assessed. Summative assessment involves a synthesis of the separate steps and an integration of specific criteria into some kind of coherent, purposeful activity. The final, summative assessment is more than just the simple sum of all the separate assessments which have been involved in the formative stage. This is discussed further in the section on feedback to teachers.

> Return now to the task suggested above concerning the main objectives which you hope to achieve in a lesson or in a series of lessons. This time state the objectives in terms of specific criteria, making quite clear what it is you want your students to do and why you want them to do it.

## Validity and reliability

### *Validity*

An assessment is valid if it does what it is intended to do. For example, an end-of-topic test which is intended to test students' *understanding* of the topic will not be valid if it only asks students to *recall* formulae, definitions and descriptions of experiments which they have done. Understanding involves more than just recalling information; it involves, among other things, being able to make use of the information in a variety of ways, such as applying knowledge to solve problems and explaining phenomena. Examinations often measure irrelevant things such as the ability to write clearly and succinctly when we want to measure the ability to remember something.

Validity must always be related to purpose because a test which is valid for one purpose may not be valid for another. For example, a valid test of achievement in mathematics at school does not necessarily indicate those who will become good accountants.

There are different kinds of validity, some of which are easier to check than others. Four common ones are dealt with here:

1 face validity
2 content validity

3 construct validity
4 criterion-related validity

1 **Face validity** is concerned with the appearance of a test. At the simplest level this can be checked by seeing that, say, a chemistry test actually contains questions on chemistry. At a more complex level it requires a check to be made on the kinds of question which are asked and what the student is required to do. For example, it is unlikely that an examination to check on a student's competence in chemistry would be valid if it contained only multiple-choice questions, or did not have a practical test of some kind, or did not have any diagrams and graphs. This is because being competent in chemistry, or any other subject, involves being able to do many different things in many different ways. In such circumstances lack of variety means lack of validity.

2 At some stage face validity runs into **content validity**. This is the extent to which the test reflects what has been taught. There are two aspects to this:

(a) coverage
(b) balance

(a) As an example of coverage, an end-of-topic test on current electricity should not contain questions on electrostatics or on magnetism unless these have been a part of the topic. Similarly one expects an external examination to be based on the syllabus which has been published.

(b) Balance is concerned with the relative importance of the different parts of the subject and the emphasis which has been given in the teaching. One expects more questions on important parts and fewer questions on the less important parts; and one expects these to have been reflected in the teaching.

It can be seen, therefore, that content validity is related to the teaching which has taken place and also to the image one has of the subject.

The achievement of both face validity and content validity are matters of judgement. There is no actual measure which enables you to say that a test has 90 per cent face validity or 80 per cent content validity. (Hoste (1981), however, has proposed a content validity coefficient which is based upon calculating chi-squared between the number of items specified for each cell of a content/objectives specification grid and the number which actually occurs.) The construction of such a grid without doing the calculation does help content validity to be achieved. Table 4.1 shows an example for an end-of-topic test on current electricity in which the teacher has attempted to cover the objectives of:

recalling facts and terminology
observing
translating
interpreting

TABLE 4.1 **Content/objectives grid for a test on current electricity**

| | *Units* | *Effects of current* | *Series circuit* | *Instruments* | *Total* |
|---|---|---|---|---|---|
| Knowledge | 2 | 6 | 2 | 4 | 14 |
| Observing | | 8 | 2 | 6 | 16 |
| Translating | | 2 | 6 | 2 | 10 |
| Interpreting | | 4 | 8 | | 12 |
| Total marks | 2 | 20 | 18 | 12 | 52 |

The grid not only enables a check to be made on the coverage of the content, but also ensures that the weighting given to different parts of the content and to the different objectives is what was intended. Such grids are increasingly common in the 16+ examinations but are not used often enough in school-based tests.

> Choose a recent test which you have used in school and construct a content/process grid on the lines shown above. Is the result what you expected or wanted? Did the test reflect the emphases of your teaching?

**3** Content validity eventually runs into **construct validity**. Constructs are abstract qualities which are made understandable by definition and example. For example, as a part of your teaching philosophy you might believe that students' confidence is improved by constant approval. If you wished to put this to the test, you would have to define what you meant by 'confidence' and 'approval', both of which are constructs. Similarly, *intelligence* is a construct; so are *co-operation* and *courtesy*. The names themselves give some idea of what is being talked about because you have met them before but, to be sure that everyone means the same thing by such things as intelligence or courtesy, it is necessary to give the behaviours which someone would exhibit when they were being intelligent or courteous. Similarly, *understanding* is a construct, and we need to be clear what it is a student must do if he or she is to show understanding. The idea of a construct is discussed further in the section on the assessment of attitudes (page 166).

> Choose a topic which you have taught recently. List the things which a student should be able to do if he or she understands the topic. Ask a colleague to do the same for the same topic and then compare notes.

We can see how content validity and construct validity overlap when we ask students to apply their knowledge to solve a problem. Being able to do this is a part of the construct *understanding*, but it also depends upon the students having covered the necessary content and having been given opportunities during the teaching to solve problems. Recent changes in emphasis in assessment have made construct validity more important than in the past. As we have seen, it is becoming common to make clear statements about aims and objectives. It is evident that, if a test is to reflect the aims and objectives which were mentioned earlier, it must involve constructs such as curiosity, interest, understanding and knowledge, and hence the test must have construct validity.

There are ways of measuring construct validity but they are rather complex and are unlikely to be used by teachers in schools. A little more is said about this in the section on assessing attitudes.

**4 Criterion-related validity** measures the relationship between the scores on a test and the achievement of some other criterion, such as the results of another test or performance in a job. There are two kinds of criterion-related validity:

(a) Concurrent – in which test results are compared with another measure of the same thing at the same time. You would be involved with concurrent validity if you wanted to check whether practical ability measured through a written paper produced similar results to those measured through a practical test. It would make sense to do this because, if the written paper turned out to be valid, it would be easier and less expensive to use than the practical test.

(b) Predictive – in which the test results are compared with another criterion in the future such as success in a job or at university. Typically the 16+ examinations are used as predictors of performance in jobs and at A level; similarly, A-level results are used as predictors of performance at university. However, an examination which is a valid test of understanding of a subject at school is not necessarily a valid predictor of performance at university or in a job. Yet many school examinations attempt to serve both purposes without any real evidence that they are valid for either. In fact results at A level are poor predictors of class of degree at university. There are many reasons for this such as the length of time between one test and the other, the different circumstances in teaching and learning, and the change in the nature of the subject between school and university. The so-called 'mock' A-level examinations are, however, reasonable predictors of performance at A level because the situation does not have the defects listed above.

Criterion-related validity, particularly concurrent validity, can be measured rather more easily than can construct validity. It is done by calculating the correlation coefficient between the results obtained from the test (e.g. a written test of practical ability) and the results obtained from the criterion (e.g. a practical test of practical ability). If a correlation coefficient of 0.7 were obtained, you would be able to say that the written test was 70 per cent valid. You would then have to make judgements as to what level of validity is needed for the test to be acceptable. There are no rules about this, and a thorough approach to the problem would require a consideration of the level of certainty at which you wish to work and an understanding of statistics. For most purposes a validity of 70 per cent or more is usually considered to be satisfactory.

All this assumes, of course, that the criterion itself is valid! In general a criterion will have been developed over a long period of time and will have been subject to checks of face and content validity as well as measures of construct validity where appropriate. A criterion which has not been subjected to this kind of rigorous checking should not be accepted as a criterion.

## *Reliability*

There are two main meanings of reliability:

1 reproducibility
2 internal consistency

**1** Reproducibility is concerned with the stability or consistency of results. If different results are obtained each time a measurement is made, then the measurement is unreliable because it lacks reproducibility. Reproducibility and validity are closely connected; a measurement can be reproducible without being valid, but it cannot be valid without being reproducible. For example, measuring a person's height with an elastic ruler will give un-reproducible (unreliable) results, and as a consequence the results cannot be accepted as a valid measurement of the person's height. If measured with a steel ruler the results become reproducible, and they are valid as a measure of height but not as a measure of, say, scientific ability. So, one can have a reproducible (reliable) measure but it is not valid if it is used to measure something which it was not designed to measure.

An obvious way to check on the reproducibility of measurements is to take them several times to see if the values stay constant. If several things (people) are being measured, then the scores from one set of measurements can be correlated with the scores from another set, and the correlation coefficient gives a measure of the reproducibility. This **test-retest** method is satisfactory if the quantity being measured does not change between the successive measurements. However, this is not the case with measurements of ability in science because changes take place between one measurement and the next. The person being measured might have learnt more, or have forgotten something, or feel less well, or not be able to concentrate in the same way as before because of an argument at home. In addition, the markers may not be consistent in the way they allocate marks in the two administrations of the test; and if two different but supposedly equivalent tests are used so that students do not carry over answers from one test to the other, the two tests are unlikely to be exactly equivalent. Apart from which, retesting of groups of students is usually very inconvenient.

An alternative is to split the examination into two equivalent halves and to treat each half as two separate measurements of the students. This **split-half** method of measuring reproducibility is much more convenient and hence is more common. It is usually done with each paper separately and is more commonly done with multiple-choice papers than with other types of paper. The reason for this is because it is easier to split a multiple-choice paper into two equivalent halves, for example by putting all the even-numbered questions into one half and all the odd-numbered questions into the other half. With other kinds of paper, getting equivalent halves is much more difficult. This will be discussed further in the section on internal consistency below.

There are, of course, many different ways of splitting a paper of multiple-choice questions into two halves; the odd-even split is only one, and each way will give a different value for the reproducibility (reliability) coefficient. Examination boards do not normally use a simple split-half method. Instead they use the formulae devised by Kuder and Richardson (KR 20 and KR 21) which effectively find the average of all possible split-halves. Further discussion of these is beyond the scope of this chapter.

**2** Internal consistency is concerned with whether all parts of the examination measure the same thing. A biology examination might be said to be internally consistent if all the questions were about biology and reflected the aims of the course. If some of the questions were written in French, or there were some questions on the Old Testament in the Bible, then one could argue that the examination was not internally consistent.

A more sensible example would be to argue that the biology examination would not be internally consistent if it examined two different domains such as theoretical ability and practical ability, because one could expect students to behave differently in each, i.e. a student who is good at theory is not necessarily good at practical. Another way in which the examination could be considered to be internally inconsistent is if there were some questions which required students to describe experiments and others which required them to do calculations.

If students *do* behave differently in different domains then, for an examination to test overall competence in a subject which has several domains, the demands of validity require that the examination be *not* internally consistent. Internal consistency is only necessary if one is examining behaviour in a single domain. The KR20 or KR21 formulae may give a low value for internal consistency because there may be several domains in the test; but the repeatability of the results could still be high. A failure to realize this could result in a rejection of the scores from the test or in a great deal of work being done to try to 'improve' a test which is already satisfactory.

Finally, if students *do* perform differently in different parts of an examination, it makes sense to report these performances separately and not to combine them into a single mark or grade. This is dealt with in the section on profiles on page 171.

# Feedback to students

Assessment is not an end in itself; it is done for a purpose. Some action should take place as a result of the assessment, and the process of assessment should provide data for decision making. It is therefore essential to be clear about what sorts of decisions need to be made because these will govern the nature of the data which are required.

Feedback to students has two main purposes:

1 to influence patterns of work;
2 to help in making selections.

## Influencing patterns of work

For this purpose the assessment is almost certainly formative since it must come part of the way through the teaching in order to influence future patterns of work.

This chapter deliberately makes only a small mention of the *informal* assessment which we do, consciously and unconsciously, all the time we are with our students. This kind of assessment makes itself felt in a large variety of ways. e.g.

the attitude we adopt when we are with the students;
the kinds of oral questions we ask;
how we accept the answers which students give;
how much attention we pay to individuals;
the amount of preparation we do;
the care we take over marking;
our willingness to help after lessons are over.

All these, and more, give back messages to the students which tell them something about our assessment of them. They are important, not only because of the effect they have, but also because, for many of them, we are not aware of what we are doing. It seems that good teachers do the right things unconsciously; the rest of us have to work hard to develop the right approach.

Most of this section is concerned with the more *formal* aspects of assessment, which involve the marking of classwork and homework, and the use of diagnostic class tests which should be set from time to time. It is convenient to consider two broad overlapping areas which are differentiated mainly by whether the feedback is norm-referenced or criterion-referenced:

(a) The first area is concerned with motivating students and confirming that satisfactory progress is being made. The feedback can, in fact, be either norm-referenced or criterion-referenced but, if it is the latter, it can also cover the second area.
(b) The second area is concerned with revealing errors and misconceptions so that something can be done about them. The feedback *must* be criterion-referenced.

(a) Norm-referencing can be of several different kinds. For example, it can be a simple statement of order of merit, i.e. first, second, third etc.; or it can be based on percentiles, e.g. in the top 10 per cent, average, in the bottom half etc.; or it can be expressed as a grade where each grade covers a certain percentage of the students, e.g.

| Grade | A | B | C | D | E |
|---|---|---|---|---|---|
| Per cent | 15 | 20 | 30 | 20 | 15 |

These methods reveal whether a student is maintaining his/her standing with respect to other students, and are more concerned with motivation than with any of the other purposes mentioned above.

It is unusual with ordinary marking of classwork and homework to make use of percentiles or of grades in any precise way. Some teachers award grades instead of marks in a subjective way along the following lines:

A Very good
B Good
C Average
D Poor
E Very poor

This is clearly norm-referenced and can cause problems in deciding what is meant by such things as 'Very good' and 'Average'. A teacher of a good group will be reluctant to give D to work which is below the average of the group but which is good in absolute terms. There is, in fact, a general problem of decision making and interpretation which is related to the group of students on which the norm is based. If it is the set in which the student is placed for teaching purposes, then the best work should always get a grade A no matter how poor it is in absolute terms, and the worst work should be given a grade E no matter how good it is in absolute terms. If the group is the whole of the year group in the school, then, with a setted organization, students in the top set should normally get As and Bs which is quite encouraging for the students. However, students in the bottom set should normally get Ds and Es which is *not* very encouraging. Whether a setted organization or a mixed-ability organization is in use, the bottom students always get the bottom grades even though they may be making progress.

The group is unlikely to be the national year group since data cannot normally be obtained in a form which is useful to individual students. (The Assessment of Performance Unit of the DES has information about the performance of various *groups* of students, but it cannot identify individuals.)

An order of merit may reveal that a student is either improving, keeping the same position, or falling back. Even the student who is falling back may, in fact, be making progress in absolute terms, although it may be difficult to convince the student, the parents and, frequently, the teachers involved that this is the case. A student who is at the bottom of a group may be doing perfectly satisfactory work. A student who is at the top of a group may be doing poor work. It all depends on the progress being made by the group as a whole and on the ability of the student being considered. Keeping one's position in a good group may be better than improving it in a poor group. Being at the top of a group is good for one's morale, but being near the bottom of a better group might push one into doing better work in order to stay with the group.

Of course, dividing students into groups is an unreliable exercise, and the students at the bottom of one group are unlikely to be better than the students at the top of the adjacent, but supposedly poorer, group. However, putting students in a particular set tells the students something about your assessment of them, and this will affect the way they behave. Remember that we are dealing at the moment with feedback to students, and with the interpretation and use which students make of the information. The problems involved in interpreting the different kinds of data mentioned above are large; and different students will interpret the same data in different ways. It all depends on the psychological make-up of the student.

> Ask some of your students about their understanding of the assessments which are made of them. For example, ask them what a mark of 5/10 for homework means. See if they would prefer to have comments instead of marks; and if they want marks, ask why. Put the same or similar questions to some of your colleagues.

Classical methods of norm-referencing are much more likely to be used on a departmental or school basis where the number of students is larger than that in an individual class. Under such circumstances the feedback is likely to concern other teachers, and so will be dealt with in more detail in the next section on feedback to teachers.

(b) If the feedback is criterion-referenced, then it says something about what it is the students can do. It relates to what is being taught and hence to objectives. This has particular and important consequences for the students because, not only must we as teachers be clear about the objectives and associated criteria, but so also should the students. This means the students can see that they are not being measured against the performance of other students but against their own achievement of clearly defined goals. It also means the students can assess their own progress and take more of the responsibility for their own education. Increased student involvement in course planning and in assessment is one of the corner-stones of the TVEI and CPVE schemes. Its success will depend upon developing an attitude of mind in which assessment is seen to be a help, and not a threat.

Consider the following two sets of comments written on students' books:

*Set 1*
Careless work and atrocious spelling.
Repeat this diagram and label it properly.
Do these two questions again and set them out properly.
This is poor, untidy work. If there is not an improvement, I shall have to put you in detention.

*Set 2*
You work quickly, which is good. Please now try to be more tidy so that your work looks good.
The diagram is correct but you did not label it. I have put in one label, please put in the rest yourself.
Both questions were right except for two simple mistakes. If you set out your work neatly, you will not make these mistakes.

The difference between the two sets is obvious. The first set of comments is all negative and discouraging. The second set is positive and encouraging. It is a matter of simple psychology that reward is more effective than punishment. You should always try to find *something* to praise at the same time as showing how improvements can be made. Making written comments is time-consuming. You may not be able to do it every time but it should be done periodically for every student.

Where numerical marks are given, most teachers employ an uneasy and ill-defined mixture of criteria and norms in their day-to-day marking. Frequently it is impressionistic, based on a hazy idea, influenced by past experience, of the standard they require and of the standard they think the students are capable of achieving. Often they are reluctant to award full marks because of a vague feeling that full marks mean perfection and no student can possibly be perfect. According to a French adage quoted by Clignet (Rowntree, 1977) for a piece of work marked out of 20:

20 is given to God,
19 to his saints,
18 to the teacher's teacher,
17 to the teacher himself,
and therefore the pupil cannot expect more than 16!

This attitude is mainly norm-referenced because it compares students with other (past or ideal) students.

Straightforward calculations are more likely to earn full marks than are descriptive pieces of work, but even then a correct answer will be penalized if the derivation is missing or is not clear. Some teachers make the basis of their marking clear to themselves (and sometimes to their students) by allocating a certain number of marks to specific aspects of the work, e.g.

Heading and statement of purpose of experiment – 2 marks
Diagram – 3 marks

Description and tabulation of results – 4 marks
Interpretation and conclusion – 3 marks
Neatness – 2 marks

or, for numerical problems:

Statement of formula or relationship – 2 marks
Clear working – 3 marks
Correct numerical answer – 1 mark
Correct units – 1 mark

This is much closer to criterion-referencing. Such approaches avoid awarding too many marks to neat nonsense and encourage the untidy genius to pay more attention to presentation. They also lead to more objectivity, consistency and speed in the marking. Consistency (or reliability) of marking is important because it leads to fair treatment of students who will then take the feedback more seriously. More importantly, however, it is more informative to the students; it lets them know what you consider to be important and what you are looking for. The choice as to which aspects should be 'listed' and the balance of marks between them can be a matter of personal preference. However, over a period of time all the objectives which you have decided are important should be covered, and it makes sense, therefore, to choose aspects which match your objectives. This now begins to move out of the realm of personal decision making into that of departmental policy because the achievement of objectives is linked with aims (as we have mentioned earlier), and so concerns other teachers covering a range of subjects and a long period of time.

> Choose an occasion in the near future when you are going to do some marking of classwork or of homework. Decide upon those aspects of the work which you consider to be important (such as those suggested above) and organize a mark scheme. Tell the students what you have decided *before* you set the work. Mark the work yourself and then get them to mark their own and also that of one of their neighbours. Discuss the decisions made and be prepared to make changes to the marks you have awarded. The real benefit, however, is not in arriving at an agreed set of marks but in getting the students to see how they could have done better.
>
> Now give the same set of work to a colleague, without the marking guide, and ask him or her to mark it using their own scheme. (You will probably have to agree to mark a set of *their* books in exchange!) Compare the marks with your original set and ask how they were arrived at.

These kinds of activity are difficult to do because they are so time-consuming. However, something along these lines is necessary if a coherent policy is to be arrived at in a department or in a school, so that the students can understand what is happening. Frequently students get many conflicting messages which are presented to them in a variety of ways. The result is confusion which they deal with by ignoring the messages. This applies especially to the slower students and to the less motivated students, who are just the ones who *need* to understand what is being said to them.

There is at least one school which finds the time for staff discussions etc. by changing the time at which school ends. They finish at 4.00 on Monday, Tuesday and Thursday, and at 3.15 on Wednesday and Friday. The Friday finish is an early start to the weekend. The Wednesday finish provides an opportunity for a variety of voluntary activities to take place (for both staff and students) including team training and staff workshops.

## Making selections

This is the second main purpose of giving feedback to students. There are four main occasions when students need to make selections:

In the third or fourth form if the school runs an options system. This involves a choice between subjects.

In the fifth form when making examination choices. In the past this has sometimes involved a choice between the GCE and the CSE, but with the merging of these two systems the choice is now likely to be between two papers in a differentiated papers examination.

In the fifth form if the student is going into the sixth form. This involves a choice between subjects.

When leaving school and making decisions about the next stage, e.g. further education or job, which job, which university.

The last of these is concerned with careers advice and falls outside the scope of this chapter. The others are concerned with either a choice between papers or a choice between subjects.

### *Choice between papers*

The GCSE General Criteria (DES 1985b) which are applicable to all subjects state:

> All examinations must be designed in such a way as to ensure proper discrimination so that candidates across the ability range are given opportunities to demonstrate their knowledge, abilities and achievements: that is, to what they know, understand and can do. Differentiated papers or differentiated questions within papers will be required accordingly in all subjects.

There are three main ways of doing this:

1 A common paper taken by all candidates, and alternative papers at varying

levels of difficulty to cater for different needs and interests of candidates. The common paper is usally of medium difficulty, but it can cover the full range instead. This is sometimes referred to as the 'petal' or 'daisy' examination pattern.

2 A common paper taken by all candidates, and an optional paper intended to be taken only by the more able candidates. This is similar to the above pattern but it has only one petal.

3 A series of papers of escalating standard. No candidate takes all the papers. In a four-paper examination, with 1 the hardest and 4 the easiest, the top group of candidates would take papers 1 and 2, the middle group papers 2 and 3, and the bottom group papers 3 and 4. This is sometimes referred to as the 'chain' pattern.

At first sight it would seem that the way out of the problem of choice generated by these examination patterns would be to let all candidates take all the necessary papers to enable them to be considered for any of the grades. This is particularly so if a grade limit applies, as is most likely for those candidates in (2) who only take the common paper. (Obtaining even full marks on this paper may result in the award of only a grade C.) However, not only might a weak candidate put in for the top two papers in (3) not get any grade at all, but also some of the examination patterns, particularly (1), involve different syllabus choices because the different papers are based on different areas of content and are not just harder questions on the same area of content.

There are considerable technical problems involved in deciding what grades should be awarded. (See, for example, Backhouse, 1976; Wood, 1978; Kingdon *et al.*, 1983). There are other problems involving applying the grade criteria to candidates in the same examination who do not all take the same papers. The problem of making a choice remains with the students and the teachers, and will differ depending on the examination pattern being used. For a fuller discussion of the issues involved, see Tattersall (1983).

## *Choice between subjects*

Subject choice revolves around the following kind of problem:

> The fourth form option system in a particular school requires students to select between biology and geography. One student, who has no idea about a future career and likes each subject the same, gets 55 per cent for biology and 60 per cent for geography in the end-of-year examinations. The student argues that, because she got more marks in geography than in biology, then she is better at geography and ought to continue with that subject and drop the other one. What is your advice?

A similar situation can arise in making subject choices for the sixth form. One student gets a grade B in biology in the 16+ examination, and a grade C in physics. 'I am better at biology, so I will do it for A level instead of physics', she argues. Is she right in her reasoning?

The problem is about making comparisons in order to make choices, and hence one must make sure that the comparisons are fair. In both of the above examples the measuring instruments which were used to provide the data were not the same. In the options-choice problem, one instrument was a geography examination and the other instrument was a biology examination. In the sixth-form problem, one instrument was a biology examination and the other was a physics examination. In both cases the measuring instruments were almost certainly written and marked by different people, tested (measured) different things and were answered by two different, but probably overlapping, groups of students. In neither case is there a basis for fair comparison and fair choice.

There are ways of reducing the problems. They involve making certain assumptions and presenting the information in a different way. The major assumption is that the group of students taking the two examinations in each case is the same. This makes the group of students the common link between the two measurements, and the assumption is made that the group will do equally well, or badly, in each examination. In the options-choice case the two groups could easily be the same because this is the way many schools work. In the sixth-form case the two groups are unlikely to be identical because different students enter the two 16+ examinations which give the data. However, there will be some overlap of candidature, and this common group of students can be used to make comparisons between subjects.

If these various assumptions are valid, then the mean mark, for example, in each examination should represent the same standard even though its numerical value may be different. To make other marks in the two examinations directly comparable we must refer them to these mean marks in some way. This is done by making use of standard scores.

## *Standard scores*

Consider the two sets of (hypothetical) marks for a biology examination and for a physics examination given in Table 4.2 overleaf. With a mean mark of 60 per cent biology appears to have been an easier examination than physics which has a mean mark of 55 per cent. However, the range of marks in biology is only 28 (from 42 to 70), while in physics it is 53 (from 30 to 83). In order to compare individual marks in the two examinations we must take into account this difference in the spread of marks. This is done using a statistic known as the **standard deviation** (s.d.).

TABLE 4.2 **Marks and ranks for a group of students in biology and physics**

| | *Biology* | | *Physics* | |
|---|---|---|---|---|
| *Student* | *Mark* | *Rank* | *Mark* | *Rank* |
| Abdul | 60 | 4 | 51 | 3 |
| Bob | 56 | 5 | 83 | 1 |
| Carrie | 64 | 3 | 36 | 5 |
| Damon | 68 | 2 | 80 | 2 |
| Enid | 70 | 1 | 30 | 6 |
| Floyd | 42 | 6 | 50 | 4 |
| *Mean* | 60 | | 55 | |

$$\text{s.d.} = \sqrt{\frac{\sum(x-\bar{x})^2}{N}}$$

$x$ = the raw mark
$\bar{x}$ = the mean of the marks
$N$ = the number of marks
$\sum$ = the sum of

Many pocket calculators have a built-in program which will calculate s.d. with a single key. Programs for microcomputers are available which will calculate a large number of statistics and will tabulate data and display it graphically. Most simple books on statistics give information on how to calculate and interpret s.d. Figure 4.3 illustrates the meaning of a standard deviation.

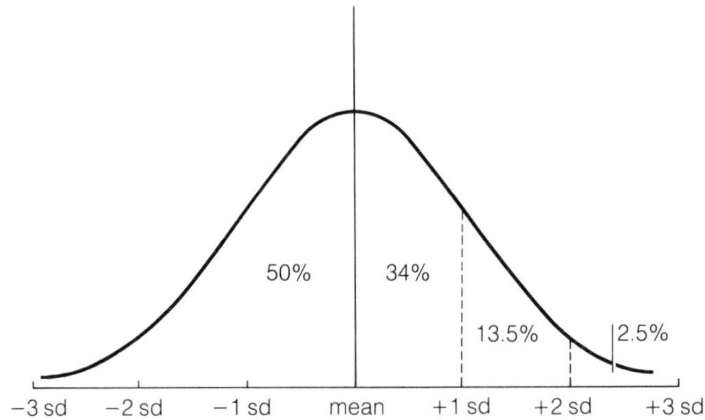


FIG. 4.3

If the marks follow a normal distribution, then several things can be said about the marks and their relation to the standard deviation:

Approximately 3 standard deviations will cover the full range of marks.

1 s.d. above and below the mean occurs at the point of inflection on the curve (i.e. where the curve changes from convex to concave).

Very nearly 34 per cent of students will have marks which lie between the mean and 1 s.d. above the mean. Another 34 per cent will have marks which lie between the mean and 1 s.d. below the mean.

This means that two-thirds of all the students have marks which lie within $\pm 1$ s.d. of the mean.

Other percentages are marked on the graph. It can be seen that 95 per cent of students have marks which lie within $\pm 2$ s.d. of the mean, and 99 per cent lie within $\pm 3$ s.d. of the mean.

We can now comment on individual marks. For example, someone who has a mark which is 1 s.d. above the mean will be doing better than 84 per cent (50 per cent + 34 per cent) of the students in the examination. Someone who has a mark which is more than 2 s.d. below the mean is in the bottom 2.5 per cent of the students in the examination.

The standard deviations for the two sets of scores above are:

Biology 9.3
Physics 20.1

With a mark of 70 per cent in biology, Enid is very nearly 1 s.d. above the mean and so has done better than about 84 per cent of the other students doing the examination. (With the small numbers involved in the illustration, this statement does not make much sense. However, it illustrates the principles, and also gives a warning about trying to apply them unthinkingly to small numbers.) In the physics examination 1 s.d. above the mean would give a mark of 75 per cent. A student with this mark would have done as well in physics as Enid did in biology; both Bob and Damon did better than this.

Abdul was third in physics with a mark of 51 per cent. What is the equivalent mark in biology, and who got it? Well, 51 per cent is four marks below the mean. This is $4/20.1 = 0.2$ s.d. below the mean in the physics examination. This fraction of s.d. in the biology examination is $0.2 \times 9.3 = 1.86$, and the corresponding mark is $60 - 1.86 = 58.14$, i.e. 58 per cent. The closest to this is Bob with 56 per cent.

We have been calculating what is known as *z-scores*. This is the mark expressed in standard deviations from the mean.

$$\text{z-score} = \frac{\text{Score} - \text{Mean}}{\text{s.d.}}$$

Abdul's z-score in physics is $-0.2$ s.d.; Enid's z-score in biology is $+1.1$ s.d. The marks for all the students in the two examinations expressed as z-scores are as shown in Table 4.3 overleaf.

For many purposes z-scores are sufficient. They enable us to compare the performance of students in two, or more, examinations. For example, we can see

TABLE 4.3 **z-scores for the biology and physics tests**

| *Student* | *Biology* z-score | *Physics* z-score | |
|---|---|---|---|
| Abdul | 0 | − 0.2 | |
| Bob | − 0.43 | + 1.4 | |
| Carrie | + 0.43 | − 0.94 | z-scores |
| Damon | + 0.86 | + 1.24 | |
| Enid | + 1.07 | − 1.24 | Mean = 0 |
| Floyd | − 1.93 | − 0.25 | s.d. = 1 |
| *Mean* | 0 | 0 | |

that Bob's mark of 56 per cent in biology is worse than Floyd's mark of 50 per cent in physics. However, for conveying information to students it has the disadvantages that the mean mark is zero, marks below the mean are negative and most marks are expressed as fractions. The way out of this is to convert the marks to any convenient mean and any convenient standard deviation. This is done by multiplying the z-score by the required s.d. and then adding the required mean. The result is a standard score. You can choose your own standard score to suit your own convenience. Most IQ scores are converted to a mean of 100 and a s.d. of 15. Since most examination results are expressed as percentages, it is usually more understandable to convert to a mean of 50 and a s.d. of 15. The standard score then becomes:

Standard score = (z-score × 15) + 50

Applying this to the above z-scores gives the standard scores shown in Table 4.4.

TABLE 4.4 **Standard scores for the biology and physics tests**

| *Student* | *Biology* standard score | *Physics* standard score | |
|---|---|---|---|
| Abdul | 50 | 47 | |
| Bob | 44 | 71 | |
| Carrie | 56 | 36 | standard scores |
| Damon | 63 | 69 | |
| Enid | 67 | 31 | Mean = 50 |
| Floyd | 22 | 46 | s.d. = 15 |
| *Mean* | 50 | 50 | |

The scores are now directly comparable. For example, we can see that Floyd's original mark of 42 in biology is worse than Enid's mark of 30 in physics. Note also that the rank order in each of the examinations remains unaltered.

However, what would happen to the overall rank order obtained by adding together the two sets of marks? Try it first for the raw marks and then for the standardized marks.

You will find that there is a slight change in the rank order. The wide spread of marks in the physics examination has more effect on the rank order than does the relatively narrower spread in the biology examination.

Holford (1980) gives another, fictitious example involving four footballers who have taken examinations in science, English, humanities and mathematics (Table 4.5):

TABLE 4.5 **Hypothetical results in four subjects**

| | *Science* | *English* | *Humanities* | *Mathematics* |
|---|---|---|---|---|
| Shilton | 20 | 56 | 66 | 70 |
| McGovern | 40 | 50 | 60 | 65 |
| Robertson | 63 | 45 | 50 | 60 |
| Frances | 95 | 43 | 35 | 50 |

What is the rank order in each subject?
Who should get the form prize based on performance in all four subjects? See what you get when you add rank orders, and then see what you get when you add raw marks.
You could also see what you get when you standardize all the marks first to the same mean and standard deviation.

One of the classic, but again fictitious, examples of what happens when marks are standardized was given in the Journal of the Assistant Masters Association in November 1958. In this example the rank order of a class of pupils given by adding the raw marks from examinations in a number of subjects was completely reversed when the marks were standardized. The story starts:

Towards the end of last term the Head suddenly asked for the examination marks of 12 Fourth Form boys who came from the parish of Hardgrind.

TABLE 4.6. **Effect of unequal standard deviations when marks are added**

| X | Y | X + Y |
|---|---|---|
| 50 | 60 | 110 |
| 50 | 50 | 100 |
| 50 | 40 | 90 |
| 50 | 30 | 80 |
| 50 | 20 | 70 |
| 50 | 10 | 60 |

Hardgrind's greatest son, for many years the chairman of our school governors, had endowed a prize to be awarded to the Fourth Form boy from his parish who showed the greatest academic promise. 'I want these boys to take the same eight subjects; I want all the subjects to be given equal esteem, and I want them all marked out of 100.' The staff were agreed that this was a reasonable idea, and were full of admiration at this evidence of perspicacity in their late chairman.

There is no room here to give the full story. The situation is familiar to many of us, and probably continues to take place in one guise or another in many schools now. The heart of the problem is giving all the subjects 'equal esteem', in other words giving them equal weight. The *weight* of an examination depends on its standard deviation. This can be seen in Table 4.6 above which shows an extreme example in which the X marks have zero standard deviation. You can see that the rank order is determined entirely by the Y marks.

As an additional point, if you want to encourage students to take up your subject in an options system, make sure you give them high marks in their examinations, but do not tell them, or other teachers, about standardized scores! Comparing performance in different subjects is, in fact, a complex issue. You can read more about it in Bardell *et al.* (1978); Forrest and Vickerman (1982); and Nuttall *et al.* (1974). For more information about standard scores read Tuckman (1975).

## Feedback to teachers

There are two main purposes of feedback to teachers, which are the same as those in the previous section on feedback to students:

1 to influence patterns of work;
2 to help in making selections.

All of what has already been said is relevant to this section also. Indeed, there is little more to add to (2) so this section will concentrate on (1). It will look at the issues with a different emphasis, and it will extend further the discussion on formative assessment, criteria and making diagnoses.

TABLE 4.7 **Satisfactory (✓) and unsatisfactory (×) performance in five tests**

| Student | P | Q | R | S | T |
|---|---|---|---|---|---|
| Abdul | ✓ | ✓ | ✓ | ✓ | ✓ |
| Bob | ✓ | × | ✓ | × | ✓ |
| Carrie | ✓ | × | ✓ | ✓ | ✓ |
| Damon | ✓ | × | × | ✓ | ✓ |
| Enid | ✓ | × | ✓ | × | × |
| Floyd | ✓ | × | × | × | × |

It is necessary to repeat what has already been said about success and failure being a joint responsibility between students and teachers. Consider, for example, the situation in Table 4.7 which shows satisfactory performance (✓) and unsatisfactory performance (×) in five end-of-topic tests: P, Q, R, S, T. The criterion for satisfactory performance might be 70 per cent or more in the test. This tells us something not only about the students but also about the tests and our teaching. For example, Abdul seems to be doing very well and Floyd seems to be in difficulties. Topic P was taught well or the test was very easy (but if the objectives were clear and the test was valid, then both the teacher and the students did well).

However, what about topic Q? Something has gone wrong with the teaching because too many students have done badly. It looks as though topic Q should be taught again. If this is the case and some improvement takes place, then Carrie will be doing well also. With the exception of Floyd, a little extra help for the other students might be in order. Floyd seems to present a different problem which needs closer investigation and will depend upon the particular circumstances involved.

Arriving at a criterion of satisfactory performance is either a matter of doing some research or of using professional judgement. In the example given above we would be looking for a **criterion score**, and this score would tell us whether or not the students had mastered the topic. The mastery would need to be for a particular purpose, e.g. to be able to cope with further work. A research approach would attempt to establish a score below which it is found that students *cannot* cope with future work. Except for very specific applications, this is so unreliable (as well as being too complex and inconvenient) that decisions about a suitable criterion score usually rely on the professional judgement of teachers. This judgement is largely subjective but guided by arguments which say something like: ‘It is unreasonable to expect a mark of 100 per cent (even the best of us make mistakes sometimes); on the other hand, mastery surely means more than half marks. It seems we are talking about a mark between 60 per cent and 90 per cent.’ Midway between these limits gives a mark of 75 per cent, and most criterion scores seem to be in the range 70 per cent to 80 per cent.

It is becoming common to talk about 80–80 tests. These are tests in which 80 per cent of the students get 80 per cent of the marks. Provided the group of students for whom the test is intended is clear, this kind of definition sets the overall standard of the tests. Within this standard one is able to introduce criterion scores for several purposes, e.g. to award a range of different grades.

This illustrates how closely inter-related are criteria and norms. The criterion part is getting a mark of, say, 80 per cent; the norm part is 80 per cent of a particular group of students. Professional judgement about what constitutes a suitable criterion score is influenced by our previous experience with many students as to what it is reasonable to expect students to be able to do, i.e. the criterion is influenced by norms.

## Diagnostic assessment

Influencing patterns of work in a positive way involves encouraging students to improve their performance. They need, therefore, to know where they are going wrong and how to put it right. This is what diagnostic assessment is about. The kinds of question which are used are little different from those used in conventional attainment testing. Provided they are capable of revealing misconceptions, misunderstandings and lack of knowledge and skills, then they can be used as diagnostic tests.

Probably the two biggest differences between diagnostic testing and conventional attainment testing lie in the way that the questions are grouped and in the way that the results are used. For example, if multiple-choice questions are used, one would not only add up marks for all the correct answers in order to get a measure of achievement, but would also look at which distractors were chosen because these reveal evidence of what kinds of difficulty the students are having. This could not occur at the very end of the teaching otherwise there would be no opportunity to do anything about the faults revealed by the test. In addition, since the results do not count towards some final judgement, the test can be a part of the teaching and learning, with the students checking their own results.

A diagnostic test can be anything from a quick, five or ten minute oral test with written or oral responses which checks on recall of essential facts, to a more formal examination lasting half an hour or an hour which tests a wider range of abilities and/or content. In a well designed scheme the tests will be planned as an integral part of the teaching, checking on the understanding of essential concepts as they are developed, and on the acquisition of skills.

## Reliability and domains

Thinking of testing as aiming to help students out of their difficulties, and as keeping a check on the progress being made, emphasizes the criterion-referenced nature of diagnostic testing. We want to check on the achievement of particular objectives. For example, we want students 'to communicate scientific observations, ideas and arguments logically, concisely and in various forms'. This is a complex objective which involves students in many different processes, such as writing, speaking, tabulating, drawing diagrams, graphs and charts, and making models. As we teach, we concentrate on one or two of these at a time, and we move from simple to more complicated situations as the students' competence improves.

Assessing just one of these processes with just one question would be an unreliable assessment of the achievement of the objective. **Reliability**, in this context, concerns the repeatability of results. Generally speaking, the more questions you ask about something, the more reliable is the assessment. Asking a student to display the results of one of his experiments in a neat table is one small part of this objective. If he makes a poor attempt at it, it does not mean he cannot display the results in the form of a neat graph. It does not even mean that he could not tabulate the results of another experiment, or of the same experiment on another occasion when he was not upset about a row at home, or was less tired, or was more co-operative etc.

There are two points arising out of this. The first is to recognize that *any* assessment of a student is subject to error or unreliability. As scientists we realize that *no* measurement is free of error; many other people do not appreciate this to the same extent and will argue that 60 per cent in an examination is definitely better than 59 per cent. The second point is to try to assess the same process several times. However, if the processes are defined with the level of specificity which avoids ambiguity, this is not feasible because of the very large number of processes which would result. This problem of proliferation was mentioned earlier when we discussed processes, criteria and skills. A way out of the difficulty, and of ameliorating the associated problems of triviality and disintegration which were also mentioned, is to group related processes into a **domain** and to sample from within the domain.

The contents of a domain are related in some way so that the domain has some kind of coherence or homogeneity. A domain can be based on subject matter (content) or on processes. A topic on water is an example of a content domain; biology and science are examples of increasingly large content domains. Handling information and applying knowledge and skills are examples of process domains. It is obvious that a domain can be very large or very small and that large domains can consist of smaller domains. Large domains are usually **open** and small domains are usually **closed**. This can be illustrated by thinking about a domain concerned with adding numbers:

| | |
|---|---|
| Closed domain | Add two single-figure numbers, no carrying involved. |
| ↓ | Add any two single-figure numbers. |
| | Add any two double-figure whole numbers, no carrying involved. |
| | Add any two double-figure whole numbers. |
| | Add any two whole numbers. |
| Open domain | Add any three whole numbers. |

It is possible to specify all examples of two single-figure numbers which, when added together, involve no carrying, e.g.

$1+1,\ 1+2,\ 1+3,\ \ldots\ 1+8$
$2+1,\ 2+2,\ 2+3,\ \ldots\ 2+7$
and so on, there being 36 in total if we count 1 + 2 as being different from 2 + 1 etc. This is, therefore, an example of a closed domain. (Actually, where young children are concerned, there are even more examples because presenting a question in a line as above is not the same as presenting it in a column, e.g.

$$\begin{array}{r} 2 \\ +3 \\ \hline \\ \hline \end{array} \quad \text{or} \quad \begin{array}{r} 7 \\ +2 \\ \hline \\ \hline \end{array}$$

but, in principle, all possible questions can be listed.) On the other hand, there is an infinite number of whole numbers and hence an infinite number of examples in which any two of them are added together. This is therefore an open domain, and when assessing it we have to sample from the infinite number of possibilities.

## The practical domain

The GCSE National Criteria for Science (DES, 1985a) say:

All schemes of assessment must allocate not less than 20% of the total marks to experimental and other practical skills. At least half of these marks must be awarded on the basis of experimental and observational work in the laboratory or its equivalent.

Doing practical work involves activities ranging from the use of specific, intellectual and manipulative skills to general problem solving through scientific experiment. These two ends of the range of activities form the basis of two of the domains suggested by the Grade Related Criteria Working Parties in biology, chemistry and physics. We will use the first, specific one to illustrate how the definition of a domain can take place and describe two schemes which show how one might assess this particular aspect. The second, more general one will be dealt with in some detail in the next section on feedback to others.

### *Intellectual and manipulative skills*

A start to the definition of this domain is obtained by going back to the assessment objectives for science which were mentioned at the beginning of the chapter. We see that the following are relevant:

1.3 Knowledge and understanding of scientific instruments and apparatus, including techniques of operation and aspects of safety;
2.1 ability to observe, measure and record accurately and systematically;
2.2 ability to follow instructions accurately for the safe conduct of experiments.

> You will no doubt say there are others. List them, remembering that we are concerned about abilities directly related to the practical domain and that we are dealing with a sub-domain involving manipulative and associated intellectual skills. You may prefer to use the assessment objectives for your own specialist subject rather than those for science.

To get to the stage where we can be fairly sure what it is we are trying to assess, we must become more specific in our statements. For example, we can identify in assessment objective 1.3 the need to use basic laboratory measuring instruments and we can attempt a definition along the following lines:

The safe, accurate and appropriate use of a metric rule, vernier calliper, micrometer screw gauge, measuring cylinder, burette, spring balance, semi-automatic chemical balance, stop watch (analogue or digital), mercury-in-glass thermometer, voltmeter, ammeter, CRO to measure voltage and frequency.

Note that this list is concerned with *measuring* instruments. It does not include the use of common apparatus such as bunsen burners, tripods, beakers, retort stands etc. Note also that it is biased in the direction of physics; a list for biology will have much that is common to this one but with one or two deletions and additions. Differences between subjects become more apparent when we broaden the definition to include more than just measuring instruments. Compared with physics, biology will put more emphasis on such things as the safe use of scalpels, on the setting-up and use of a microscope and on techniques of sampling and the use of control experiments.

> Expand the above ideas in order to define this particular sub-domain for your own subject. You will find that the list gets quite large and you will have difficulty deciding what should be included and what should be excluded. You may decide that the use of a control experiment, say, does not belong in a domain concerned with manipulative skills. In such cases decisions are a matter of personal judgement as to how important the particular skill is and whether it could more conveniently be included in another domain. In this case, we have to remember that there is another sub-domain involving the solving of problems through scientific experiment.

Assessing every single skill in your list for every student may turn out to be an impossible burden. Remember, however, that the assessment can be progressive and accumulative, i.e. it can be spread over several years. For most students you are unlikely to need to assess their ability to use a metre rule when they are in the fifth form. You will have checked on this some time in the past and will have provided opportunities for them to continue to use metre rules in the intervening period. In the fifth form, you are more likely to be concerned with such things as using voltmeters and CROs. A characteristic of assessment in this sub-domain is that it can arise directly out of the teaching and takes place as the teaching progresses. It is much more closely linked to specific skills than is the sub-domain on problem solving, and it enables an accumulation of formatively assessed processes and skills to count towards the summative assessment. A student can be asked to show that she can measure the diameter of a piece of wire and, if she does not succeed, can be given instruction until she does succeed.

The successful assessment of the students will depend upon good organization and good record keeping. The growth of graded assessments is making this apparent.

## Graded assessments

Graded assessments are a means of giving credit to students in stages for what they can do. There are several reasons behind the growth of this movement, not least of which is the realization that students currently attend school from age 5 and reach age 16 before getting any external acknowledgement of their achievements. A not insignificant number do not even get any recognition at that stage, and leave school apparently not having achieved anything in their 11 years of full-time education. This is not the place to debate the merits or otherwise of the movement, nor to describe the several different schemes which are being established. I shall give a summary of one scheme which originated in Avon as an example of what is involved. For full details, contact The Senior Adviser, Mathematics, Science and Technology, Education Department, Avon House North, St James Barton, Bristol BS99 7EB.

This science certificate is designed to provide a summary of the level of basic scientific attainment for students in secondary schools. The award of the certificate is given to all students over the age of 13, but it is primarily designed for those below the sixtieth percentile for whom it is likely to be the only form of certification of their progress in science. (The ILEA graded assessment scheme is aimed at students of all abilities, it being argued that to limit it to the bottom ability students will automatically make it a second class qualification and debase its market value.)

The scheme is structured to provide objectives at different levels. Each level can be achieved by the target group of students in less than one year, and the achievement is acknowledged by the award of a certificate. The whole purpose of the scheme is to increase the motivation of the students.

Level I is defined by four domains (although the scheme does not refer to them as such) which are practically-based:

Manipulative skills (Ma)
Recording skills (Re)
Observational skills (Ob)
Measurement skills (Me)

Each domain is then defined by listing the activities required. For example, the recording skills and the measurement skills are as follows:

## *Recording skills*

Every pupil should be able to:

1 draw diagrams (with labels) of familiar, individual items of equipment;
2 identify items of equipment;
3 draw diagrams of simple photo-reduced geometric shape as viewed through a microscope (minimum $\times 40$);
4 tabulate a given set of results with one column of results already completed;
5 answer simple questions given a drawn pie chart;
6 construct a bar chart from a set of figures with both axes already labelled;
7 record the results of experimental investigation on sheets provided.

## *Measurement skills*

Each pupil should be able to:

1 make measurements of mass to an accuracy of one scale division;
2 measure lengths less than 1 metre to the nearest millimetre;
3 measure lengths over 1 metre to $\pm 1$ per cent using a ruler or measure too short for the task;
4 use a stop clock to an accuracy of 1 second;
5 read volume in a measuring cylinder to an accuracy of one scale division;
6 measure + and − values of temperature to the nearest scale division;
7 read an analogue meter to the nearest scale division (ten divisions).

The domains are assessed by the teachers in the schools using tasks provided by the LEA. Question sheets are provided for the students, and teachers' notes give instructions for setting up and marking the tasks. Two examples are shown on pages 146–149.

To gain an award the students are asked to do about 14 tasks, each task typically assessing several of the activities in the domains. You can see that Station E assesses Ob4 (the fourth activity in the Observation domain), Me7 and Re2; Station F assesses Me5, Ma4, Ob1 and Re1. Schools can assess students individually when they are ready, or they might assess a small group of students on one station in a week, or they may operate a more formal 'circus' in which all the stations are set up in one session. When all the stations have been attempted most, if not all, of the activities within a domain have been covered and a student's performance in each domain is assessed about eight times. The testing and marking is criterion-referenced, the student either gets a tick for successful

| Pupil Number |
| --- |
| |

1984/85 Series

QUESTION SHEET: STATION E

TEACHERS ONLY

1. Look at the electrical circuit which has been set up in front of you.

   DO NOT TOUCH IT

   Study the four cards showing diagrams of electric circuits. Which diagram shows the real circuit on the bench?

   Answer:Diagram _______________ Ob4

   What is the reading shown on the meter?

   Answer _______________ Me7

2. Here are the names of some pieces of electrical equipment.

   Socket Plug Fuse Wire Switch

   There are three items on the bench. They are labelled A, B and C. Name these electrical items

   A is ______________

   B is ______________

   C is ______________ Re2

Pupil Number

1984/85 Series

QUESTION SHEET: STATION F

TEACHERS ONLY

. Look at the measuring cylinder marked X which has water in it. How much water is in the measuring cylinder?

Answer ____________

Me5 [ ]

. Use the empty measuring cylinder and the beaker with water in it. Pour the water into the measuring cylinder so that it holds 55 $cm^3$.

ASK YOUR TEACHER TO CHECK THIS FOR YOU.

When it has been checked by the teacher, pour the water back into the beaker.

Ma4 [ ]

. Look carefully at the test tubes in the rack. You may pick them up.

BUT DO NOT OPEN THEM

Describe what you see in each test tube.

First test tube ______________________________

______________________________

______________________________

Second test tube ______________________________

______________________________

______________________________

Ob1 [ ]

Draw and label a diagram of Flask F which has a coloured liquid in it.

Re1 [ ]

STATION E 1984/85 SERIES

TEACHERS' NOTES

Station will need:

(a) Provided by School:

1 cell or battery, 1 switch, 1 bulb and holder, set of labels, connecting wire and an ammeter or volt meter (single scale analogue type). A broken meter with a fixed reading would be ideal.

The scale should have 10 equal divisions between each whole number. The meter should read, say, 2.3 rather than 2.0 (too easy) or 2.18 (too difficult).

(b) Provided with Question Pack:

4 prepared circuit diagrams, labelled 1, 2, 3 and 4.

3 lettered cards A, B and C.

To set up Station:

1. Set up a circuit using the cell or battery, switch and two of the remaining items of equipment. Place the appropriate label beside each item. Lay out the 4 numbered cards. Use the broken or fixed reading meter in the circuit.

2. Set out the three pieces of domestic electrical apparatus. Beside (or on) each, attach the cards A, B and C.

Successfully completed if:

1. Correct card (diagram selected) - tick box Ob4

2. Correct reading on meter, to nearest scale division - tick box Me7

3. All three items correctly identified - tick box Re2

| For guidance only; estimated duration of Station 5 - 8 minutes. |
|---|

STATION F 1984/85 SERIES

TEACHERS' NOTES

Station will need:

(a) Provided by the School

1. Two $100cm^3$ measuring cylinders, one marked X. A beaker holding at least $60cm^3$ of water.
2. Two sealed, half-filled test tubes, contents should be:
   i) mixture of marble chips and copper sulphate crystals (the fact that there are two different solids should be obvious);
   ii) car oil and coloured water allowed to settle.

   Test tube rack.
3. A conical flask holding coloured liquid.

(b) Provided with Question Pack:

Nothing.

To set up this Station:

1. Fill measuring cylinder X to a suitable height, say, $64cm^3$.
2. Fill the beaker with enough water to carry out the task, say, $60/70cm^3$.
3. Place the two half-filled test tubes in a rack at the Station.
4. Half-fill the conical flask with coloured water (say, dilute potassium permanganate solution).

Successfully completed if:

1. Correct reading $\pm 2cm^3$ (units not important) - tick box Me5
2. Correct filling of measuring cylinder to $\pm 2cm^3$ - tick box Ma4
3. Any valid observation which includes at least four key words drawn from the categories of colour, physical state, quantity, named chemical or particle size, ie. yellow and black, solid, mixture = 3 - tick box Ob1
4. Diagram of reasonable likeness, at least one label. At least one 'key' word "flask", "pink", "liquid" used - tick box Re1

For guidance only; estimated duration of Station 4 minutes.

completion of an activity or not. A final mark is determined which is the percentage of the total possible number of ticks.

A silver certificate is awarded to a student who gets between 60 per cent and 85 per cent of the total marks; a gold certificate for marks over 85 per cent. The certificates are professionally produced to a high quality and contain on the back a summary of the domains and their component activities. They are awarded three times a year at the end of each term.

Level II is defined by three other domains:

Skills (S)
Problem solving (PS)
Prediction interpretation (PI)

These domains are not entirely practical. For example, the Prediction/interpretation domain is defined as follows:

### *Prediction/interpretation*

PI1 Use a graph to answer simple questions.
PI2 Extrapolate from a graph for prediction purposes.
PI3 Use raw data to identify patterns and predict outcome of actions.
PI4 Matching data to draw a conclusion.

There is no room here to give further details. It can be seen that the heart of the scheme involves the identification of domains which form the basis of the assessment. Each domain is defined by specific activities (or processes), and questions or tasks are given to find out if the students can do these activities. The answer is either 'Yes' or 'No'. Mastery for the purpose of obtaining a certificate is determined by summing the Yes's, the criterion scores for mastery being arbitrarily set at 60 per cent for the silver certificate and 85 per cent for the gold certificate. Summing the individual performances helps to overcome the inherent unreliability of the individual measurements.

It should be noted that, while domains are identified, they are not a part of the decision making process nor of the reporting process. Their main purpose lies in defining a range of activities on which the assessment is based. They help to ensure a spread of activities and hence to increase the validity of the assessment process. Note also that the scheme can be diagnostic and formative as well as summative. The students know as well as the teachers what is required of them and they can practise the skills, assessing themselves and each other if they wish, until they think they are ready for formal testing.

The domains could be used as the elements in a profile if it were thought that the assessment of each were sufficiently reliable and that reporting on them separately would add useful information. A student's certificate might then contain the following:

| Ma | Me | Re | Ob | Total |
|---|---|---|---|---|
| 65 | 55 | 60 | 70 | 63 |

This shows that the student is rather weak in measurement skills, strong in observation skills and qualifies for a silver certificate overall.

A similar but more comprehensive scheme for the assessment of practical skills has emerged from the Government's development programme in Scotland (Munn and Dunning, 1982). The internal assessment of practical science skills is an important part of this programme, and a practical test item bank (TAPS, Techniques for the Assessment of Practical Skills) to be used for the certification of 14–16 year olds in the bottom 30 per cent of the ability range has been developed. (See Bryce *et al.*, 1983.) The bank provides full details for assessing students in six skill areas as follows:

| | *Skill area* | *Ability to . . .* |
|---|---|---|
| O | Observational skills | identify, classify, detect changes and differences. . . |
| R | Recording skills | present findings using spoken and written summaries, diagrams, tables and graphs. . . |
| Me | Measurement skills | read scales, measure and supply units, estimate values. . . |
| Ma | Manipulative skills | handle apparatus, co-ordinate movements, adjust and control, assemble and attach. . . |
| P | Procedural skills | choose and use particular pieces of apparatus, implement a procedure or technique. . . |
| F | Following instructions | follow demonstrations, spoken, written, or pictorial instructions. . . |

As with the Avon scheme, the skill areas are defined by statements as to what the students should be able to do, e.g.

O5 classify objects from given information.
R3 label a diagram accurately.
Me1 recognize or supply the correct units for common measurements.
Ma2 demonstrate fine motor control in a variety of ways including making precise movements or adjustments. . .
P10 use a test paper or test solution.
F2 set up apparatus or carry out a procedure from spoken instructions.

The statements tend to be less precise than do those in the Avon scheme, but their exact meaning is conveyed by the bank of tasks which are available to the teachers. A description of the tasks is also available to the students, even if the teachers do not tell them, because the teacher's guide is freely obtainable from bookshops. Any student who wishes to do so can therefore practise the tasks at home. In most instances this does not matter because he would be practising those very skills which he needs to acquire. For some items the response can be learned without there being any understanding, e.g. some of the observation tasks. However, it is unlikely that a student will practise all the 315 tasks which are available. Nevertheless, there is an important principle involved: there is nothing wrong in making clear to a student what it is he or she has to do, and then the student going away and practising to make sure he or she can do it.

The assessment of practical abilities at level I in the Avon scheme does not require the teacher to observe and mark how the student does a particular task. If the correct reading is obtained within the prescribed limits of accuracy, it is assumed that the student has performed the operation correctly. This is also the case with the vast majority of the 315 TAPS items. There are, however, a number of items which require some kind of check either during the performance of the task or immediately afterwards. For example, when assessing a student's ability to use a Celsius laboratory thermometer, the following seven criteria must be satisfied:

1 Removes thermometer from case.
2 Holds by correct end (during experiment).
3 Places bulb under water.
4 Waits for mercury level to stabilize.
5 Keeps bulb under water while reading.
6 Eye-level reading.
7 Dries and returns thermometer to case.

These must be observed by the teacher while the task is being attempted. Suggestions for coping with these situations, and for the general organization of the assessment procedures, is given in the teacher's guide.

### Summary

The DES (1983) gives a plan which shows how a subject department in a school can implement a coherent assessment scheme. This is shown in Figure 4.4.

The plan is followed by a description of a series of 'tracking exercises' which have been done by some schools in order to interrelate aims and objectives, lesson planning and lesson evaluation, including assessment of students. It involves making clear statements about aims, objectives, skills, attitudes, concepts and knowledge which are involved in a lesson or in a series of closely linked lessons, and setting out how they will be dealt with in the lessons. A key element in each exercise is an evaluation by the teacher and, sometimes, by the students also.

## Feedback to others

We begin now to be more concerned with the interests of other teachers in the school, with parents, employers and admissions tutors to institutions of further and higher education. External examinations and school reports are of particular concern.

The arrival of the GCSE has brought with it several changes. Notable among them, because they affect teachers directly in the way they work, are differentiated examinations, which have been mentioned already, and grade-related

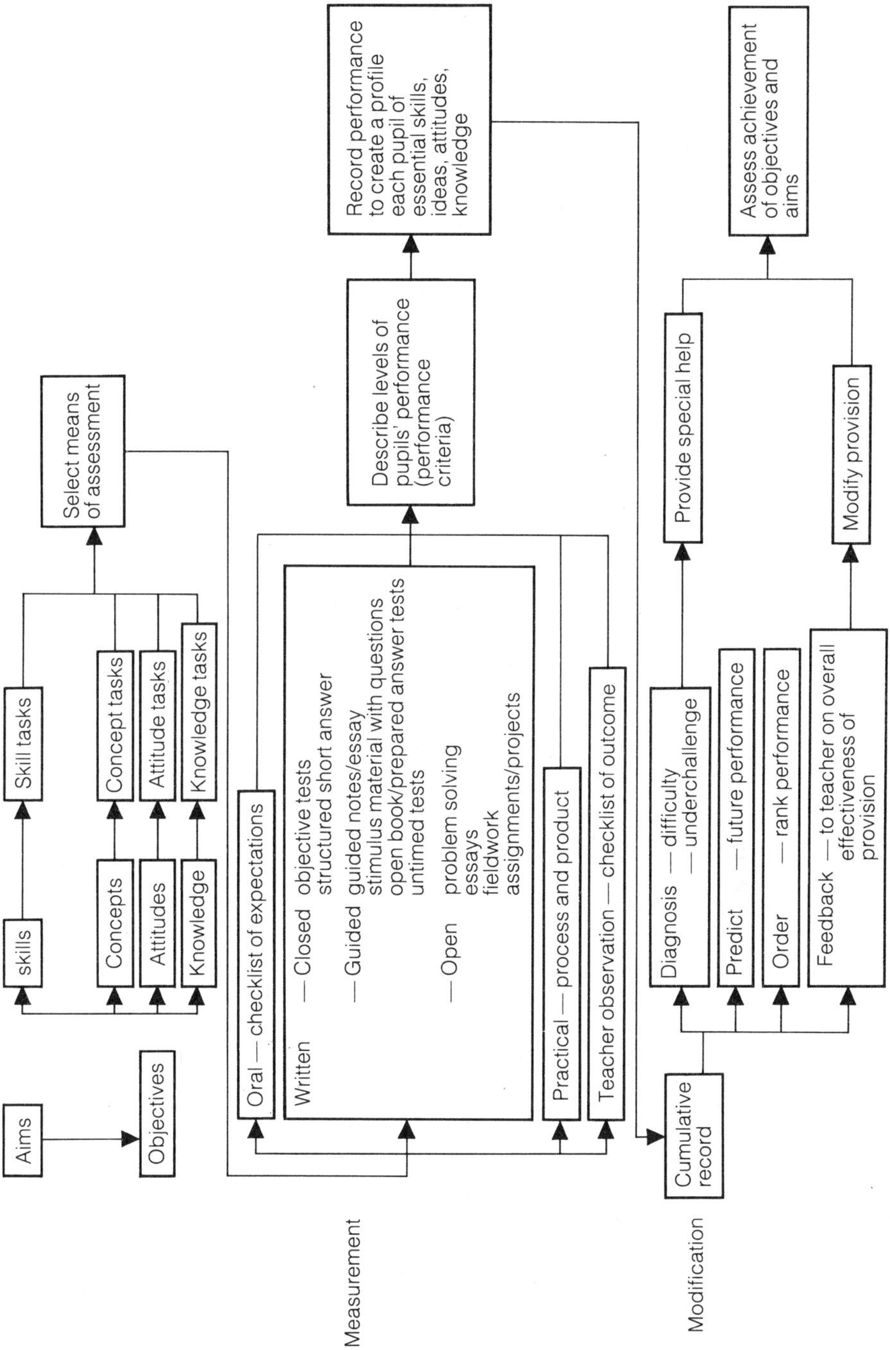


FIG. 4.4 **Subject disciplines: sequence of assessment implementation.** (From DES, 1983)

criteria. The grade-related criteria devised for the GCSE are based on process domains such as recalling and understanding knowledge, handling information, and doing investigations. No more than six domains are used to define a subject and so each one is large and open. The assessment of a student's ability within a domain thus entails sampling from the domain; and the sampling must not only be representative of the domain but also, until true criterion-referenced grades arrive, must enable a range of competencies to be displayed so that the full range of grades involved in the GCSE will be awarded. (There is some argument as to whether each domain should separately cover the full range of abilities in the GCSE target group. Provided all the domains taken together cover the full range, it does not seem necessary that each domain separately should do so. Indeed, with true criterion-referencing, it must be possible for all candidates to get full marks in any domain provided they satisfy the necessary criteria. Arguments about covering the full range of grades do not apply; if the effect of no candidates falling into the bottom grade results in making the examination more difficult so that they do, then this is a retreat from the principles of criterion-referencing.)

It is not possible in this chapter to deal in detail with all the issues and consequences of criterion-referencing of grades, although some of them have been discussed in previous sections. The decisions made by the Secondary Examinations Council affect not only the examination boards but also teachers in schools because, particularly with the assessment of practical abilities, it is the teachers who do the assessing. For this reason this section will take further the assessment of practical work and will deal particularly with open-ended practical investigations.

## Practical investigations

The kind of work involved in this domain is more familiar at A level than at 16+. For example, it is seen in the investigations which are a part of the Nuffield physics examination. Perhaps somewhat surprisingly it is also becoming familiar in junior schools, particularly those involved in the British Association Award Scheme. The main characteristic of the work is its open-endedness; and it is encouraging for the main body of teaching that it is being attempted successfully at both ends of the age spectrum in schools.

Open-ended practical work is aimed at giving the initiative to students for finding the solution to a problem. With its emphasis on autonomy in making decisions and integration of several bits of knowledge and skill, it contrasts with the specific, 'unitary' nature of simply using measuring instruments and exhibiting manipulative skills which were discussed earlier. Yet it involves these skills, and probably the main reason for separating out the two domains is so that students can be given credit for being able to show competence in fairly clearly defined and important skills such as reading a thermometer and focusing a microscope.

Working in open-ended situations is often seen as being what science is all about. As such, the ability of students to perform satisfactorily in such situations is thus an important part of a valid assessment of a student's ability in science. From the point of view of a public examination, one of the biggest problems associated with open-ended questions is that they lead to open-ended answers which are difficult to mark reliably. This will be discussed further later on.

Open-endedness is not, of course, confined to practical work, but this section concentrates on this area. The range of possible activities is very large, and they do not all require a great deal of time, space or apparatus. Nor need they make great demands on the students.

*Example 1*

Do all leaves from the same tree have the same shape?

Apart from the leaves themselves, this requires little more than a small amount of bench and storage space, a ruler and a calculator. There is a particularly crucial decision to be made about the meanings of same shape and different shape which can make a considerable demand on some students. However, the problem can be solved at different levels varying from qualitative enlargements using an OHP to the use of sophisticated statistical techniques involving cluster analysis and discriminant analysis. Similarly, the time involved can be variable, but a satisfactory exploration can be started and finished within the space of a double period.

*Example 2*

Two kinds of paper clip are common:

(a) Curly

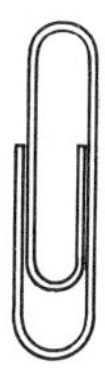

(b) Cross-over

Find out whether one of them is more effective than the other.

Although chosen with the idea of eventually involving students in the measurement of forces, several quite different approaches are possible. One method could use a constant number of pieces of paper subjected to a standard vibration, with the criterion for effectiveness being the time taken for the papers to fall apart. Another could pull the papers apart, with the criterion for effectiveness being the force needed.

In this area of work, expectations are constantly being confounded by the lateral thinking of students who are not constrained by a particular kind of science education into working along conventional lines. This is particularly apparent in junior schools, although it may be less so by the time the students reach age 16.

The effect of our conventional, rather academic science teaching is illustrated by a remark made by a 14 year old boy after his first experience of being allowed to take the initiative in an open-ended problem solving session, 'It's good fun, but it's not really science is it?'

It is unreasonable at age 16 to ask students for the first time to take the initiative in solving an open-ended problem. They need time and practice to develop confidence and to acquire the necessary knowledge and skills. This means a range of problems is needed which makes gradually increasing demands both in terms of subject knowledge and in terms of techniques. A problem which asks a student to find out how fast ants move is difficult if the students have never timed anything over a measured distance. It becomes a great deal easier if it follows some instruction on measuring speed and the student is already competent in using a metre rule and a stop watch. However, it is not as easy as finding the speed with which a colleague walks across the laboratory because the colleague will start and stop when asked whereas the ant will not!

Make a list of open-ended investigations which might be suitable for one of the groups you teach. For each investigation:

say what subject matter is involved;
indicate some alternative approaches;
list the apparatus which you think might be needed;
estimate how long your slowest student will take to do the investigation.

Now give the group one, or more, of the problems. Tell them that they have to decide what to do themselves. This includes deciding what apparatus is needed, what measurements to take and what to do with the measurements when they have taken them. Tell them also that it is not an examination of any kind.

The exact organization will depend upon the time, space and apparatus you have available. This will govern whether they all do the same investigation, or all do different investigations, or work in pairs etc. (It is better to work as individuals, or at the most in pairs.)

What you do with the final results is also a matter for your own judgement. You can ask the students to write an account of what they did and what they found out. (But if they have never done this before, they will need some guidance.) At the minimum you should perhaps insist that they keep sufficiently good records to be able to tell their colleagues, verbally, about their work.

Needing to find the average of several measurements, being sensitive to intervening variables and needing to use control experiments are all factors which can increase the complexity and hence the demands of an investigation.

## *Marking and mark schemes*

The variety of approaches which is possible even in the same exploration (the open-ended answers mentioned earlier) means that, if the activities are to be assessed, the mark scheme must be sufficiently broad to enable all sensible approaches to be properly judged. That is to say, the mark scheme must embrace those aspects of doing science which are common to every good exploration. At the same time the marking must be capable of being done without making unreasonable demands on time, organization and cost. A balance must be struck between a scheme which ignores these requirements and hence becomes impossible to apply, and one which concentrates too much on reliability thereby distorting the scientific activity.

One way to do this is as follows:

Clarify the processes involved in the domain.
Devise an assessment scheme which enables the competence in each of these processes to be assessed.
Define an open-ended exploration as one which enables students to demonstrate their level of competence in each of the processes.

This is at odds with those who say the decision making process should put the assessment scheme last but, provided the assessment scheme matches the objectives, this approach will drive the teaching in the direction we want. It will require an interplay between processes and assessment because not all desirable processes will be capable of being assessed, either because we do not have the techniques to do it or because there are too many processes. With a careful choice, however, one will not only assess a majority of the important processes but will encourage others to be developed even though they are not assessed.

Choose one or two of the explorations you devised above and decide what processes the students have to use when doing them. Are any important processes missing from any one exploration?
Do you think it matters if there are?
Would you expect a student to do only one exploration?
Would it be possible to involve all the important processes if students did several explorations?

## *Tight assessment and loose assessment*

The nature of open-ended work is such that its assessment is best done by teachers in the schools. To ensure as much uniformity of standards as possible, the boards have to issue guidelines. At one extreme the guidelines can be so explicit that the teachers will have little doubt about how to award marks. This is what might be called tight assessment. It produces the greatest reliability and the least need for moderation of standards, but it constrains the open-endedness of the activity.

At the other extreme, the guidelines can be very general thereby encouraging a wide variety of activities, but leading to uncertainty about commonality of standards. This is what might be called loose assessment. These two extremes are discussed below.

1 **Tight assessment.** There are basically two kinds of tight assessment. One is content-driven, the other is process-driven.

(a) *Content-driven assessments* In this scheme the activities of the students are constrained along certain pre-determined paths to which are allocated particular marks. There is a variety of possibilities, two of which are given below for illustration.

**Example 1** (Adapted from TEC example)
*Title*: An Exploration of Thermometers

*Summary*: This assignment requires some background reading, some experimentation and the production of a report. It should occupy no more than five hours of work including the writing of the report.

*Tasks*

1 Taking a mercury-in-glass thermometer as an example, why is it useful to:
(a) have a large bulb containing a (relatively) large volume of mercury, and
(b) have a very narrow bore tube?

2 Look up the maximum temperature glass can be heated to yet retain its 'rigid' characteristics (there is more than one sort of glass).

3 Look up the boiling and freezing points of mercury and ethanol.

4 Could pentane be used as the liquid in a liquid-in-glass thermometer and, if so, over what range?

5 Estimate the useful operating ranges of mercury-in-glass and methanol-in-glass thermometers.

6 Look at a mercury-in-glass thermometer. Is the scale linear?

7 Heat a beaker of water to near boiling point and then place a thermometer in it. Why is it difficult to say how long it takes for the reading on the thermometer to become stable?
Illustrate your answer with a sketch graph.

8 Suppose you were using a mercury-in-glass thermometer to monitor the temperature of a component. The component's temperature, initially at

room temperature, rises very rapidly to 80°C in 5 min and then falls back to room temperature. Sketch a graph showing this variation.

On the same axes, sketch another graph showing how the thermometer reading would change over the same time interval.

9 What is meant by the response time of a thermometer?

10 Warm a beaker of water to about 60°C and place four mercury-in-glass thermometers in it. Note as exactly as possible the reading on each.
How accurately can you read the thermometers?
Do they agree to within these limits?

11 What is the current price of a mercury-in-glass thermometer designed to cover the range −10°C to about 120°C?

12 To monitor a temperature using a liquid-in-glass thermometer clearly needs an operator to watch it and note temperatures at set intervals of time. At current rates, what is the cost per hour of such an operator?

In an industrial environment, it may be necessary to monitor temperature over a full working day for 1 year. How much would this cost using a mercury-in-glass thermometer?

*Report*
You should prepare a report including graphs, sketches, tables and experimental results with conclusions and comment where appropriate.

In this particular example the marks are not shown, but it is clear that a fairly tight mark scheme could be constructed.

**Example 2** (from the JMB – for Physics A level)

*Design and construction of a thermometer*
The thermometer you are required to design and make has to cover the range 0°C to 40°C, to have a sensitivity of about 3mm per °C and to use methylated spirit.

Before attempting to construct the thermometer from the capillary tubing supplied you must first do some preliminary experiments on both the tube and the methylated spirit. This should provide you with the information you need to design the thermometer required. (Be sure to include your design calculations in your report).

Having decided on the dimensions of your thermometer, construct it – some notes are available to help you to do this.

Calibrate the instrument using a commercial thermometer – it will be yours when you have made it.

*Assessment* (30 marks)

1 Has the diameter of the capillary tubing to be used, been satisfactorily measured? (0–3)

2 Has the coefficient of expansion of methylated spirit been satisfactorily measured? (0–3)

3 Has the diameter of the thermometer bulb to give the required sensitivity of 3mm per °C been calculated? (0–5)
4 Has the thermometer been successfully constructed? (0–5)
5 Did the thermometer have the required sensitivity? (0–3)
6 Have adequate details of apparatus and procedures been given in the written report to enable someone else to repeat the work? (0–5)
7 In the written report are the results and conclusions presented in a clear and concise manner? (0–5)
8 Is there any feature of special merit which deserves a bonus mark (e.g. ingenuity)? (1)

This example is one of a package of assignments all of which were pre-tested and all of which have a mark scheme which gives a total of 30.

(b) *Process-driven assessments* Process-driven assessment schemes attempt to identify the steps or processes which it is thought all open-ended explorations will go through and to award marks for each. One such series of processes might be:

observing
repeating observations
recording
controlling variables
analysing and deducing
assessing experimental error
producing a report

Such lists purport to summarize 'scientific method' and imply a rather tidy view of the way in which scientific research takes place. A list of headings like this, while better than nothing, is not really good enough on its own and is usually accompanied by statements (sometimes called criteria) of the behaviour required of candidates in order to be awarded certain marks, e.g.
*Analysis*
In analysing the observations and data, the candidate:

| | |
|---|---|
| drew well reasoned deductions from all the data; | 3 |
| made reasonable deductions from most of the data; | 2 |
| made a significant attempt to draw a conclusion; | 1 |
| made no significant attempt to arrive at a conclusion. | 0 |

(From the JMB.)

The problem with this particular example is the imprecision of such words as 'reasonable' and 'significant'. Another example which attempts to give a more detailed description of behaviour in a hierarchical form is as follows:
*Possession of appropriate manipulative skills*
10–9 Very good general ability to carry out a full range of skills. Good appreciation of the appropriateness of apparatus. Able to make correct

decisions as to the accuracy required for a specific operation and to apply the necessary techniques to achieve such accuracy.

8–7 Good general ability but limited in certain skills.

6–5 routine worker who does not vary his degree of precision in accordance with the requirements of the particular situation. Does not always appreciate the precision or delicacy of apparatus or the variations which may occur in results as a result of faulty or inappropriate techniques.

4–3 Rather careless in handling material and apparatus.

2–1 Careless in handling material and apparatus. Quantitative results contain numerous errors which have not been recognized.

(From the JMB.)

The difficulty with this kind of list is that many students exhibit behaviour which samples from more than one mark band.

A way out of these problems is to avoid the attempt to categorize students into bands which are defined by specific behaviour statements. This can be done by modifying the example given above for the assessment of analysis so that the different grade bands are more precise in their meaning and at the same time allowing students to fall into a band by virtue of the *number* of criteria they satisfy. One example of this is given below:

4 Excellent, meets all the criteria.
3 Very good, meets well over half of the criteria.
2 Good, meets about half of the criteria.
1 Fair, meets well below half of the criteria.
0 Poor, meets none of the criteria.

This can be tightened even further if the performance of the candidates can be measured either in terms of achievement of each criterion in the process (1 mark – achieved, 0 marks – not achieved) or in terms of increasing proficiency within the separate statements which define the domain (perhaps with a range of marks from, say, 0 to 5). In both cases the individual marks can be added and the sum used to arrive at an overall mark for the process, e.g.

5 Excellent, achieved 81–100 per cent of the marks.
4 Good, achieved 61–80 per cent of the marks.
3 Satisfactory, achieved 41–60 per cent of the marks.
2 Poor, achieved 21–40 per cent of the marks.
1 Very poor, achieved 0–20 per cent of the marks.

It should be noted that these are criterion-referenced decisions, not norm-referenced, because they result from the summation of a series of criterion-referenced judgements. It is possible for *all* candidates to get full marks for the domain if they satisfy the conditions.

**2 Loose assessment** Loose assessment is at the opposite end of the data-gathering process from tight assessment. In a loose assessment very little or no data are gathered in any formal way. One simply requires that students be involved in a programme of activities without attempting to measure the achievement of specific objectives. The reward comes from being involved, from participating.

Reporting is of the form:

Mary Smith has completed an exploration on 'Finding out what snails eat'. The exploration involved planning, experimenting, observing, drawing conclusions and writing a report. The work was done on her own but she had free access to reference books and the advice of anyone she cared to consult.

A copy of her report is attached.

A series of carefully chosen explorations, perhaps graded in order of difficulty according to the number of variables involved in the exploration, or the amount of guidance given to the candidate in the initial statement of the problem, would enable a range of behaviours to be assessed at various levels of difficulty. Achievement of the higher grades in the examination would be conditional upon a certain number of explorations at certain minimum levels of difficulty.

The big advantage of loose assessment is that it makes the minimum of demands on teachers. Some commonality of standards can be achieved by requiring teachers to attend standardizing meetings (as with AEB/SCISP) at which case studies are discussed. This does put a demand on teachers, but it can be spread over a period of time.

## Attitudes

### *Introduction*

Giving the initiative to students for finding the solution to a problem, which is the key element in open-ended work, requires some commitment on the part of the student which goes beyond just the application of knowledge. It requires such things as perseverance, co-operation and dependability. These are characteristics which reflect upon the attitude of the student. Most teachers see them as important in the education of young people, and some believe they should be assessed as a part of the normal assessment of students.

The assessment of attitudes is, in fact, a part of some examinations at 16+. (See, for example, the AEB/SCISP examination.) Also, some comment on attitudes is usually made in reports which are sent home to parents, and there is invariably a section on attitudes in most references written by a school in connection with applications for jobs. For example, the following are the headings in a confidential reference required to be completed by a school for students who are applying for sponsorship to university/polytechnic by a large firm:

Acting responsibly
Dependability

Attitude to authority
Appearance
Attitude to work
Relationship with peers
Working in groups

Once in employment, another large firm requires its management trainees to be assessed by their immediate supervisor under the following headings:

Communicating
Planning
Problem solving
Decision making
Innovation
Initiative
Data analysis
Team work

It is easier to decide what aspects of a person's performance should be assessed in a firm than it is in a school where no specific job is in mind. In a school, therefore, it is probably more important to concentrate on broad characteristics which are capable of generalization rather than on specific 'skills' which are more job-specific.

## *Some basic principles*

Firstly, it is important to be clear what is to be included under the heading of attitudes. It should be noticed that the second list of headings which was given above does not include such things as dependability and attitude to work which appeared in the first list. The list refers to aspects of a person which, while personal, are not character judgements. They are 'skills' which are judged to be important for doing a particular job, and their absence is not a reflection on the (good or bad) character of the person. However, the distinction between 'skills' such as communicating and problem solving, and personal characteristics, such as honesty and dependability, is not always clear; for example, team work appears to have an element of both. This lack of distinction is part of the problem about assessing such characteristics; they all tend to be listed under the heading of attitudes. Strictly speaking the second list does not constitute a set of attitudes.

> Make a list of some general skills and personal attributes which you think should be developed in students in school. Decide which are attitudes, which are personality characteristics and which are cross-subject skills.

Discuss the list you have compiled above with other teachers. Do they agree with it? Do they think that all, some or none of the items in the list should be assessed?

For each item what sort of behaviour would they expect from a student in order to get a high score, and what sort of behaviour would get a low score?

Secondly, it is important that the assessment of attitudes be co-ordinated across the school. This is because the characteristics involved not only cut across subject boundaries, but a student may behave differently in different situations and the same behaviour may be assessed differently by different teachers. It is necessary, therefore, for everyone to be clear about what is happening and to be aware of the basic principles behind the assessment of attitudes.

Some rather more detailed points about attitudes are given below. An understanding of these will reduce confusion and enable discussions to take place more amicably.

• Attitudes are concerned with people. A statement about attitudes is a statement about people. (This is part of the controversy about the assessment of attitudes; we are trying to say something about the student himself or herself, and not about the student's knowledge or understanding of a subject. We are dealing with what is commonly called the *affective domain* as opposed to the *cognitive domain*.)

• Attitudes may be related to:

Feelings or emotions, e.g. enjoyment, likes, dislikes, interests, happiness;
Personal characteristics, e.g. self-confidence, open-mindedness, willingness to co-operate with others, loyalty, truthfulness.

These are closely connected with value judgements. Feelings or emotions tend not to have value because we cannot reasonably expect all students to enjoy, like, or even have an interest in, all the subjects which are taught. However, we do expect all students to be open-minded, loyal and truthful, and so these have value. The assessment of an attitude towards a subject is less controversial than the assessment of personal characteristics.

• Attitudes have:

Context, e.g. peace and war, science, smoking. Attitudes, particularly feelings and emotions, tend not to exist in isolation. One has an attitude *towards* something or somebody.
Intensity, e.g. different people enjoy the same thing differently; the same person enjoys different things differently

Linearity (we assume this for ease of use), i.e. strongly positive ... strongly negative, e.g. like very much ... dislike very much. We frequently assess on a scale from 1 to 5 and assume that 3 is in the middle or is average. This can lead to the further assumption that a score of 4 means liking something twice as much as when the score is 2. The absurdity of this is apparent when we try to think of the meaning of someone being twice as honest or twice as beautiful as someone else. We have to be careful that we do not try to deal with measurements (such as attitudes) which are on an *ordinal* scale as if they were on a *ratio* scale (like length and weight).

## *What attitudes?*

Attitudes can be general, i.e. applicable to any subject in the curriculum and hence assessable by all teachers in the school, or they can be subject-specific.

Some examples of **general** attitudes are:

integrity (honesty, trustworthiness, loyalty)
courtesy (consideration for others)
industry (perseverance)
resourcefulness
self-respect (self-confidence, emotional stability)
leadership

Some examples of attitudes which can be **specific** to science are:

to be concerned about the application of scientific knowledge in the community;
to be willing to work individually;
to be willing to work as part of a group;
to be willing to search for and to test for patterns;
to be unbiased in reporting scientific work.

Attitudes which are required to be assessed as a part of a formal examination are likely to be subject-specific. The more general attitudes are likely to be a part of a school's programme of monitoring students' progress.

Brown (1975) draws attention to the problem of finding the right level of specificity for stating an objective:

For example, an objective:
'to appreciate the economic implications for the community of scientific and technological progress'
is broad, somewhat ambiguous and difficult to translate into classroom procedures, but may well be an important and relevant objective. On the other hand, the objective:
'to appreciate the economic implications for the community of scientific and technological progress as evidenced by the naming from memory of five inventions of the last fifty years that are now in general use as home appliances'
leads easily to teaching procedures and test items, but may well be meaningless and trivial in the development of the desired attitudes.

This problem was discussed earlier in the section on reliability and domains on page 140.

Note that one would normally approach a person directly in order to find out their attitude towards, say, the Government or energy conservation. This would usually be done by way of a questionnaire, either written or verbal. When assessing such things as personal attributes, however, this is not the way it is done; mainly because it is too easy for the respondent to fake the result. In education one person (the teacher) is asked to give his or her opinion about the attitudes of another person (the student). As mentioned earlier, however, it is becoming increasingly common to involve the students in their own assessment. The area of attitude assessment is particularly appropriate for this kind of move. In the armed services and in business it is common for the person being assessed to see the assessment and to make their own comments.

## *Assessing attitudes*

There are three basic ways for assessing attitudes which are open to teachers:

1 observing behaviour;
2 asking students to write essays;
3 using questionnaires.

The first of these, observing behaviour, involves being clear about what aspects of attitude one is looking for and having indicators of behaviour which can be observed by teachers in the classroom or laboratory and are interpreted in the same way by all teachers. This can be done by having descriptors which define the attitude *construct* under consideration as outlined below, or by having 'comment banks' as described in the section on profiles on page 174.

Asking students to write essays on how they feel about particular aspects of science is, as mentioned above, open to faking. In addition, the marking of essays is particularly unreliable and it would be very difficult to get from them any approach to an objective measure of student attitude.

The third method of using questionnaires, whether answered by teachers about students or by the students themselves, is probably the most fruitful. It must be realized, however, that in order to complete a questionnaire or rating scale about a student, a teacher needs to have the necessary evidence. Many teachers wrongly interpret academic achievement as being indicative of attitude. A good attitude scale can help to overcome these problems, and it will be helpful to understand something behind the construction of such scales. It involves being clear about constructs as mentioned in the section on validity on page 122.

**(a) Constructs** Attitudes are examples of what psychologists call **constructs**. You cannot point to an attitude and put a ruler against it in the same way that you can point to and put a ruler against a length. Attitudes (as with all constructs) have to be defined by description and example, and a good scale for measuring an attitude would normally go through some complex process of validation. Central to this process is the composition of statements which describe the construct. Most worthwhile constructs are not narrow in the behaviours which they cover, and so the description of a construct will usually include a range of behaviours which typify the construct. For example, 'being willing to work as part of a group' might be described as follows:

contributes effectively as a member of the group;
interested and involved in group and class discussion;
tolerant of the views of other members of the group;
persists to ensure that the purpose of the group is achieved;
conforms to the role assigned within the group;
able to organize and direct others without being overbearing.

A person's overall position within the construct is an amalgam of the separate behaviours which constitute the construct.

One cannot be sure that all the statements contribute to a measure of the same construct. For example, 'being able to organize and direct others without being overpowering' might be more concerned with a construct about leadership, i.e. this statement might not be a *valid* part of the 'working as part of a group' construct. *Construct validity* can be checked statistically using a process known as factor analysis. This is beyond the scope of most schools (although programs for use on microcomputers are becoming available), and the best way to proceed at the moment is to agree through discussion about the statements which should define a construct. This ensures that the construct has *content validity*.

> For each of the attitudes which you decided on above as important, compose a set of behaviour statements which define the attitude. (It is impossible to judge a person's attitude, or anything alse about a person, if it does not give rise to something which is observable.)
>
> Check with your colleagues about their agreement with the statements.

**(b) Attitude scales** There are several ways of attempting to quantify the assessment of attitudes and hence of constructing an attitude scale. Probably the most common are:

the semantic differential;
Likert scales;
Guttman scaling.

Rather more will be said here about the first two and not so much about the last since it seems to be less widely used.

(i) The **semantic differential** was developed by C. E. Osgood (see Osgood *et al.* 1957). To use the semantic differential one first decides upon the **construct** (or

**concept**) to be evaluated, e.g. physics, school, doctors. Sets of **polar adjective pairs** are then chosen, e.g. good–bad, strong–weak, pleasurable–painful. Finally the respondent is required to indicate on a **scale** from 1 to 5 or 1 to 7 his feelings about the construct within each adjective pair, e.g.

*Biology*

| | |
|---|---|
| Good | Bad |
| Clean | Dirty |
| Important | Unimportant |

With the correct choice of adjectives, feelings about a construct (or concept) can be summarized using any or all of three factors:

1 evaluative (e.g. good–bad)
2 potency (e.g. hard–soft
3 activity (e.g. fast–slow)

The three adjective pairs given above for biology are all evaluative.

One can compare the attitudes of different individuals or groups towards the same construct, or the attitudes of the same individual or group towards different constructs. One could compare the attitude of a group of pupils to science before they have been taught a particular topic to their attitude after they have been taught the topic, for example:

*Science is*

| | | |
|---|---|---|
| 1 | Good | Bad |
| 2 | True | False |
| 3 | Interesting | Boring |
| 4 | Useful | Useless |

The analysis of each adjective-pair would be as follows (using the useful–useless adjective pair as an example.)

| | *Value*(V) | *Frequency*(F) | V × F |
|---|---|---|---|
| Extremely useful | 1 | 2 | 2 |
| Quite useful | 2 | 18 | 36 |
| Slightly useful | 3 | 14 | 42 |
| Neither useful nor useless | 4 | 5 | 20 |
| Slightly useless | 5 | 8 | 40 |
| Quite useless | 6 | 0 | 0 |
| Extremely useless | 7 | 3 | 21 |

Total reponses = 50 Weighted sum = 161

$$\text{Weighted mean} = \frac{\text{Weighted sum}}{\text{Total responses}} = \frac{161}{50} = 3.2$$

A profile of the responses could then be produced as follows:

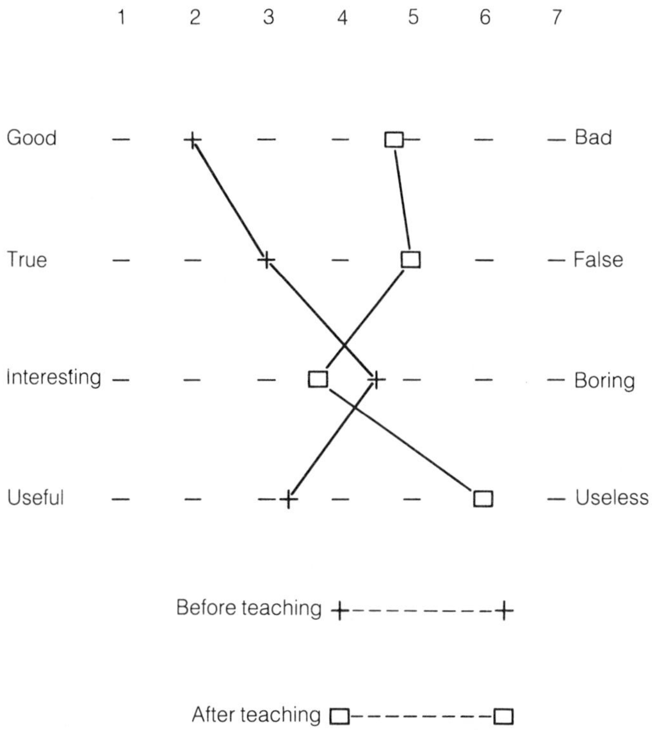


(ii) With **Likert** scales, statements are made which have approximately equal loading on attitude or value, and the response is made to indicate the degree of intensity of feeling with respect to the statements. For example:

| *Statement* | *Response* | | | | | | |
|---|---|---|---|---|---|---|---|
| Most pupils like science | Strongly agree | | Strongly disagree | | | | |
| | 1 | 2 | 3 | 4 | 5 | | |
| Mathematics | Like | | | | | | Dislike |
| | 1 | 2 | 3 | 4 | 5 | 6 | 7 |

The numbered points on the scale are usually described in words, e.g.

| Strongly agree | Agree | Uncertain | Disagree | Strongly disagree |
|---|---|---|---|---|
| 1 | 2 | 3 | 4 | 5 |

To avoid 'sitting on the fence' the middle choice can be omitted, e.g.

| SA | A | D | SD |
|---|---|---|---|
| 1 | 2 | 3 | 4 |

Several statements are usually made about one construct, e.g.

*Authoritarian*

| | SA | A | D | SD |
|---|---|---|---|---|
| Caning pupils helps to keep discipline | 1 | 2 | 3 | 4 |
| Pupils should not talk during lessons | 1 | 2 | 3 | 4 |

Scores are then added and the average found. A low score from the above statements would indicate an authoritarian person, a high score would indicate an easy-going person.

A good scale would provide opportunities for the respondents to disagree as well as to agree, e.g.

| | SA | A | D | SD |
|---|---|---|---|---|
| School rules are not necessary | 1 | 2 | 3 | 4 |

(Reverse the scoring before adding.)

The treatment of the scores is much the same as with the example given with the semantic differential.

(iii) With **Guttman** (or cumulative) scales, a set of homogeneous items (e.g. statements) is chosen which measure one attribute or construct, e.g. self-respect, leadership, tolerance. The items are then arranged in order from low to high according to their value loading or complexity or difficulty etc., depending upon what you are interested in.

*Example*

I want to ask you some questions about a man known to have been a convicted criminal and to have served some time in prison:

1. Would you object to such a person living in your community?
2. Would you object to him working where you are employed?
3. Would you object to inviting him into your home socially?
4. Would you object to him marrying a member of your family?

Answering 'Yes' to 1 implies answering 'Yes' to 2, 3 and 4 etc.

We adopt the same principle when trying to allocate test questions to an incline of difficulty, e.g.:

| | |
|---|---|
| $3 \times 5$ | easy |
| $7 \times 9$ | ↓ |
| $4 \times 23$ | ↓ |
| 15% of 160 | hard |

### *A word of caution*

Attempts to quantify the measurement of attitudes can give rise to a false sense of precision about something which, in the present state of the art, is fundamentally not very precise. There is unreliability in all measurements, and the scores obtained from attitude measurements are particularly suspect and should be tempered with judgement. The main value in defining a construct with behaviour statements lies in making clear to everyone concerned just what is being considered.

## Profiles

### *Introduction*

If students perform differently in different parts of an examination, then combining the different results into a single mark or grade represents a loss of information. A profile is a way of attempting to overcome this problem by setting out what is known of someone under separate headings. As the NUT(1983) says, 'A profile is not a method of assessment, but a *record* of information about a pupil, which may be presented in a variety of ways.' A 16+ certificate which sets out the grades awarded to a student in different subjects is a profile. So is the report which is sent home at the end of each term or each year. This typically contains information about achievement and effort in different subjects together with a comment written by the subject teacher. More recent developments in profiling (see, for example, Balogh, 1982; Goacher, 1983; Harrison, 1983; Mortimore, 1984) attempt to give more detailed information about performance within a subject; more particularly, however, they aim to cross subject boundaries and also form a bridge between the academic and the pastoral side of education in an attempt to give a picture of 'the whole student'. For this purpose they are not motivated so much by the need to find areas in which students perform differently but by the need to report on performance in significant areas of the education process.

A further, key feature of profiles is to be clear whether they are for **formative** purposes or for **summative** purposes. For formative, parochial purposes a profile can be more lengthy and detailed and can contain 'shorthand' statements which need discussion for their proper interpretation. The content and format of a formative profile can be different at different stages in the student's education; earlier information may become irrelevant or may be incorporated in later information as the teaching covers different areas of content and develops different skills and processes.

For summative purposes a profile needs to be easily used and understood by 'outsiders'. This puts constraints on the detail which can be presented, the language which can be used and hence on the length of the profile. By its very nature it must attempt to give a useful summary of the detail which may be contained in various, earlier, formative profiles. It is also becoming common to distinguish between a **record** and a **report**. A record gives details of what a student has done without attempting to mark or grade it, or interpret it in any way. Any interpretation is left for the user to undertake. A report interprets the information before presenting it. The dichotomy which exists is that, on the one hand, a record is likely to be more flexible and informative but is necessarily rather long and more time-consuming to use while, on the other hand, a report on a student is interpreted by a third person (usually the teacher) before being presented to the user. This makes it easier to use but less informative. It is also subject to the idiosyncrasies of the interpreter; for example, behaviour which is seen by one person as independence of mind is seen by another person as argumentative.

The uses and advantages of profiles are summarised by McGregor (1985) as follows:

*Formative*
Shows achievement
Shows progress
Identifies goals

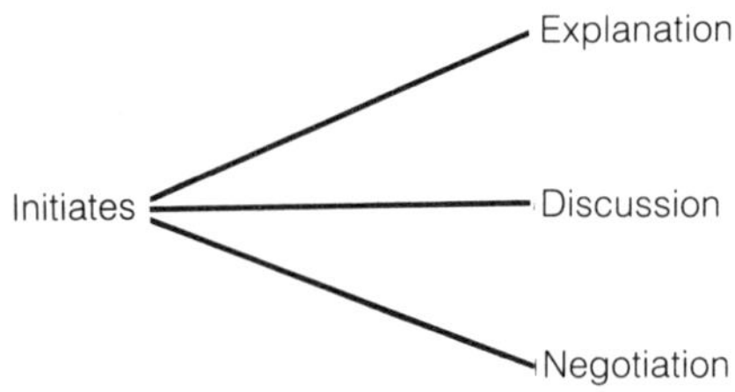


*Summative*
Produces information required by employers
Presents data in a way people understand
Shows achievement in areas normally omitted
Provides a focus for discussion at interview

*Other roles*
Gives cohesion to different activities
Gives cohesion to course team
Gives 'national recognition' to life work skills

## *Elements of a profile*

**1 Within subjects** There are two basic ways of categorizing performance within a subject; one is in terms of content, and the other is in terms of processes. A content split which fits into a formative profile can be based on successive stages (i.e. topics or modules) of work, such as 'Water', 'Cells', 'Gears and gearing', 'The weather', and is convenient because it fits neatly into the teaching scheme. A content split for summative purposes can be based on traditional major subject divisions such as, for Physics, 'Heat', 'Optics', 'Electricity', 'Mechanics' etc.

A process split is more generally useful because processes are often common to several subjects and the information obtained can thus be amalgamated to form an overall profile. The processes listed in the section on processes, criteria and skills (see pages 118–119) can be used for both formative and summative profiles.

Neither the content split nor the process split necessarily has domains in which students perform differently. Attempts can be made to identify such coherent domains by using statistical methods such as factor analysis, but the results of attempts which have been made so far have not been as clear-cut or as useful as one might wish. (See Harrison, 1983.) An alternative is to decide rather more arbitrarily in what parts of an assessment scheme it might be sensible and useful to know about student performance. The domains suggested by the SEC to be used as criteria for the award of grades are examples of this approach. An alternative example is suggested in the section on graded assessments on page 144.

**2 Across subjects** Process domains which are common to more than one subject vary according to the level of detail at which they are presented. Goacher (1983) gives four main headings:

1 Basic skills
2 Personal characteristics
3 Life skills
4 Personal achievements

Each of these is subdivided. For example, 'Basic skills' includes language, numeracy, and study skills, and these are further subdivided so that numeracy, for example, contains (a) accuracy, (b) calculation, (c) measurement, (d) graphicacy and (e) 3-dimensional structures. Of particular note is the section on personal characteristics. This includes not only the more 'traditional' items such as attendance and punctuality, but also more controversial ones such as initiative, leadership, reliability and perseverance. These are covered in more detail in the section on attitudes on pages 162–171.

The Schools Council Committee for Wales (1983) has proposed that a profile should contain:

(a) A personal comment by the young person's tutor at school.
(b) Teachers' comments on
  (i) Personal qualities
  (ii) Communication skills – oral, written and graphic.
  (iii) Practical skills
  (iv) Numerical skills
(c) A personal contribution written by the pupil, detailing interests, activities, awards and certificates gained.

This Welsh initiative sees some advantage in having a national profile:

On a national scale it should be possible to offer schools an even wider range of expertise and shared resources. Although rigorous moderation is neither feasible nor desirable, coordination of the development of profile systems, and associated in-service provision, will ensure the optimum use of resources. A major role of any external body established to coordinate the scheme would be to offer assurance of comparability by endorsing and therefore widening the currency of the profile awarded.

The South-Western Profile Assessment Research Project, however, believes that each school needs to establish its own profile to suit its own purposes. There is obviously a dichotomy between the need to allow individual schools the freedom and flexibility to develop their own profiles and the need to have some kind of standardization in order to give confidence to the users of the profiles. This problem is particularly pressing at the summative stage, but it also influences profiles which are produced for formative purposes. The Welsh group believes it can avoid rigid uniformity by including personal comments from the personal tutor and from the student.

Involvement of students is a key feature of many profile schemes. The South-Western Project says there should be active involvement of the student at all stages in the production of his or her profile. This is also a key element in the proposals for the Certificate of Pre-Vocational Education which is dealt with in more detail in Chapter 7(e).

## *Formats for presenting profiles*

There is not enough space in this chapter to give details of the wide range of formats which exist. A short summary will be given here, but for more information you should look at the references which are given in this section.

**(a) Single mark or grade** For example:

| | Theory | Practical | Total |
|---|---|---|---|
| A. Einstein | 75 | 25 | 65 |
| R. Ohm | 25 | 75 | 35 |

The marks or grades may be norm-referenced or criterion-referenced. The temptation to give a total mark or grade is either irresistible or, as in the case of the GCSE, a requirement, and so rules for combining have to be devised. The above example indicates how unequal weighting of the components of the profiles can give apparently strange results. This is discussed further in Fairbrother (1977).

**(b) Written records and reports** The nature of these has been discussed earlier. In an attempt to achieve some kind of objectivity and standardization, headings and sub-headings can be given along the lines mentioned above. In addition, descriptors or 'comment banks' can be supplied which not only help to define

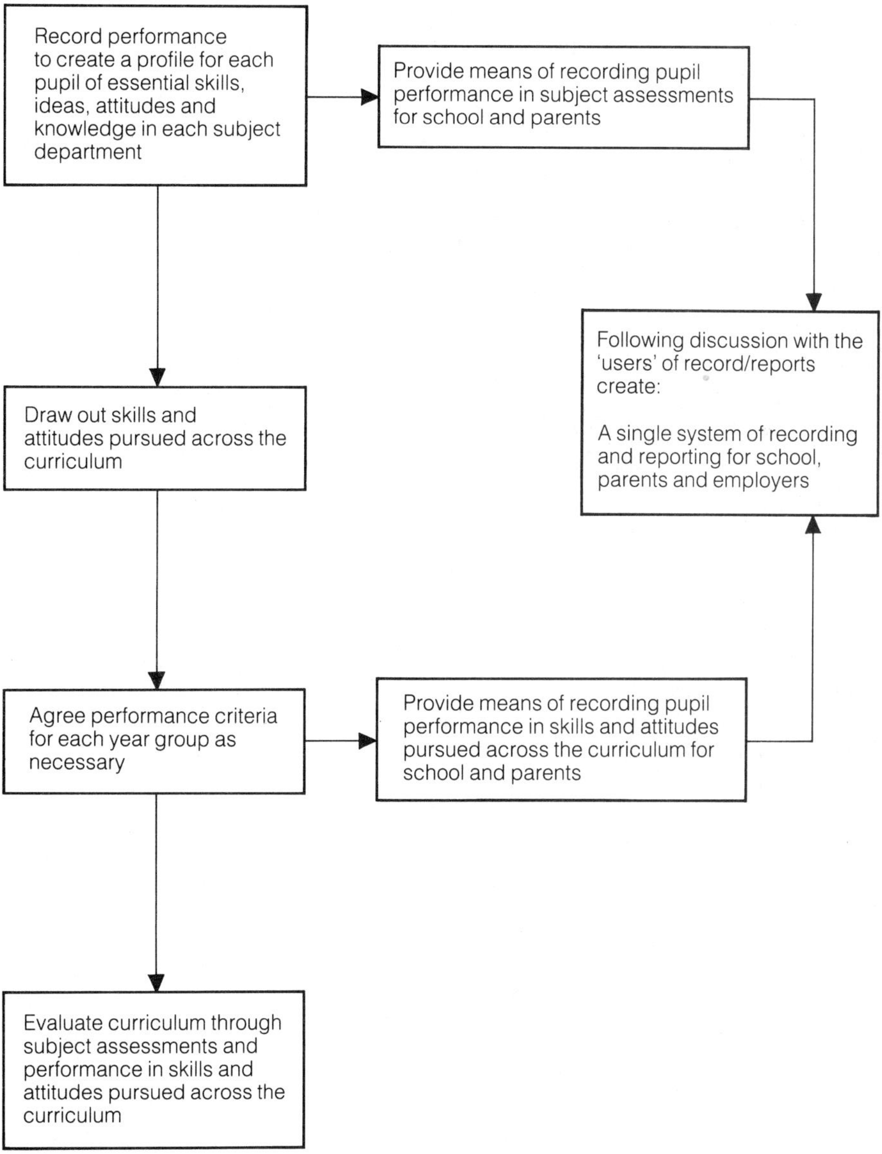


FIG. 4.5 **School assessment: sequence of recording and reporting.** (From DES, 1983)

the meaning of the various headings but also provide a common vocabulary for use by the people making the record or report. For example:

Communication skills – Graphic
1 He/she can interpret intricate graphs/plans/maps/tables/patterns/ diagrams.
2 He/she can interpret simple graphs/plans/maps etc.
3 He/she can interpret simple graphs/plans/maps etc. with some assistance.

**(c) Grids** These come in many different forms but the main characteristic is that of putting a tick in a box. In addition, most of them attempt to indicate a position in some kind of continuum or progression:

*Example 1*

| | *Good* | *Average* | *Poor* |
|---|---|---|---|
| Confidence | | | |
| Leadership | | | |
| Common sense | | | |

*Example 2* Manual dexterity

A Highly skilled in use of hands
B Skill level satisfactory
C Has limited powers of dexterity

*Example 3*

| | | | |
|---|---|---|---|
| Dexterity and co-ordination | No opportunity to assess | Did not achieve basic level | Can use everyday implements, can lift, carry and set down objects as directed |
| | 0 | 1 | 2 |
| Measuring | No opportunity to assess | Did not achieve basic level | Can read graduated linear scales and dials |
| | 0 | 1 | 2 |

## *Constraints*

McGregor (1985) identifies four serious constraints in attempting to introduce and use a profile system:

1 Staff time
2 Staff development
3 Format – different functions, i.e. formative v summative
4 Three different audiences
   (i) Student
   (ii) Instructor/Tutor
   (iii) Employer

The resolution of these constraints lies in a thorough understanding of the aims, objectives and details of the profiles in use, a programme of education and training for all those involved and an increase in the use of modern techniques, such as computer storage and retrieval of information. The DES (1983) outlines a plan for arriving at a profile of student performance within a school; the suggested sequence of recording and reporting is shown in Figure 4.5, p. 175.

| | | |
|---|---|---|
| Can reliably perform basic manipulative tasks | Can perform complex tasks requiring accuracy and dexterity | Can perform tasks requiring a high degree of manipulative control |
| 3 | 4 | 5 |
| Can measure out specified quantities of material by length, mass, etc. | Can set up and use simple precision instruments | Can set up and use complex precision instruments |
| 3 | 4 | 5 |

## Bibliography

Backhouse, J. K., 1976, 'Determination of grades for two groups sharing a common paper', *Educational Research*, 14, No. 1

Balogh, J., 1982, *Profile Reports for School Leavers* (Schools Council/ Longman, Harlow)

Bardell, G. S., Forrest, G. M., and Shoesmith, D. J., 1978, *Comparability in GCE: A review of Boards' Studies, 1964–1977* (Joint Matriculation Board, Manchester)

Brown, S., 1976, *Attitude Goals in Secondary Schools* (University of Stirling)

Bryce, T. G. K., McCall, J., MacGregor, J., Weston, R. A. J., and Robertson, I. J., 1983, *Techniques for the Assessment of Practical Skills in Foundation Science* (Heinemann Educational Books, London)

DES, 1983, *Curriculum 11–16. Towards a Statement of Entitlement* (HMSO, London)

DES, 1985a, *General Certificate of Secondary Education, The National Criteria: Science* (HMSO, London)

DES, 1985b, *General Certificate of Secondary Education, The National Criteria: General Criteria* (HMSO, London)

Fairbrother, R. W., 1977, 'Profiles in examinations', *Physics Education,* January

Forrest, G. H., and Vickerman, C., 1982, *Standards in GCE: Subject Pairs Comparisons*, 1972–80 (Joint Matriculation Board, Manchester)

Goacher, B., 1983, *Recording Achievement at 16+* (Schools Council/ Longman, Harlow)

Harrison, A., 1983, 'Profile reporting of examination results', *Schools Council Examinations Bulletin 43* (Evans/Methuen, London)

Holford, D., 1980, Implications for teacher training, In *Assessment and the Curriculum*, edited by R. W. Fairbrother (Chelsea College, London)

Hoste, R., 1981, 'How valid are school examinations? An exploration into content validity', In *The British Journal of Educational Psychology*, 51, 10–22

Kingdon, J. M., French, S., Pierce, G. E. and Woodthorpe, A J., 1983, Awarding grades on differentiated papers in school examinations at 16+, *Educational Research*, Vol 25, No. 3 (NFER/Nelson, Windsor)

McGregor, S., 1985, An occasional note from the City and Guilds of London Institute, In *An Approach to Profiling in Life and Work Skills* (GCLI, London)

Mortimore, J. (ed.), 1984, *Profiles in Action*, Further Education Unit, DES (DES, London)

Munn and Dunning Reports, 1982, *Framework for Decision*, Scottish Education Department (SED, Edinburgh)

NUT, 1983, *Pupil Profiles: A Discussion Document* (NUT, London)

Nuttall, D. L., Backhouse, J. K., and Willmott, A. S., 1974, 'Comparability in Standards between subjects', *Schools Council Examinations Bulletin 29* (Evans/Methuen, London)

Osgood, C. E., Suci, G. J., and Tannenbaum, P. H., 1957, *The Measurement of Meaning* (University of Illinois Press)

Rowntree, D., 1977, *Assessing Students: How Shall We Know Them?* (Harper and Row, London)

Schools Council Committee for Wales, 1983, *Profile Reporting in Wales*, A discussion paper issued by the SCCW

Scottish Council for Research in Education, 1977, *Pupils in Profile* (SCRE, Edinburgh)

SSCR, 1984, *Towards the Specification of Minimum Entitlement: Brenda and Friends* (Secondary Science Curriculum Review, London)

Tattersall, K., 1983, 'Differentiated examinations: a strategy for assessment at 16 + ?', *Schools Council Examinations Bulletin 42* (Evans/Methuen, London)

Tuckman, B. W., 1975, *Measuring Educational Outcomes* (Harcourt Brace Jovanovich, New York)

Turner, E., 1980, *Criterion Referenced Assessment: An Annotated Bibliography* (University of Stirling)

Wood, R., 1978, Placing candidates who take different papers on the same mark scale, *Educational Research*, Vol. 20, No. 1 (NFER/Nelson, Windsor)

# 5 How is science teaching organized?

**Brian Nicholl and John Nellist**

- ★ An analytic approach to the employment of the school's finite resources can lead to their being used most effectively.
- ★ The laboratory/room provision should be analysed.
- ★ Teaching and technician staff should be deployed to best meet the needs of the department, bearing in mind the whole curriculum.
- ★ The varieties and styles of student grouping, the influence of option patterns and the grouping within teaching sets should all affect the organization of the teaching.
- ★ Improving the organization of the department involves considering people and their influences, expectations and staff development policy.

## Introduction

The organization of students and teachers is a critical factor in establishing effective programmes of work in a school science department. As noted in earlier chapters, the overall curriculum must be planned to take account of the broad aims of the school, but within each subject and each teaching group, it is essential that the curriculum is matched to the development of each young person. There will be school policies on matters such as curriculum, student groupings, examinations, allocation of time between different subject departments and the like, but individual departments – and teachers within these departments – will have the ultimate responsibility for translating these policies into agreed and acceptable outcomes. Organizational frameworks must be established at all levels by the school, by the department and by each individual teacher. External constraints such as LEA policies, the influence of governors, the views of parents and, of growing importance, the local community, must all be taken into account. A school has finite resources which include laboratories, workshops and other teaching spaces; staff, both academic and ancillary; and funds. Central to the thinking of all teachers should be employment of such resources to meet, as effectively as possible, the developmental needs of the individual youngster.

The key questions posed in this chapter must be:

Are organizational frameworks designed to match teaching requirements and intended outcomes, or is the reverse true?
Are resources and teaching strategies too heavily dictated by external constraints?

In short, a thoroughgoing review of departmental practice is an essential pre-requisite both for efficient day-to-day operation and for the effective management of change. Such a review will provide data for both an 'as it is' and an 'as it could be' analysis. One dimension of a review concerns resource allocation. Schools do not control the size of their total entitlement. Building provision, staffing allocations and capitation allowances are all externally set. However, sharing out the total cake, albeit sometimes within LEA guidelines, is properly within the remit of individual schools. Departments then have a responsibility to argue their case for an equitable share, presenting within a whole curriculum framework a carefully researched and documented rationale for staffing, financial and other provision. Curriculum and timetable-related issues are important too and demand a similar analytical approach.

This chapter seeks to encourage review through providing possible frameworks for analysis, and offers, in some cases, examples of national or local data against which individual school findings can be tested. It deals particularly with:

1 laboratory/room provision;
2 staffing allocation and deployment;
3 student organization and grouping.

Examining the match between organizational and curriculum intention is at the heart of the matter and well worth time and effort.

## Laboratory/room provision

This is an obvious starting point, routinely addressed by science departments. It requires the simplest of analyses and is included here as an integral part of any full survey of resources.

The number, size and design of laboratories and ancillary rooms will vary considerably from one school to another, and may well reflect the economic and

Complete the following check-list (Table 5.1) as an inventory of all the facilities used in your department:

TABLE 5.1 **Provision of accommodation**

| *Laboratories* | | | | | *Lecture theatres* | *Workshops* | | *Prep. rooms* | | | |
|---|---|---|---|---|---|---|---|---|---|---|---|
| *Gen.* | *Biol.* | *Chem.* | *Phys.* | *Others* | | *Science dept.* | *Others* | *Gen.* | *Biol.* | *Chem.* | *Phys.* |
| | | | | | | | | | | | |
| Total teaching spaces available | | | | | | | | | | | |

educational climate prevailing at the time when the school was built. In an ideal world teaching accommodation will relate to both the kind and style of curriculum provision intended. For many existing schools this is a counsel of perfection since the design and building of schools can rarely keep pace with shifting education philosophies. See Table 5.1 on p. 181.

If the totals for columns 1–6 are combined, they can be compared with the maximum number of teaching groups in operation at any one time during the timetable 'week'. (In this connection a timetable 'week' is taken as the cycle period for the operation of the timetable. In many schools this will be the normal five-day week, but numerous other variations will exist.)

The quotient

$$\frac{\text{maximum number of teaching groups in operation at one time}}{\text{total number of teaching spaces available}} \times 100\%$$

describes the 'maximum utilization factor' for your accommodation. You have problems if your MUF is greater than 100 per cent!

However, and more likely, you may well find a significant discrepancy between the availability of specialist laboratory provision and the demand for it. If such a mismatch exists, then consider the following:

Can the problem be eased, at justifiable cost, by:

1 changes in the whole school timetable?
2 shifts in internal arrangements within the department?
3 negotiations with other subjects who have access to 'specialist' rooms?

To get some sense of how your department's provision matches national norms, work through the following section making equivalent calculations and compare your results with the statistics presented in Figure 5.1 by the Assessment of Performance Unit (APU).

The APU (1982) presented a survey of laboratory facilities. The criterion used to assess the adequacy of laboratory accommodation, drawn from a sample of over 550 schools, is based on a formula developed by members of HM Inspectorate. The following assumption are made:

That pupils aged from 11 to 16 will study science for about a sixth of their curriculum time (ie. 6 periods in a 35 period week) and that their science work will be practically based. Allowing one period per day for general laboratory maintenance, there will be available in each laboratory about 30 hours of teaching time in a 35-period week or 35 hours in a 40-period week. An n-form entry school with y year-groups within the age-range 11–16 would then need 6ny/30 or 7ny/35 (ie. ny/5) laboratories in order to accommodate such a practically-based science teaching load.

Applying this criterion, a 5-form entry 11–16 comprehensive school would need 5 laboratories, while a 3-form entry 13–16 school would need about 2 laboratories to be considered adequately provided. HMI considered that schools with sixth forms would need one further laboratory over this basic number to meet their extra requirements.

(It is interesting to note that this criterion appears to ignore the wide range of science options offered, at least in upper forms of many secondary schools.)

On the basis of the above formulation, the APU (1982) survey reports the position in the sample schools being as shown in Figure 5.1.

You may also wish to check your school laboratory provision against any existing LEA formula. In the final analysis, however, the adequacy or otherwise of your school's specialist accommodation can only be judged against the requirements of the science curriculum; the qualitative (the use made of laboratories) is as important as the quantitative (how many laboratories are available for use).

This next section turns briefly to this issue.

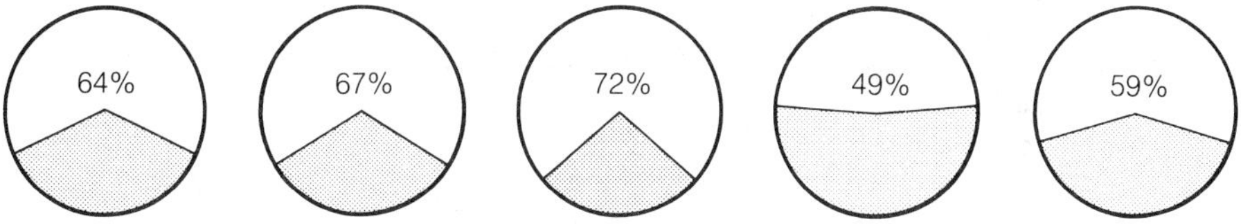


FIG. 5.1 (a) **Adequate laboratory accommodation (% schools within region)**

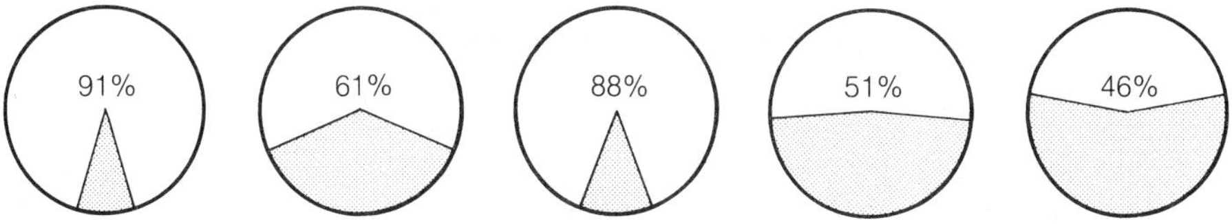


FIG. 5.1 (b) **Adequate laboratory accommodation (% schools within type in England)** (From APU, 1982)

## Using laboratory accommodation

Begin by completing an analysis on the lines indicated in Table 5.2.

TABLE 5.2 **Utilization of accommodation during a timetable week.**

| | | *No. of periods timetabled* | | | | *Totals/year* | |
|---|---|---|---|---|---|---|---|
| *Year group* | *No. of science periods/'week'* | *laboratory* | *lecture theatre* | *class-room* | *other* | *in lab no. %* | *outside lab no. %* |
| 1 | | | | | | | |
| 2 | | | | | | | |
| 3 | | | | | | | |
| 4 | | | | | | | |
| 5 | | | | | | | |
| 6(i) | | | | | | | |
| 6(ii) | | | | | | | |

If this analysis reveals clear causes for dissatisfaction, it may be well worth looking at the matter in more detail; a departmental meeting would provide a first forum.

The following are suggestions for the style and kinds of questions which might be addressed:

1 Is the available specialist rooming equitably and sensibly shared across (a) year groups; (b) teaching groups within year groups; (c) staff?
2 Is the spread of laboratory use a good match to course requirements?
3 Are the laboratory and other specialist rooms used in a flexible way to accommodate peaks or troughs in demand within particular courses or at particular times of year?
4 Does the existing timetable pattern result in particular constraints in relation to the effective use of rooms?

There is a strongly held belief among many science teachers that all science teaching must take place in a laboratory. Indeed, some practitioners would claim that teaching science without a laboratory is akin to learning to swim without water. Such views are defensible but their defence should not be taken as self-evident. We do need to ask questions about the purpose and place of practical activities within the variety of courses offered. It is not appropriate to deal in detail with such issues here, but once again we can look analytically at what we offer and its match to existing provision.

1 Devise a way of putting into categories the 'practical' activities offered within the department. For example, those centring on conventional apparatus, those demanding facilities available only within one or two teaching spaces, lecture demonstrations, those requiring extensive audio-visual resources, activities of a project nature dependent upon 'string and sealing wax' resources etc.
2 How are such categories of activity spread across courses and laboratories, and is there a good fit between available spaces and the styles of practical work engaged in?

Chapter 3 of this handbook argues persuasively for a variety of teaching/learning approaches well matched to intended outcomes. The aim here is to promote an analysis of room provision informed by such considerations. Science department accommodation requirements may not begin and end simply with access to large numbers of conventionally specialized and expensive laboratories. There can and should be variation. Activities of a technological kind, for example, may require only a limited range of the usual laboratory resources but, on the other hand will perhaps require access to some facilities usually associated with workshops. Teaching the social and historical aspects of science may be much more dependent upon the effective deployment of audio-visual and paper resources.

The message then is not simply 'Have we enough laboratories?' but 'Do the teaching spaces available to the department lend themselves to the kinds and styles of learning we seek to promote?'

Analyses conducted against this latter criterion are likely to raise more issues of importance and interest than a simple count of the total number of rooms available. Such analyses may also result in more potentially purposeful solutions within a whole school framework, for it should be remembered that it is possible to share resources. Much of what is said elsewhere and in this section points to changes both quantitative and qualitative in the science curriculum.

As a final accommodation exercise, assume, if you are not already so committed, a departmental shift to 'science for all' in line with DES (1985) for your school. Calculate against this new base the room requirements for science both in terms of the number of rooms required and the types of room. The outcome of such an analysis could well inform your implementation of the policy statement.

# Staffing allocation and deployment

In this section, like the last, it is worth dealing separately with the quantitative and qualitative aspects. 'How many staff?' and 'How shall we use them?' are the issues. A split between teaching and technician staff is also made, as a matter of convenience, though clearly there are elements of overlap.

## How many teachers?

Schools rarely have direct control over the total number of teachers they employ. Staffing in this sense is usually a matter of local authority policy, albeit mediated in a growing number of instances by negotiations at individual school level. As might be anticipated, there is considerable variation in the shape and detail of staffing policies across the range of LEAs, but two broad styles of working are common. The first of these is structured around the concept of 'pupil teacher ratio' (PTR). The second, and increasingly popular, system can be described as 'curriculum led staffing' (CLS) or by some other terminology which conveys the same sense.

Science teachers, and teachers in general, are not always familiar with local staffing policies. Many might argue they have no need to be so. 'We cannot control the total number of staff employed, so why be concerned as to how that number is derived?' There is a contrary case to be made. Schools do control how the total staff employed are distributed across curriculum areas and across special interests and responsibilities. Curriculum and other priorities shift, rolls alter and internal staffing changes do need to be made. Such changes demand negotiation. If departments are properly to contribute to such debates (in some cases perhaps 'to defend their corner'), it is at least helpful and, we would argue, vital to know something of the rules determining the global staffing allocation made to the school. Are there age-related criteria, for example? What assumptions are made about class size? Is there a remedial entitlement designed to help cater for those students with special educational needs? And so on. Many staffing formulae will contain these and other elements, all of which may inform how a department should view its own position relative to other departments, and indeed relative to other schools, and how it should negotiate for change.

But to return to common systems. The idea of staffing on the basis of pupil teacher ratios is familiar and generally well understood. One LEA operating a middle and high school system has used the following PTRs to determine the staffing complement of a high school.

| | |
|---|---|
| Years 3 and 4 | 1 teacher for 20 pupils |
| Year 5 | 1 teacher for 15 pupils |
| Year 6 | 1 teacher for 11 pupils |

Using these figures, an eight-form entry school would be allocated total staffing as follows:

| | | |
|---|---|---|
| Year 3 | 240 pupils | 12 staff |
| Year 4 | 240 pupils | 12 staff |
| Year 5 | 240 pupils | 16 staff |
| Year 6 | 88 pupils | 8 staff |
| | | Total 48 staff |

PTRs are also used to make national comparisons between local authorities. Such league tables make interesting reading but do need careful interpretation. A large rural authority (in geographical terms) with a scattered population and many small schools is likely to appear better served than a more compact and densely populated neighbour.

As noted earlier, there has been a shift from PTR-derived staffing to more sophisticated methods. In large part this shift has been encouraged by the now well documented problem of falling rolls. Once schools fall below a certain size, the maintenance of a suitably varied and differentiated curriculum becomes

TABLE 5.3

| *Form entry of school* | *No. of pupils in year group* | *No. of teacher periods required in each of* | | | *No. of f.t.e. staff required in each of years* | |
|---|---|---|---|---|---|---|
| | | *yrs 1–3 (11–18)* | *yr 3 (13–18)* | *yrs 4–5 (all schools)* | *1–3* | *4–5* |
| 3 | up to 90 | 172 | 172 | 184 | 5.38 | 5.75 |
| 4 | 91–120 | 212 | 212 | 236 | 6.63 | 7.38 |
| 5 | 121–150 | 256 | 256 | 292 | 8.00 | 9.13 |
| 6 | 151–180 | 299 | 299 | 348 | 9.34 | 10.88 |
| 7 | 181–210 | 342 | 342 | 400 | 10.69 | 12.50 |
| 8 | 211–240 | 385 | 385 | 460 | 12.03 | 14.38 |
| 9 | 241–270 | 429 | 429 | 512 | 13.41 | 16.00 |
| 10 | 271–300 | 477 | 477 | 569 | 14.91 | 17.75 |
| 11 | 301–330 | 516 | 516 | 624 | 16.13 | 19.60 |
| 12 | 331–360 | 564 | 564 | 680 | 17.63 | 21.25 |

Investigate the staffing policy operating within your own authority. List the assumptions it makes about:

1 group sizes;
2 special needs entitlement;
3 pupil age;
4 the science curriculum.

increasingly difficult; group sizes become uneconomic, option systems and minority subjects come under pressure, and staffing compensations need to be built into any calculations. Curriculum led staffing attempts to combat such pressure, usually by defining, perhaps through negotiation with the school, the minimum staffing level required to sustain an agreed curriculum. Schemes vary in detail and implementation but the common intention is to staff so that the basic curriculum needs of the school are met. Departments then have a role in defining and justifying such needs.

Table 5.3 on p. 187 shows the method used in one authority to calculate staffing ratios, based on CLS.

> Use the information in Table 5.3 to calculate how many staff your own school would have, based upon this system. How does this compare with your actual situation?

## Deploying the teachers

As a generalization, schools do determine how their staffing establishment will be distributed to meet the variety of needs defined by the curriculum offered. (Curriculum led staffing policies may imply or demand particular structures and priorities.) The task is not easy. Historical accident, changing priorities and local enthusiasms all make their demands. What is clear and is argued elsewhere in this text is that individual subject/department contributions need to be set in the framework of the whole curriculum if the best working decisions, even though there are usually compromises, are to be made. Few schools have the luxury of staffing from a clean slate.

That there are particular concerns for science departments in the deployment of staff will be evident. Two are worth particular mention.

1 Science educators in England have long argued for reduced maximum class sizes, say to 20, i.e. for science to be given the standing of a practical subject (a goal already achieved in Scotland).
2 DES (1985) and many LEA documents direct us to the provision of balanced science for all. For most schools, this will mean more rather than less science lessons in total.

> Calculate for your school
>
> 1 the number of staff required to teach science if no group can be bigger than 20 pupils;

2 the number of staff required to teach a programme of balanced science for all pupils as recommended in DES (1985) (assume 'normal' class sizes).

Assuming either or both calculations require an increase in the number of science staff, how would you adjust the school's curriculum to accommodate the new priorities within the confines of the existing staffing establishment?

The above exercise highlights sharply the difficulty of decisions often faced by headteachers and senior management teams. Careful analysis by science departments of their staffing requirements is essential if such decisions are to be appropriately informed. Hull and Adams (1981) suggest, in chart form, factors to be considered in such a staffing requirement analysis (Figure 5.2). They suggest, that 'the basic task facing the head of department when considering the staffing of courses for the following year is to ensure that every class has a teacher for every timetabled science lesson. In terms of Figure 5.2 this means that the total number of periods required (A) must equal the total number of periods available (B).'

## Who does what?

Beyond the relatively straightforward logistics of 'How many science teachers?', there remains the critical issue of deploying teachers within the departmental team. The following simple exercise suggests a way into what might be termed 'first level issues'.

List the staff in the department, noting alongside each, specialist subject interest and teaching programme in terms of the year groups taught, subject taught to that group and ability level within the group (if appropriate).

Then check the following:

1 Are all staff deployed widely across the age and ability range?
2 Do subject specialisms match teaching requirements? Are staff appropriately qualified?
3 Are discrepancies in teaching loads (contact ratios) consistent with additional responsibilities or can they be explained in other ways?
4 If (1) and (2) reveal inconsistencies, are these deliberately engineered as serving the best interests of the department as a whole?
5 How do the patterns revealed in (3) compare with other departments in the school?

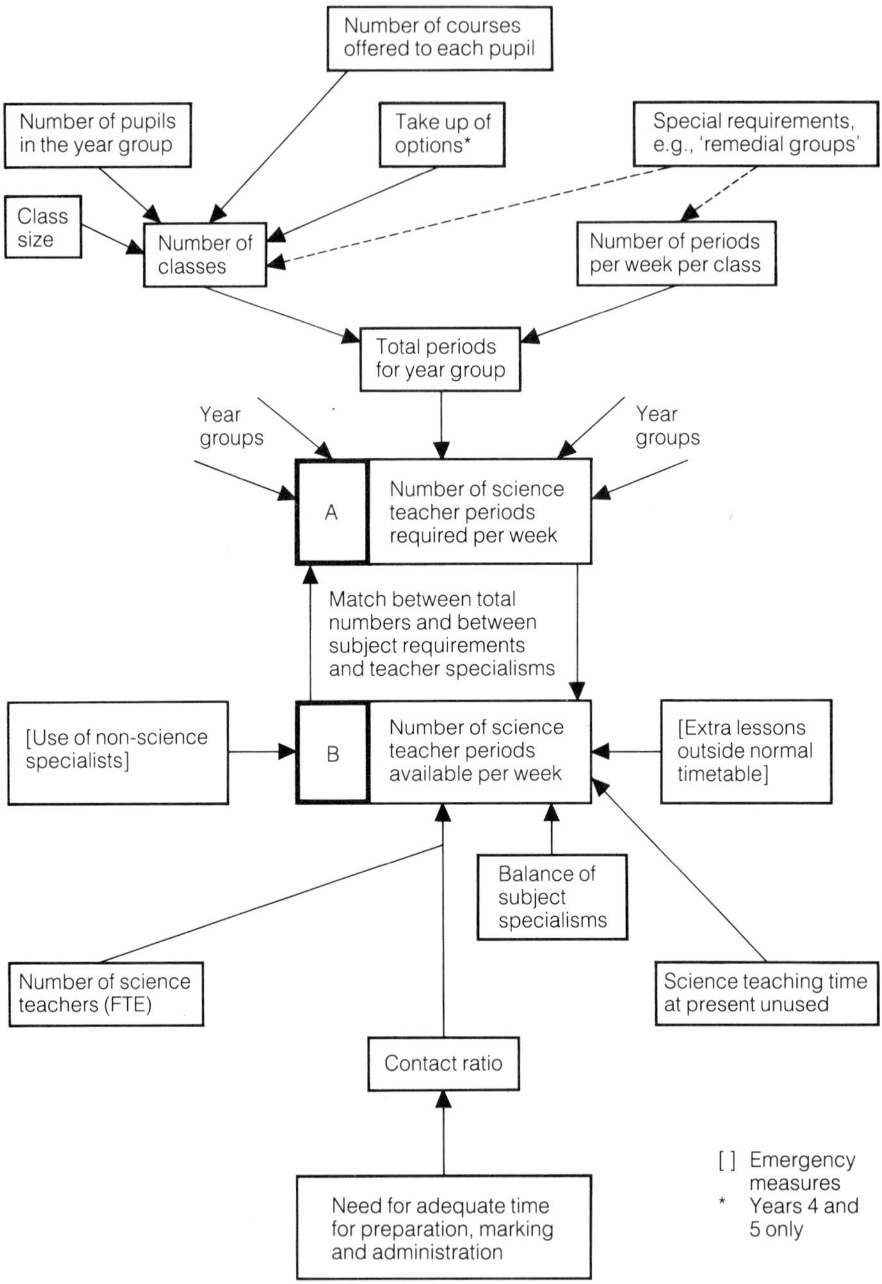


FIG. 5.2 **Staff allocation.** (From Hull and Adams, 1981)

A simple analysis of this sort reveals, particularly to an outsider, something of a department's style of working and its values. It can raise other interesting questions but certainly should lead into a set of second level considerations related to departmental responsibilities.

It would be naive to ignore the issue of promoted posts. As with staffing establishments, the number of scale points available is a function of school size and, within strictly defined limits, it is determined by LEA policy. Again the internal distribution of points falls within the remit of individual schools. Such distributions also give an indication of a school's purpose and priorities.

> All structures convey a message. Staffing structures in schools are no exception and the particular message which they convey is concerned with hierarchy. This message is a public one. It will reveal a great deal about what a school views as important and in particular, it will suggest an order of importance of the subjects which the school offers. A school's hierarchical structure thus gives an indication of its curricular priorities.
>
> (DES, 1977)

The extent to which the allocation of points for particular responsibilities is a matter for general debate and discussion does vary from school to school. Increasingly and, it might be argued, beneficially, schools are becoming more 'open' in this sense. Science departments once more need to be clear about their share of a scarce resource and to see their internal structure in the whole school context.

> List the posts above Scale 1 held by departmental staff. Identify those which are science specific (i.e. not assigned for responsibilities outside the department).
>
> Alongside each such post, note:
> 1 the general scope of the additional responsibility as you see it;
> 2 any additional non-teaching time allocated to the post-holder to enable her/him to discharge the responsibilities.
>
> Compare the department's total points allocation with other equivalent curriculum areas.

For most departments, such an exercise will be entirely straightforward, even trivial, but if the exercise reveals that you are not clear about who does what then there are problems! There may be other messages too to be drawn from such a review.

Clarity about formal responsibilities, recognized by payments above Scale 1, is important but it is not the only issue. It can be argued that assigning some responsibility to all staff, from probationer to 'old-hand', promotes both the efficiency and the corporate health of the department. Such responsibilities may

List for your department a set of areas of responsibility which you feel are either neglected or, in the time sense, under resourced. Classify your list under the headings: maintenance or development (i.e. to do with keeping the system going or to do with moving it forward). Devise a departmental plan suggesting how such gaps might be filled.

well shift from person to person and from year to year. For the individual they provide scope for initiative and enterprise, for professional and, possibly, career development. For the department, they offer clear practical benefits and help to sharpen the idea of the working team. The allocation of task is best negotiated with the individual and needs to fit her/his skills, aspirations and professional readiness. The range of possible responsibilities is very considerable and shifts over time. For example, liaison with feeder primary schools or local industry did not have the same status as an issue ten years ago as it does today. Not all tasks identified need to be quite so global in scale; the maintenance of displays, fish tanks or the department's safety file all contribute to departmental ethos and effective day-to-day working.

This section on teaching staff has dipped into establishment and deployment concerns. Some of these are briefly revisited in later sections. Your own departmental review will and should raise other questions of importance.

## Ancillary staff

Laboratory technicians are an essential part of the staffing of any science department. This section, following the pattern of the last, considers the questions 'How many technicians?' and 'How should we use them?' No distinction is made between the types and grades of ancillary support. Many technicians are well trained for their role, others less so. Both the fully trained technicians and the less specialized laboratory assistant each have their place. Clearing and cleaning is as much a part of day-to-day efficiency as the repair of the cathode ray oscilloscope.

## How many technicians?

As is the case for teaching staff, so too for ancillary staff there is no national standard. Local policies rule. Four examples of local formulae used to calculate a school's technician establishment are given below. The first three are largely science specific, dealing only with the number of science technicians. The fourth follows, in a limited way, the increasingly popular policy of assigning a school a points quota. This last approach aims to take account of the growing demands for technician support in curriculum areas other then science.

**1 By school roll**

| *Roll* | *Senior technician* | *Technician* | *Asst. technician* |
|---|---|---|---|
| 2000 + | 1 | 2 | 3 |
| 1600–2000 | 1 | 2 | 2 |
| 1200–1600 | 1 | 1 | 2 |
| Under 1200 | — | 2–3 | 0–1 |

**2 By number of practical areas**

$$\text{Number of technicians} = \frac{\text{Number of practical areas}}{4}$$

**3 By national formula**
A formula derived by the Laboratory Technicians' Sub-Committee of the Association for Science Education in 1979 is also roll-related and recommends:

$$\text{Number of FTE technicians} = \frac{\text{Unit total} + (\text{four times number on roll})}{3000}$$

**4 By points establishment**
In this system three factors are seen as important:

the facilities for all practical subjects;
the dispersement of these facilities;
their utilization;

(a) *Allocation of points* — *points/room*
- laboratories, workshops, AV reprographics: 4
- art, drama, home economics, needlework, technical drawing, language laboratories: 1
- farm (or equivalent): 10 points

(b) *Dispersement factor*
- no layout problems: 0 points
- layout with some difficulties: 2 points
- layout with acute difficulties (split buildings, split-level rooms): 4 points

Then the appropriate level of staffing is calculated according to the formula:

$$\text{Technician allocation} = \frac{\text{Total points}}{18.4}$$

In some authorities, all ancillary support, clerical, librarian, school nurse, bursar and so on count against an agreed points quota, each post carrying a points weighting related to its status and salary. Such global systems have the advantage that they properly recognize the range of support required by schools and allow individual establishments to determine their own priorities. On the other hand, under such a scheme, science departments may have their 'traditional' technician provision challenged or even reduced.

> Using the first three of the above formulae, calculate theoretical technician establishments for your school.
>
> How do these formulae and their predictions for your department compare with your own authority's policy?

## The deployment of technician staff

Technicians are a valuable and scarce resource. Few science departments would claim to have too many and, after the analysis above, not a few departments may feel badly done by. Since there seems little immediate prospect for a real growth in numbers then the effective use and management of the technician or the technician team is vital.

In some schools, technicians, like teachers, are designated by science subject, the chemistry technician or the biology technician for example. Such designations have obvious merit. Individual laboratories, preparation rooms, stocking systems become well known, and the technician also becomes familiar and secure with the nuances and esoterics of the discipline, and skilled in the specialist techniques it demands. However, designation by subject should not preclude team operation. There are peaks of demand in particular areas of the department and some tasks, often the dreary ones, are best done in company. Furthermore, particular courses require co-operative working, such as pulling resources from a range of stockrooms and laboratories. A too strongly developed sense of 'territory' on the part of the technician can actually hinder the effective teaching of such courses; using the chemistry balance for physics should not be seen as a hanging matter!.

Arising from this issue of designation in the sense used above, there is the larger question of job description and lines of responsibility.

> • Before reading on, record for your school:
>
> 1 the 'management lines' for the technicians. To whom are they finally responsible? Who manages and programmes their day-to-day working?
> 2 six key aspects of their role.

You might now test your perspective against that of the laboratory technician. The diary extract below based on contributions from serving technicians (ASE, 1976) gives a flavour of the technicians' view of the world.

'The Secret Life of Anne Sillary'

10.40 Made coffee.
10.42 Emergency call from Geog. Dept. for projector in R.12 next period.
10.43 Picked up coffee.
10.44 Put coffee down to provide brush and shovel for Mr. A.
10.45 Call from R10 . . . water dripping through ceiling in R22 again! Took remedial action.
10.55 Bell for break. Wheel trolley of apparatus to E34, E21 and R9. Collect dirty glassware from E21. Carry microscopes upstairs. Get out Boyle's Law apparatus for Mr. B. who forgot to order it. Set up projector in R12. Received 'phone call re. TV recordings for History and Economics Departments.
11.15 End of break – reheat coffee.
11.17 Urgent message with profuse apologies from Geography Department. It should have been R11. Mrs. C. is very nice albeit scatty . . . take big breath and transfer projector.
11.24 Supply new thermometer.
11.25 Set automatic recording for Schools' Broadcast.
11.28 Start to dismantle power supply with burned out rectifier.
11.30 Supply extra 4 mm plug to Mr. D. Does he eat them? Must make up some more.
11.31 Undid two more screws.
11.32 Nuffield L. T. Unit not working. Find it is only a loose connection.
11.36 Phone call for Mr. D. 3Q can be awkward so I stay with them whilst he answers it.
11.43 Supply copper sulphate. Make note that we are getting low.
11.45 Mr. E. brings in films. Could I parcel them up so that he can post them at lunchtime?
11.55 Third period ends. Wheel trolley to E21 and put out more apparatus. Collect projector from R11. It hasn't been used!!
12.00 Mr. F. is breathing fire and fury because I have given him the wrong apparatus. He should learn to write! Get out the other apparatus with bad grace.
12.10 Respond to emergency call from new French teacher. Point out that the wall socket has to be 'on' as well as the tape recorder.
12.14 Pour cold coffee down sink.
12.15 Lunch in school canteen (official break is 12.10 to 12.55).
12.30 End of morning school.
12.31 Bump into The Head who wants some distilled water for his battery.
12.36 Put feet up.

12.37 Put feet down. Duty staff would like a pin for a boy who has split his trousers.
12.41 Telephone message from Mr. A. Did he leave his keys in R23? Yes he did, and a lot else besides! Why don't Departments of Education teach the basics of class control? Clear away the mess against my better judgement. Will have another word with the Head of Department.
12.53 Mrs. G. wonders whether I can get a cow's eye for Wednesday.
12.56 Discuss new test-tube racks with Mr. D. Will make them if I have time.
1.00 Clear apparatus from other rooms, store as necessary and put out as per requisition slips.
1.45 Bell for afternoon school.
1.46 Start work on the power supply again.

> Using the diary extract and your own criteria drawn up previously, decide which tasks realistically might be expected to fall within a technician's job description and which not.

Clear expectations, role definitions and job descriptions are of real value. Properly agreed and understood, they minimize dispute and reduce the risks of role overload. Clear lines of management too are important (in any department, a technician can potentially have as many bosses as there are teachers). A specimen job description for technicians has been prepared by the Gloucestershire Education Committee in its document 'Help for new Heads of Science' (currently being revised prior to publication by ASE in 1986).

**Specimen Job Description of Laboratory Technician/Assistant**

1 The Lab. Technician will be responsible to the Head of Science, under the Senior Technician, and will be assigned particular daily duties and general routine duties.

2 **Particular Daily Duties**

Preparation of specific lesson materials for designated areas of the department to include, as appropriate:

collecting apparatus and chemicals from storage;
preparing necessary solutions;
checking individual components in and out for class use;
arranging that apparatus including worksheets, books and audio visual aids is available, in rooms, for lessons;
preparing experiments, setting up apparatus and equipment for demonstration and practical lessons as requested by teaching staff;
liaising with staff over use of equipment and stock;
advise staff of any problem, including safety aspects;

assisting with collection of sundry worksheets, books, audio visual aids and materials;
returning apparatus, etc., and chemicals to storage as soon as practicable;
washing and drying glassware;
repairing damages or arranging for this to be done;
looking after animals, insects and plants kept by the department;
constructing simple apparatus.

All requisitions will be received at least 48 hours before required. Late requests to be dealt with as and when possible.

3 **General Routine Duties**
Laboratory maintenance including:

switching on/off main services;
testing non-standard electrical isolator;
maintaining laboratory clean, tidy (in conjunction with teacher in charge);
cleaning of sinks, chemicals on bench tops, spillages of chemicals on floor;
keeping cupboards and doors closed, storing materials tidily;
keeping equipment clean.

Other duties:

cleaning of goggles on half-termly basis;
checking plug-ends and earthing of electrical equipment on half-termly/termly/annual schedule;
cleaning of safety screens;
taking stock of chemicals, consumables, stationery, books and breakable items;
up-dating stock record books and county inventories;
advising Senior Technician/Head of Subject on stock replacement needs;
writing orders and checking arrivals.

4 **Discretionary Duties** dependent on interest, qualification and experience, usually shared between team of technicians:

construction of more substantial items of equipment;
repair of equipment;
preparation of chemicals and solutions to higher standard of accuracy;
care of audio visual equipment, tapes, cassettes;
care and maintenance of reprographic equipment;
reprographic work for the department;
development of systems of storage and stock maintenance;
development of experimental work in schemes for teaching;
assisting with appraisal of software, development and use of micro-computing resources;
maintenance of language laboratory equipment;
making video/audio recordings, cataloguing and taking bookings for use of equipment.

Compare this with your own authority or school version. The technician too might enjoy seeing it!

The Gloucestershire document also discusses other aspects associated with the management and training of laboratory technicians.

Whatever the intricacies of the job description – and such documents are needed – most teachers would agree that the core of the technician's role is to enable, in a sense, and to service effective teaching and learning in laboratories and classrooms. At the simplest level, this means providing the right apparatus, in full and in working order, in the right place at the right time. Efficient booking systems allowing adequate preparation time are essential and are referred to elsewhere in this text. A level beyond this requires the technician to 'think like teacher'; to know something of the idiosyncracies of individuals (the box of tissues – 'Johnny's nose always bleeds after swimming'), the perversity of inanimate objects (the spare fuse – 'it always blows at the critical moment'), the fallibility of teacher as demonstrator ('I've put out a cloth, it sometimes spills') and the mores and morals of groups ('please check the hand lenses, 3T like them'). Support of this quality, characterized by real empathy for the job in hand does, like many aspects of the technician's role, require a significant element of on the job training. But, above all, it stems from a high level of interest and commitment; the sense of a personal stake in the department and its workings. In short, the technician staff see themselves as full members of the departmental team and need to be recognized as such.

Use the following check-list to conduct a personal audit of your own department's use of its technician staff.

1 Do the technicians attend and contribute to departmental meetings? Regularly, sometimes, never?
2 Do the technicians have their own clearly designated areas of reponsibility? Areas in which they can exercise control, use initiative and deploy resources?
3 Do technicians ever work alongside teachers in laboratories or classrooms?
4 Are technicians encouraged to access and use relevant professional texts and journals?
5 Are efforts made to promote the professional and career development of the technicians within the department through, for example, in-service training and contact with other technicians?
6 Are the technicians encouraged to take part in school and departmental social events?

7 Does the department, and 'the technician manager' in particular, give conscious attention to the small personal courtesies and expressions of interest (apparently trivial but too important to be left to chance)?
8 Does the 'technician manager' provide occasional opportunities for more protracted conversation, a review of progress, of problems and a personal planning session?
9 How are the technicians viewed by the school community as a whole, by the Head, the staff and the students? What are your expectations for the technician staff in this context?

Reflections promoted by the list above will no doubt raise other issues. Reiterating an earlier view, effective technical assistance is a scarce and valuable resource. Careful and sensitive management, promoting job satisfaction and commitment, is needed if the optimum benefit of this resource is to be obtained/achieved.

## Organizing the students

Without students, issues relating to accommodation and staffing are meaningless. We now turn to the methods of organizing students' teaching and learning activities. If for a moment, we look at a science department as a system, rather like a factory, it can be described on an input-activity-output basis. The key input, the raw material, is the students themselves. Through the teaching/learning activity, value is added and better educated students emerge as output. Such an analogy, while somewhat mechanistic in approach and limited in many other respects, does provide a way of drawing attention to interesting issues and shifts. Firstly, departments have only limited and now declining control over the quantity of input, i.e. the total number of students they teach. Science for all up to 16, if implemented, will make the total school population the determining factor. Where, and at a time when, science for all is not the accepted policy, then some degree of control remains. Particularly enterprising departments, which optimize the activity part of the system (effective teaching and learning), recruit well to science courses even though these are optional. In some instances, such success can generate its own particular pressures. (It is worth noting in passing that under the impact of falling rolls and recent legislation, schools as a whole are subject to market forces in this sense, and science departments now have a role in the battle to maintain rolls.) In the same way that the number of students entering science courses is largely externally controlled, so too is the 'quality' of the raw material; this being determined by the characteristics, propensity for education and previous history of the students. Schools, and on occasion individual departments, can dictate, however, how the students are to be grouped and organized for the teaching/learning activity.

Student grouping is thus the focus of this section. Three main issues are tackled:

1 varieties and styles of grouping;
2 grouping and option patterns;
3 grouping within teaching sets.

## Varieties and styles of grouping

The common organizational patterns adopted by schools are concisely described in 'The English Department Book' (ILEA, 1982) as follows;

There are four broad kinds of grouping a school can use, though the divisions between them can be blurred in a school's particular arrangements:

streaming, where pupils remain in the same 'narrow' ability group for all or most subjects;
banding, where pupils are arranged in 'broad' ability strata within the limits of which departments can, if they wish, arrange their own teaching groups;
setting, where departments can form ability groups of their own devising from within the whole year;
mixed ability, where each group contains a full range of ability and stays together for all or most subjects.

Each mode of grouping has its merits and de-merits, its advocates and its detractors. Grouping policies are likely to be different for young people of different ages, and there is too a variation from school to school in the degree of 'control' a department can exert on these policies.

For science departments, the key question is 'Is the composition of teaching groups well matched to the department's philosophies, teaching styles and strategies and its resource base?'

Draw up and complete a table in the style of that given below for a representative sample of groups across your school's age range.

| | | | *For learning and teaching* | |
|---|---|---|---|---|
| *Teaching group* | *No. in group* | *Description of group* | *Advantages* | *Disadvantages* |
| 1 JN | 29 | Middle group of three roughly equivalent top band classes. | (a) Class contains a significant proportion of scientifically able students. | (a) Despite banding group does have a considerable range of ability. |

| | | |
|---|---|---|
| | (b) Curriculum for all is common and staff feel justified and secure in adopting a largely class teaching approach. | (b) Teaching 'to the middle' does not serve best interests of extremes |
| | (c) Staff have high expectations of students; students have positive view of themselves. | (c) Significant overlap between 'bottom' of top band and 'top' of middle band – curriculum not entirely common – transfer difficult. |

Develop the analysis by answering the following questions:

(a) Do the forms of grouping adopted by the department have any detrimental effects on:
 (i) group sizes?
 (ii) the allocation of staff to groups?
 (iii) groups within other departments in a given year?
(b) Who determines the composition of the groups?
(c) What criteria are used and which evidence drawn up to allocate students to groups?

This kind of grouping review, as well as informing departmental practice, can have implications for other subject areas and whole school policies. In this latter context, the well made and researched case can be a powerful agent for change.

## *Non-streamed grouping – the mixed ability case*

Organizing students into mixed ability groups, perhaps better described as non-streamed groups, is the strategy which has and does provoke the greatest level of debate and anxiety. It makes very considerable demands on teachers and resources, but some of the points in favour of a mixed ability approach are succinctly put below. This is an abstract from ILEA (1982) with appropriate amendments to change the context to that of the Science Department.

For pupils:

1 Mixed ability grouping avoids overt labelling of pupils and so helps to prevent pupils making limiting decisions about their own potential as learners.

2 Mixed ability grouping encourages co-operation as opposed to competition. Pupils who show different abilities can learn from one another and gain from each other's strengths.
3 All pupils have access to the same kind of curriculum and resources. Most research shows that 'less able' pupils do better in mixed ability classes and that able pupils maintain their level of performance.

For teachers:
1 Everyone teaches the same kind of class in a given year. This means that opportunities for co-operation – developing common practices and sharing the real problems of teaching and learning – are maximized.
2 The move to mixed ability teaching can provide a department with an exciting change of direction as teachers are forced to re-examine their assumptions about the nature of science teaching. This often leads to the creation of coherent units of work offering a framework within which new and fruitful patterns of communication in the classroom can develop.
3 Teachers are invited to see pupils as members of a class possessing constellations of different qualities rather than as a homogeneous group with certain shared characteristics. This means, among other things, re-considering the criteria by which they judge pupils' performance in science and communicate that judgement both inside and outside the classroom.

Much else has been written about mixed ability teaching and this is not the place to rehearse details of tactics or further to develop the arguments. Suffice it to say that at whatever level and to whatever degree a non-streamed approach is proposed or adopted by a science department, effective teaching and learning is unlikely to be achieved without the active support of a committed team of teachers and without the development of an appropriate resource base.

Much valuable advice and thorough analysis of the issues is contained in ASE (1981). Science departments working with or planning to work with mixed ability groups are directed to this excellent text for the guidance it provides in this particular context, and also for its exposition of good practice in science teaching in other contexts.

## Grouping and option patterns

In most schools there is significant interplay between curriculum structures and student grouping.

For instance, student groupings can influence future curriculum options: members of a third year 'lower ability' set, offered a science course rather than the physics, chemistry and biology thought appropriate for their more able contemporaries, may as a consequence be restricted in their choice of fourth year programme. Conversely, the setting of physics in the same column of an option system as home economics and child care is likely to have a significant impact on group composition within these subjects! That there may be particular consequences of these kinds of interplay for science departments will be evident.

Investigate the department's present fourth year teaching groups. Are there awkward imbalances within groups, e.g. male/female, able/not so able etc?

Calculate, for boys and girls separately:

(a) the percentage of the year group studying *each* science subject offered in the fourth year curriculum;
(b) the percentage offering (if applicable)
 (i) three science subjects
 (ii) two science subjects
 (iii) one science subject
 (iv) no science;
(c) if applicable, the average number of science subjects per male and per female student.

If causes for concern emerge from these two activities, you might go on to relate these to:

(a) the science curriculum in the earlier years;
(b) the structure of the school's option system.

This kind of analytical approach to student numbers and student groupings is already routine practice in many departments. It can usefully inform both the departmental and whole school debate. (NB. The issue of girls and science is the subject of a separate section in Chapter 7.)

Science for all, as defined elsewhere in this text, should simplify matters a good deal.

## Grouping within teaching sets

Working in sub-groups is a common and well established feature of many science classes; pairs for practicals, small groups for projects and so on. On occasions, this style of working is prompted largely by practical and pragmatic considerations, i.e. it makes the best use within a given lesson structure of the resources and space available. 'There are only ten power packs and we have 30 pupils.' At other times, teachers actively seek to encourage co-operative working and the team approach, recognizing that students can learn from and help each other, that discussion and debate are key features of the learning process and that individual skills brought together can complete a complex task. (Chapter 3 tackles some of these issues more extensively.) The main purpose of this short section, as with the earlier sections, is to simulate an active review of day-to-day happenings within the department.

Consciously note, over a sequence of lessons for a given class, the pattern of student working. Record:

1 the relative proportion of whole class to small group working;
2 the factors influencing a particular pattern;
3 the composition of groups – Do they remain the same? What about male/female composition, ability distribution and the like?
4 the way in which composition of the groups is determined and who decides the composition.

It is worth, too, spending a little time observing more closely the working of one or two individual groups and noting such matters as:

whether there is a clear leader;
whether individual members invariably take on the same role, e.g. as recorder
in mixed groups, whether roles are heavily influenced by sex stereotypes – girls write, boys do, etc.
(The growth of school based practical assessment is likely to enhance the importance of just such observations.)

As before, the central issue remains: 'Do the groupings adopted match the intended learning outcomes?' If we aim to foster co-operative working, then designing tasks which demand it is a good starting point. If we look to develop self-confidence or promote discussion then careful grouping would seem to be of equal importance.

That many teachers instinctively practise such strategies is beyond dispute, but even the natural teacher who is adept in this respect can gain from close observation and analysis. The conscious recognition of key features of effective practice may well improve personal performance and will make easier the important business of sharing skills and expertise with other colleagues.

## Where to from here?

Reviewing individual or departmental practice by the techniques suggested earlier, or otherwise, can both raise issues and enable the teacher or team to define the present state of the department – the 'as it is' position. It may also help to sharpen views on the 'as we might wish it to be' state. Getting from one to the other is the difficult task. This section deals briefly with some of the issues associated with making changes. It makes use, in summarized form, of some of the ideas to be found in 'Understanding Managerial Roles' (ASE/British Gas, 1984). Inevitably, there are simplifications in this shortened form and readers are recommended to consult the original workshop packs.

## The department as a system

In an earlier paragraph, the idea of treating the department as an input-activity-output system was introduced. This can help in a number of instances. It can, for example:

1 help with appraisal review – Does an activity achieve the desired link between what comes in to the department and what goes out? ('Does this teaching strategy achieve this learning outcome with that group of pupils?' 'Does our management of the department's budget make the most of the money we get?')
2 help the individual or department to respond to new ideas. ('If we change the third year course, what will the benefits be? What will it cost?')
3 help with planning – How should an activity be changed to respond to shifts in incomes or expected outcomes? ('The feeder primary schools have started an extensive programme of primary science. What about our first year course?' or 'The Head is not happy with the O-level chemistry results. What can we do?')

> For your department, list with their 'connecting' activities, some important incomes and outcomes. Identify 'problem' activities and high priority activities.

It may be that such an approach will enable you to pinpoint causes of problems or reasons for priority, more effectively and more overtly. As noted in (3) above, problems or changes in priority may be caused by shifts in what comes into the department or changes with regard to expectations about what comes out. Analysis will not remove your difficulties but it may help you tackle them.

## People and influences

Adequate physical resources in the shape of teaching spaces, books and equipment are important but few would doubt that people are the major key to change. Part of your analysis then of the department as a system must investigate this variable. Who are the key influences? One way to engage with such a question is illustrated in the exercise below.

> Select from your input-activity-output analysis one activity (preferably, as a beginning, a fairly simple one, such as textbook selection). List the people or role holders influencing the activity (e.g. headteacher, head of department, teacher 1, teacher 2, students etc.). Assign each an arbitrary score on a 0–10 scale which represents their 'influence' on the activity. (0 represents no influence, 10 the highest possible influence. A

set involving three people all exerting equal and maximum influence would be scored 10, 10, 10, and so on). Don't agonize too much over assigning precise numbers. You are after a qualitative sense of the system.

Persuade a colleague(s) to undertake the same exercise.

Do you all view the activity in broadly the same way, i.e. recognize similar influence patterns? Is the existing influence pattern a good match for the activity in hand? Ought some influences to be reduced and others given more say? (It is interesting to reflect on the role of the students, for example, in many activities.)

This simple influence scoring system can be elaborated and developed in a range of ways. One such is to translate the numbers into a diagram, representing each role by a circle of a size roughly equivalent to that role's influence on the activity. Connecting the circle by arrows of varying thickness can then convey both the direction and extent of communications between the influential parties. A simple example is given as Figure 5.3. Such an approach cannot convey all the subtleties and nuances of many activities, but it can make clear some essential messages. If, for example, the technician and/or the teachers had little say (low influence scores) in the devising of the system, communications were poor and the head of department dictated the system to be used (high influence score), it may be that the activity would not work to its best effect. Misunderstandings and even resentment could be generated.

The construction of role-set activities can serve other purposes. It can, for example, pinpoint 'roles under pressure', i.e. those roles with lots of arrows centring on them (the probationary teacher trying to meet the often conflicting demands of Heads of department, Heads of House, teacher tutor and, of course, the students themselves). If views about role relationships are exchanged with colleagues, different perspectives on relationships can be exposed ('You always seem to be telling me'; 'I thought I always listened and took your views into account'). For change too there are implications. Shifting influence patterns may well be essential in order to improve the quality of an activity. ('Why don't we give the Special Needs department a say in devising the work cards for the bottom set?')

## Expectations

Whatever our role within the school or departmental system, that role will carry with it certain 'expectations'; expectations which make demands on us and our own expectations of others. We expect things of our colleagues and of the 'outside world', and all have a view of what we as teacher, as Head of department or as headteacher should do. Parents expect us to teach effectively; we expect

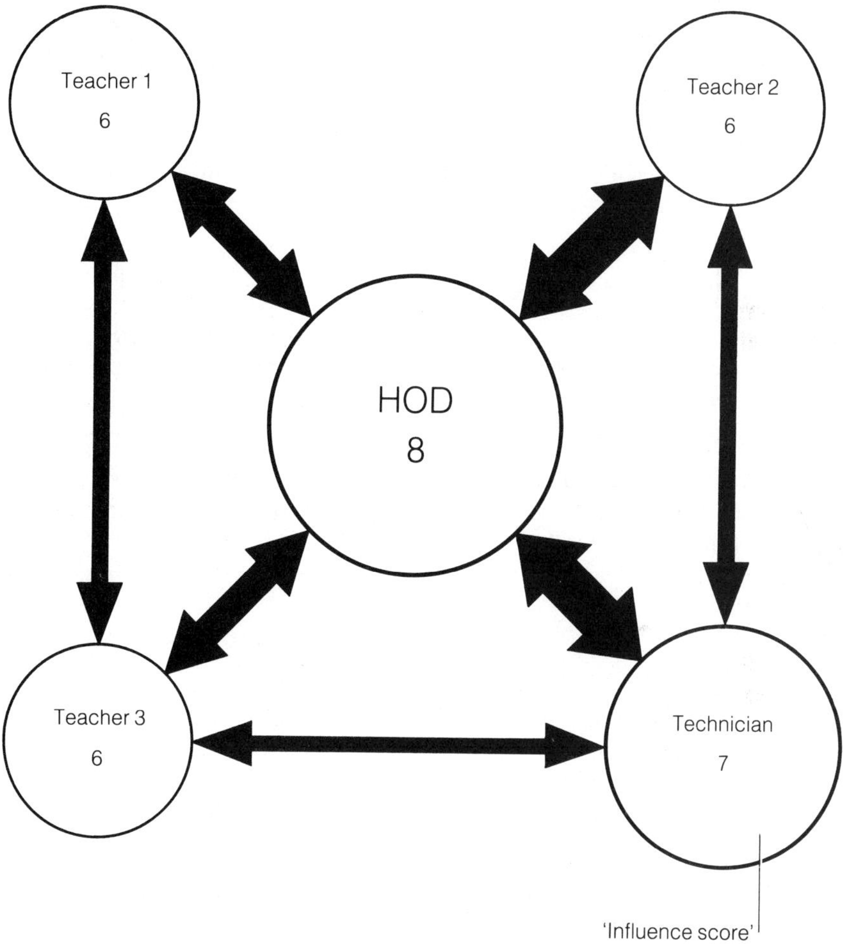


FIG. 5.3 **Simplified role set for a small science department**

parents to support our efforts to do that. We also have expectations of ourselves, of what we can do and are capable of doing in a given role.

Being clear about expectations is important. As an illustration of one aspect of this issue, try the following exercise.

> Ask a colleague, preferably a different role holder, a Head of department or technician for example, to write down what she/he expects of you in your current role. You, in turn, record your expectations of her/him Exchange pieces of paper and discuss!
>
> (The same exercise can be carried out rather less painfully, but still usefully, by role playing. You become Head of department, colleague becomes probationer and so on).

As intimated above, such expectation exchanges can be potentially threatening and require a level of openness and security not always found in schools, departments or other systems. The game is, however, worth the effort. A fully or even partially worked through expectation analysis can serve a number of purposes, helping to identify, for example:

1 role conflict, i.e. conflicting expectations. 'Headteacher says do A, Adviser says do B.' 'Head of department teaches all sixth form, you expect to extend your teaching experience.'
2 role ambiguity, unclear expectations. 'Nobody ever told me I was expected to take games.'
3 role overload/underload. 'Technicians should have three arms.' 'I could have sorted that out if they had asked me.'

Thus the important message here – in the words of ASE/British Gas (1984) – is 'expectations need to be communicated; need to be clear; need to be complementary.'

Expectation analysis and the exchange of ideas about roles can also be used:

1 as a means of beginning discussions on individual performance. (What do we expect of ourselves? What are our standards? Do they match the needs of the job and the expectations of others? Can we identify any development needs? Have we particular role problems?)
2 in helping to plan and bring about change, by clarifying matters relating to performance and 'who does what' and, importantly, by pinpointing where individuals or groups need to develop new knowledge and skills. This last issue is taken up in the next section.

## Staff development

Any school or department aspiring both to maintain the best of its existing practices and to meet changing conditions, demands and expectations (shifts in the input or output pattern) recognizes the importance of establishing a clear and explicit staff development policy.

> As a beginning, try the following. Note the last two in-service courses you attended. Who or what motivated your attendance? Did the course make sense in terms of meeting school, department or individual needs or priorities?
>
> Now, assume you can choose three areas for further training or skill development. (These might be subject centred – more knowledge; practice centred – how to teach x or y; or more general – improving management or pastoral skills etc.) List possible sources of such training (your school, other schools, the LEA INSET programme, college or university offerings, or others).
>
> Look now to the department as a whole and identify training/development needs more generally. Check your views with a colleague or, better, use the section which follows as a stimulus for a departmental meeting.

Any policy of staff development which is well worked through is likely to look to needs under the broad headings:

1 career development – looking to the individual's potential for progression through the career structure;
2 professional development – improving and developing performance in existing role;
3 personal development – offering scope for individual growth and learning.

Increasingly, such policies are set within school and local authority frameworks and influenced too by national concerns and priorities. (Science teachers and particularly Heads of science departments, for example, have been offered training opportunities under schemes promoted and substantially resourced on a national basis. The current TVEI Related In-service Training Initiative may well be a forerunner of similar developments in the future.) However, it is evident that clear responsibilities remain with individual departments. In particular it is important that the department:

1 looks actively to staff development;
2 knows about the range of opportunities available locally and nationally;
3 engages in its own on the job training, utilizing the range of skills already available within the department;
4 appropriately balances the needs of individuals and the needs of the departmental team as a whole.

Issues related to further education and training for teachers are not likely to decline in importance in the coming years given the changing shape of the science curriculum, of examination and assessment procedures, and emerging shifts in classroom practice. There is, too, that link between discussions on individual and departmental performance and training needs, a link which was noted earlier; the idea of and the demands for appraisal in this sense are not likely to go away.

## Overview

This chapter has focused on teaching spaces, student grouping and staffing. Other aspects of resources and their deployment are dealt with in Chapter 6. The intention here has been to promote and provoke a review of current provision and practice, both as an essential activity for the healthy department and as a prerequisite for change and growth. Many of the ideas will be familiar and others of significance have been omitted – there is no mention of meetings, for example. Directed use of the referenced texts will help to redress these omissions. At the heart of the matter remains the challenge of optimizing staff and other resources, and to clear curriculum ends for the benefit of the student and his or her varied needs and aspirations. The analytical approach can help us to meet this challenge.

## Bibliography


APU, 1982, *Science in Schools Age 15*, Report No. 1 (HMSO, London)

ASE, 1986, *Help for New Heads of Science* (Association for Science Education, Hatfield)

ASE, 1981, *Study Series No. 7, Non-streamed Science, A Teachers' Guide* (Association for Science Education, Hatfield)

ASE, Laboratory Technicians Subcommittee, 1976, 'The Secret life of Anne Sillary', *Education in Science* No. 67 p 28 (Association for Science Education, Hatfield)

ASE/British Gas, 1984, *Meetings on Vehicles of Communication* (ASE/British Gas, Hatfield)

ASE/British Gas, 1984, *Time Management* (ASE/British Gas, Hatfield)

ASE/British Gas, 1984, *Staff Development – Selection and Appraisal* (ASE/British Gas, Hatfield)

ASE/British Gas, 1984, *Understanding Managerial Roles* (ASE/British Gas, Hatfield)

DES, 1977, *Curriculum 11–16*, Working papers by HMI (HMSO, London)

DES and Welsh Office, 1985, *Science 5–16: A Statement of Policy* (HMSO, London)

Hull, R., and Adams, H., 1981, *Decisions in the Science Department* (Schools Council/ASE, London)

ILEA, 1982, *The English Department Book, A Guide to Organization and Resources* (ILEA, London)

# 6 How are resources organized?

**Brian Nicholl**

## Introduction

★ Careful management of funds is a high priority.
★ Resources (apparatus, textbooks and writing aids) should only be acquired after careful research.
★ Resources should be deployed systematically. An administrative stucture should exist to ensure resources are well managed.
★ Assistance with resources may come from outside the school, e.g. from industry.
★ Resources should be used safely.

This chapter is concerned more with practical advice than with theoretical considerations. Some of the suggested practices will be well known to many readers but they are considered to be worth repeating in the hope that they will offer some new ideas.

Good organization makes it possible for plans to become effective; the provision of resources in the form of space, apparatus, materials, time and staff, in sufficient quantities to allow the planned courses to be carried out, must be a high priority in any science department organization. This organization may be short-term or long-term, and range from ensuring that technicians supply each member of staff with the needs for a particular lesson, to ordering apparatus for a new course which is to start two terms hence. Whatever the resource – material or human – careful planning will improve the efficiency of the department and lead to greater job satisfaction among the staff of the department.

This chapter considers:

budgeting within the department;
how resources can be acquired and deployed;
the management and maintenance of resources;
using outside resources and professional support;
forming useful links with industry;
legal responsibility and safe use of resources.

Throughout the chapter a distinction is made between apparatus and materials and written or other audio-visual resources. While realizing that this is an artificial demarcation – all are meant to assist the learning processes of the students – it forms a convenient classification.

## Budgeting for resources

The starting point for the acquisition and maintenance of resources is the allocation of a budget to a school, within the school and within the individual departments which make up the school. The science department is probably one of the biggest spenders in a school. The careful management of funds is of the highest priority – not least in times of restricted budgets – both to ensure maximum purchasing power and to provide proper accounting of moneys spent. A system such as the one that will be described later in this chapter (page 230) should ensure that the head of department knows exactly how much has been spent by the department at any time during the year.

The absolute responsibility for the allocation of capitation within a school probably rests with the Head, but the concept of a finance committee – usually found in industry and commerce – could well be, and sometimes is, applied in schools. A likely constitution of such a body would include all senior management, heads of departments with, perhaps, representation from the general teaching staff.

Within an individual department overall responsibility for, and control over, the budget must be taken by the head of the department. However, a wise head of department will exercise this authority in consultation with the heads of subject and the senior laboratory technician. Perhaps there is even then a case for establishing a departmental finance committee.

LEA policy for the allocation of capitation to schools varies throughout the country. In one authority schools are circulated with the proposed allocation and may then apply for additional finance. Their success (or otherwise) will depend largely on the strength of the case they are able to put forward.

Within an individual school the allocation of capitation is likely to be made according to a formula – sometimes understood (or even known) only by the originator! One headteacher uses the following calculation.

Operating sum = Global sum – 10 per cent for curriculum development, furniture, administration i.e. general office, exercise books, cleaning materials, field courses

Operating sum = $\sum wpn$ (for all departments)

where w = weighting, p = pupil periods, n = pupils in group.

Examples of weightings:

| | |
|---|---|
| geography, mathematics, English | 1 |
| biology | 1.5 |
| chemistry | 2.0 |
| physics | 2.5 |
| metalwork | 2.0 |
| woodwork | 2.0 |

Sixth form weighting is increased by a factor of 2.

Allocations based on this formula form a basis for discussion with all heads of department and, in the case of the science department (or faculty), a capitation allowance is then given to each subject department within the science faculty. Table 6.1 provides some data against which science departments can

TABLE 6.1

| | ASE/EPC Survey (1984) (for 1981–2 mainly in English maintained schools) | APU (1982) *Science in Schools Age 15* Report No. 2 for 1981 in English maintained schools |
|---|---|---|
| % of LEA allowance for teaching resources allocated to science | | Grammar 17%<br>11–18 Comp. 12%<br>11–16 Comp. 8% |
| £1/student spent on teaching resources for science | With VIth form £3.15<br>No VIth form £2.47 | Grammar £3.45<br>11–18 Comp. £2.55<br>11–16 Comp. £1.85 |
| | N.B. Prep. schools £3.25 student<br>Ind. schools with VIth form £9.00/student | N.B. 40% of schools reported extra money via special LEA grants, PTA etc. (Range £30–£12 000) |
| Cumbria LEA (capitation allowance for teaching resources 1983–84) | 11–16<br>£26.11 | 17 +<br>£38.30<br>This gives an average of £27.22 if 25% proceed to sixth form |

assess the adequacy of their share of the school capitation allowance for teaching equipment and materials.

In allocating funds within the school, and the science department, it is important that the following are considered and that a fair spread of resources is determined: needs specific to the department as a whole, particular subject interests within the department, particular age groups, particular ability groups. *Help for New Heads of Science* (ASE, 1986) suggests that, in drawing up estimates for expenditure, three sections are used to cover years 1–3, 4–5 and sixth form, and that each section is sub-divided into headings which might include:

consumable materials such as chemicals etc.;
hardware – those items expected to have a long life (with the possible addition of a minimum cost);
textbooks;
stationery and duplicating materials;
audio-visual aids;
books for the departmental library or possible curriculum development;
repairs to equipment;
technicians' requirements.

Many heads of science hold back a percentage of the department's allocation as a reserve against contingencies, overspending by one section of the department, unexpected repairs or purchases and the like. Amounts remaining unspent towards the end of the financial year provide a bonus for the department – bearing in mind the loss of money if funds are not used before the end of the financial year.

Finally, a word must be said about the sometimes controversial question of the use of petty cash within the department. Local custom will vary, but a strong case can be made for the provision of modest sums of money to be used for local purchases. Not only will the existence of such a fund lead to economic gains (local hardware shops can often supply items at a fraction of the cost of those from national school suppliers) but there will be real benefits in time and convenience for the science department staff. It goes without saying that careful records (and receipts) should be kept for all expenditure from petty cash funds and that such sums of money should be part of the department's overall capitation.

Use the following questions (extracted from Hull and Adams, 1981) to encourage discussion within the department about the allocation of a budget. (Comments on the questions are provided in the original text.)

1 Does the department construct and present to the headteacher, deputy head or finance committee each year a well argued case for its allocation of money?
2 Has the department discussed the possibility of suggesting that a formula be used in allocating funds to departments within the school? What would be the advantages and disadvantages to the science department of such a scheme?
3 Have all potential sources of income, whether within the school or elsewhere, been approached recently?
4 What are the advantages and disadvantages of the present system for allocation of funds within the department? Does this system lead to an equitable distribution?
5 If heads of subject are responsible for placing their own orders for apparatus and materials, what precautions are taken to prevent duplication? Are any steps taken to encourage sharing the cost of apparatus and materials?
6 What part of the departmental allowance is set aside for repair and maintenance of existing apparatus? How much of the departmental allowance is spent on replacement, and how much on the purchase of additional material and apparatus?
7 Is sufficient money set aside for the purchase of books and other printed matter?

# Acquisition and use of resources

Many science teachers will think of resources largely in terms of bunsen burners, test tubes, oscilloscopes, skeletons, fish tanks and balances, depending upon their own academic disciplines, though all will use printed resources, whether they be textbooks, wall charts, or their own worksheets. In whatever sphere of science teaching the reader is involved, there is no lack of choice when it comes to obtaining new resources. The increasing impact of microelectronics, if anything, exacerbates the problem. What guidance can be given on acquiring resources? How do we make the 'best buy' against the blitz of information and claims from manufacturers and publishers?

## 1 Apparatus

Once the decision to purchase new equipment has been made the choice of available alternatives is often so bewildering that chance, or personal likes and dislikes, will be the main guiding factor. But, before reaching such a decision, much research needs to be done. ASE (1986) lists the following stages in procedure (Figure 6.1). For completeness the full chart is reproduced here, though some of the recommended stages will be considered later in the chapter.

The process of identifying needs requires both established departmental procedures and, on occasions, full discussion with all members of the department. Consumables, for example, can be controlled by regular checks – probably by the technicians – and repeat orders made before current stocks run out. Purchase of new apparatus, on the other hand, may be linked with a change of syllabus or the availability of new or additional funds, and will be preceded by staff debate and consultation.

If the school financial year begins in April, the purchase of new equipment should be considered at the beginning of the Spring Term (or even earlier), so that firm orders can be placed as soon as new funds become available. While the ultimate responsibility for placing orders probably rests with the head of science – or heads of subject – opportunities should be provided, probably through departmental meetings, for other staff to enter their own ideas and priorities.

There is much outside advice available on assessing available products. The Association for Science Education's two publications *SSR* and *EIS*, for example, are valuable sources of such information. The Association's annual meeting, held in early January of each year, provides what is probably the largest exhibition of apparatus (and also textbooks and other materials) ever seen under one roof. The Consortium of LEAs for the Provision of Science Equipment (CLEAPSE) gives considerable advice on the merits (or otherwise) of similar equipment offered by different manufacturers, and publishes comparative guides. CLEAPSE has also negotiated discount contracts with a number of suppliers for its member authorities. Your science adviser will be able to tell you whether these, and/or other CLEAPSE services, are available to your

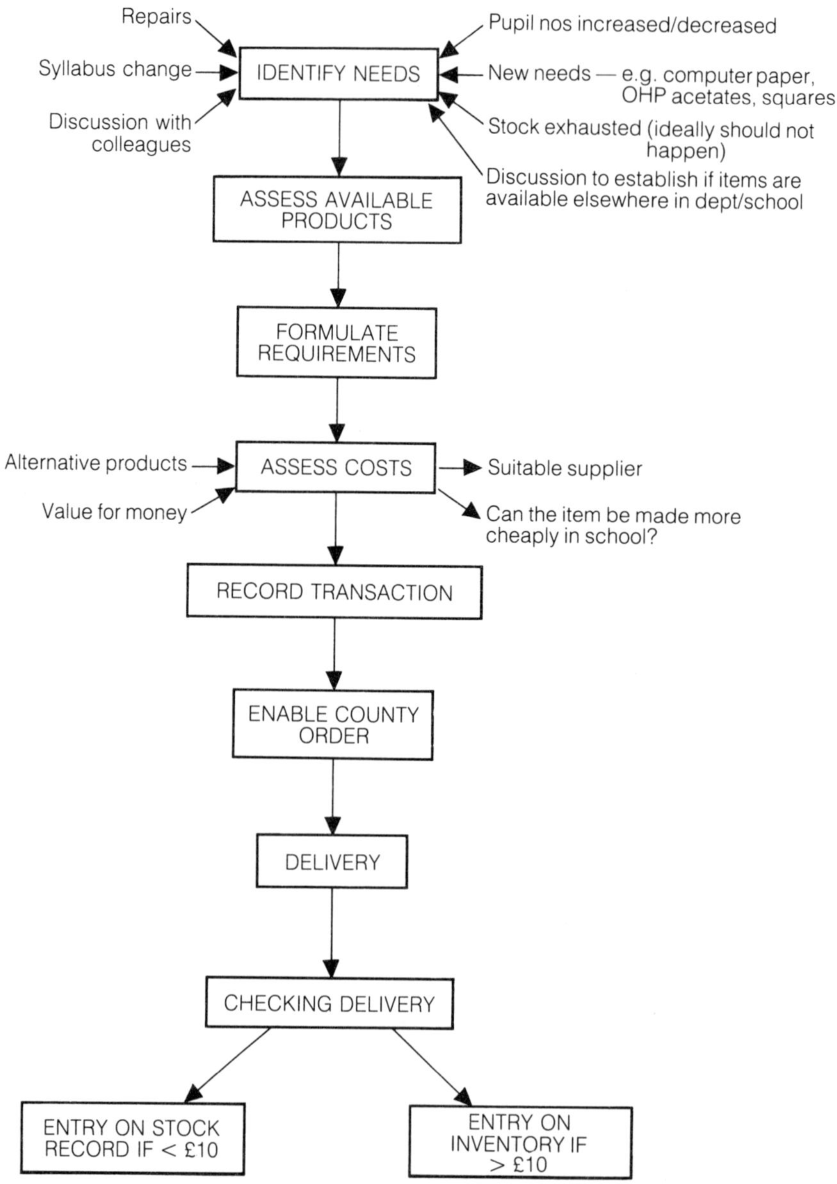


FIG. 6.1 **Ordering apparatus.** (from ASE, 1986)

school. A similar service is provided for schools in Scotland by the Scottish Schools Science Equipment Research Centre (SSSERC).

There is a growing mountain of both hardware and software available for microprocessor users, and information about what is available can be obtained from organizations such as:

Centre for Educational Technology;
Microelectronic Education Programme;
Computers in the Curriculum Project.

Your local Science and Technology Regional Organization (SATRO) may also be able to help.

## 2 Textbooks and other written material

In a world where television offers the main communication medium for many of our students, and the only reading for pleasure carried out by many children is the comic, some would question the wisdom of depending upon the written word as a teaching resource. The importance of other forms of communication – such as talking and writing – are discussed in Chapter 3 and more fully in, for instance, ASE (1980), Sutton (1981) and Bulman (1985), but few science teachers will be willing to abandon the use of class textbooks or individual reference books. Reading is a powerful method of self-instruction and of class-based learning. Much resource-based learning is totally dependent upon the ability of the individual student to read instructions, descriptions and questions. Because the material is written down, and in that sense does not go away, the student can read and re-read a particular passage until he/she is ready to go on. At its most basic level, the class textbook offers the teacher a minute or two's respite in a busy day – 'Read pages 10–15 in your textbook and answer the questions at the end of the chapter'. Examinations also continue to make considerable reading demands, and the influence of examination paper language on performance is well documented.

Much has been written about the skills required to become a competent reader, and excellent and very practical advice is given in Davies and Green (1980). This book, and indeed the whole project, offers ways in which students can be encouraged and directed toward active use of textbooks. The acronym DARTS (Directed Activities Related to Texts) captures something of the flavour. However, in this chapter, we are particularly interested in the use of resources and their initial acquisition. How then are you as teacher to evaluate the written offerings of the many authors who are convinced that they know just what is required for your students? In short, what guidance can be given in assessing a textbook – whether for class or individual reading? Direct experience would seem to be vital. Once again, the ASE annual meeting offers a unique opportunity to obtain 'hands-on' experience of a very large variety of science books, and inspection copy services make individual texts accessible. But what criteria can be applied to making a choice from the wide selection of books available? The Middle Secondary Science Review of the ILEA has produced a draft of a book review form for the assessment of textbooks. It uses the following headings:

basic information;
content;
layout;
demand on students;
support for students;
other comments;
follow-up material/reference.

The following list of questions is provided by ASE (1985) as possible criteria for the selection and evaluation of published primary science materials intended for teacher and student use, but can be modified for use with other published works. It makes a useful distinction between teachers' and students' material.

*Analysis of materials*

Are materials attractively presented?

Are they produced in monochrome, full colour or in a limited range of colours?

Are clear photographs or simple line drawings used?

If materials are sold in packs, is the supply of teacher and pupil materials adequate for the intended use?

How durable are the materials? Are they likely to last for a reasonable length of time in use?

Are teacher/pupil materials separate or combined in one unit?

*Teacher information and guidance*

How detailed are the teachers' notes?

Under what headings is guidance given?

Is there a clear statement of the aims of the publication?

Is there a clear statement of the objectives by which children might achieve these aims?

Are stated objectives mainly concerned with scientific processes, skills or scientific concepts, or has a balance been struck between the three?

Do the teachers' materials provide adequate background information on the science involved?

Is a list of resources given? How realistic is this in terms of cost, availability and storage of items?

Are there hints on dealing with problems which may arise, e.g. advance warnings, safety aspects?

Are there useful addresses for obtaining further information and resources?

Is any guidance given as to how the materials can be adapted to suit various approaches and teaching styles?

Are suggestions given as to how the activities link in with other areas of the curriculum?

*Pupil materials*

Are the pupil materials intended for a specific age range or ability group?
Can the materials be adapted for class, group or individual work?
Is the language suitable?
Is the required reading age right for the target group?
Are the manual skills necessary to carry out the practical work realistic for the intended age group?
How directive are the work cards:
Are they prescriptive?
Do they encourage children to investigate their own ideas by experimentation?
Is discussion and evaluation of tests encouraged?
Can the cards be adapted for the slow learner?
Are there suggestions for extension activities and problem solving to stretch the more able?
Can the children do some activities at home?

Another writer, John Foster (1978), sets out the following series of questions which teachers should ask when assessing the suitability of material for school use.

Is the text compelling? Will a pupil find it immediately interesting and appealing?
How clearly are the facts/ideas put across? Is the order of presentation straightforward? Are the facts/ideas easy to grasp?
How dense is the text? How many facts/ideas will the pupil reader encounter per paragraph? Per page?
Is the level of abstraction and conceptual difficulty of the text suitable for the age, maturity and motivation of the pupils who will be expected to read it?
How complex is the style of the text? Is the sentence structure simple or are complicated grammatical structures used? If so, will the pupils be familiar with them?
How difficult is the vocabulary that is used? When specialist terms are introduced, are they adequately explained? Is there a glossary?
Are pages well designed with any illustrations/diagrams suitably positioned in relation to the text? Are there too many pictures per page or perhaps too much text per page? [Newton (1984) discusses the use of pictures in science textbooks.]
Is the print size too big or too small for the age and ability of the pupils who will use it?
Are the illustrations suitable for the age range with which it will be used? Do they complement the text? Do they supplement the text adding an extra dimension to the section/chapter? Are they just decorative or perhaps even distracting?
If it is a textbook, are the activities suggested and the questions asked suitable? Do they stimulate thought? Are any instructions that are given easy to follow?

How easy is it to find information from the book? Is there a table of contents? Is there an index and, if so, is it easy to use?
How would you use the book in class? To introduce the facts/ideas that it contains? To reinforce and summarize ideas/facts presented in another way?
Would you give it to pupils to read on their own? At home? In class?
What claims do the publishers/author make for the books/materials? In the light of your examination, are these claims justified?

Perhaps three more points should be added to this list:

Does the publication match your own use of it in its contents?
At the price charged for the book, is it a good buy?
Could the same information be obtained from other sources at a cheaper price (perhaps from one of the industrial companies which produces educational material)?

Finally, and of major importance, is the publication free from bias of sex (and race or class)?

> Select a textbook used in your own department. Using the above, or other criteria, check your own impression of the usefulness of the book in the situation in which it is used.The following broad headings could also be useful:
>
> Subject matter – is it interesting to the reader?
> Printing – do you like the size and style? Does its organization on the page help the reader?
> Language – does this seem to you to be complex, simple, formal, informal?

The 'readability' of a text is a particular technical aspect of textbook selection worth further attention. Tessa Carrick (1978) considers three facets of readability:

readers' interest and motivation;
visibility of the printed word;
the language used.

She suggests that a student will read a textbook only if suitably motivated. This motivation might be provided by the intrinsic interest of the subject, the attractiveness of the book to the reader, the teacher's own attitude to books, the student's own curiosity and the tasks he/she is asked to perform using the book (note the DARTS mentioned earlier). The first impact of any printed material will be made by the front cover and the general quality of illustrations and organization of the material. Publishers are becoming more and more aware of the importance of these aspects. Since there are no suitable techniques for evaluating printed materials in these terms, their effectiveness is still a matter of subjective opinion. Perhaps the aesthetic appeal of books to younger readers is more important than has previously been accepted. It might be of interest to discuss this quality with your own students.

The visibility of print is affected by a number of factors which include: size and shape of print; spacing of lines and letters; length of line; type and quality of paper; use of italics, bold, capitals for emphasis etc. Galliland (1972) lists the range of type size, line width and spacing which may be used without loss of legibility, but this is done in the language of a printer and might be difficult for the non-technical reader. Some publishers now list the type size and face used in a particular text and this gives the reader an immediate indication of its suitability for a particular audience. Type sizes will be stated as, for example, 11 on 13 point. The first number indicates the size of the type used (where 72 points = 1 inch) and the second number is a measure of the distance between two lines of type. As a guide, this handbook is set in 10 on 12 point.

Assessing the level of language has attracted more attention, and there are many methods of 'measuring' the readability of passages of prose. The Schools Council Project DARTS has investigated the suitability of many of these methods. All involve the application of a readability formula, usually taking acount of vocabulary, particular word length or number of syllables in words and sentence structure or length. Tessa Carrick discusses a number of readability tests and applies them to a selection of school biology textbooks. ASE (1980) also provides examples of methods of assessing readability, as does ASE (1979a). Reading age can now be ascertained using various computer programs – such as *Textgrader* published by Hutchinson Education.

Most of the tests produce a 'reading age level' for the passage assessed, and it is of interest to note that one contributor to Sutton (1981) suggests that the following reading ages are required to read a selection of public documents:

| | Minimum reading age |
|---|---|
| Application form for a Family Income Supplement | 13 |
| Application to buy Premium Savings Bonds | 16 |
| Application to re-licence a motor vehicle | 17 |
| Child benefit application form | 14 |
| Application for civil legal aid | 17 |
| Divorce petition | 17 |

The interested reader should consult one of the publications already listed above for a fuller account of the use of readability tests, but one example – the Fry readability graph – is given below. It is selected because of its ease of use.

## *Fry readability graph*

This method of judging reading age is based on two factors: word length and sentence length. To use it:

1 Select three passages from the text each 100 words long. (The passages should be taken from the beginning, the middle and the end of the text.)
2 For each passage count:
the number of sentences (part of a sentence counts as a fraction of a sentence to the nearest 1/10);
the number of syllables (count numbers as single syllable words);
3 Using the graph shown in Figure 6.2, plot the average number of sentences per 100 words (for the three passages) against the average number of syllables per 100 words. The point obtained gives a reading age level.
4 Points which come above the line suggest that the difficulties will be concerned with vocabulary, while points below the line are indicative of difficulties of sentence structure.

> Apply the Fry readability measure to the following extract taken from a textbook for first year secondary science pupils overseas.
>
> What is the reading age level required for the text? Do you think the text is suitable for 11–12 year olds?
>
> You should notice that the seedling in box B continued to grow straight up. The seedlings in box A, however, bent towards the light. This is one of the ways by which plants move. They move by growing in a certain direction. In this case they grow towards the light. Box B is needed to show that it is the light which causes this effect in box B. It is needed for comparison with box A. It is called the **control**. Because plants usually move very slowly, we often don't notice their movement. In this section we have discovered . . .

**A word of caution** Most of the readability tests should be considered to predict rather than to measure how difficult a particular passage would be for a group of readers. They can only measure the features of the passage that appear on the page. They cannot take account of the students' understanding of the concepts involved; they are not sensitive to the difficulty of the ideas or vocabulary expressed in the passage. Nor can they take into account the way in which the material is presented on the page. Nevertheless, they can provide an indication of whether the text can be read by the particular age group to which the book is addressed.

Before finishing this section it is of interest to mention another kind of readability test which depends upon vocabulary and not upon word and sentence length. An example of this kind of measuring instrument is the Cloze procedure which involves taking a passage from a text and omitting words at fixed regular intervals. The student is required to read the passage and insert the

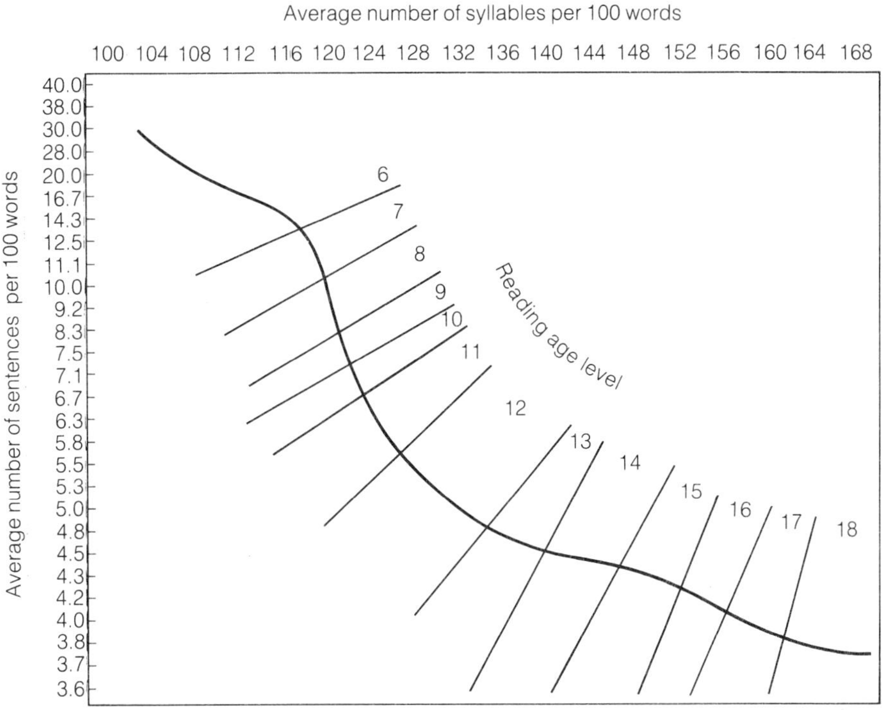


FIG. 6.2 **Fry readability graph.**

missing words. A rough guide to the interpretation of the results suggests that a 60 per cent success at filling the gaps indicates that the student will be able to use the text for independent study. If the success rate is in the range 40–50 per cent, the student will be able to use the text with help, but any score below 40 per cent has been described as 'frustration' level.

This concern with vocabulary has led some researchers to produce word lists showing the most important, useful, necessary words which a young person should know. One such list, the Dolch word list, gives the hundred most important words in learning to read, followed by the hundred next most used words – see Figure 6.3. It has been suggested that List A makes up, on average, one-half of all our reading. At the other end of the scale, DES (1977) suggests that:

The list of words overleaf should be understood by pupils as a result of their school science course. It is not a complete list and pupils will vary greatly in both the breadth and the depth of meaning they attach to the words.

Important words in learning to read

| | | |
|---|---|---|
| *a | *and | *he |
| *I | *in | *is |
| *it | *of | *that |
| *the | *to | *was |
| +all | +as | +at |
| +be | +but | +are |
| +for | +had | +have |
| +his | +him | +not |
| +on | +one | +said |
| +so | +they | +we |
| +with | +you | about |
| an | back | been |
| before | big | by |
| call | came | can |
| come | could | did |
| do | down | first |
| from | get | go |
| has | her | here |
| if | into | just |
| like | little | look |
| made | make | more |
| me | much | must |
| my | no | new |
| now | off | old |
| only | or | our |
| other | out | over |
| right | see | she |
| some | their | them |
| then | there | this |
| two | up | want |
| well | went | were |
| what | when | where |
| which | will | who |
| | your | |

These 100 words make up, on average, one half of all our reading.

Keywords (McNally and Murray, 1962)

* the first 12 make up one quarter of those we read and write

\+ the next 20

the remaining 68 follow

The hundred next most used words

| | | |
|---|---|---|
| after | again | always |
| am | another | any |
| away | ask | bad |
| because | best | bird |
| black | blue | boy |
| bring | day | dog |
| don't | eat | every |
| far | fast | father |
| fell | find | five |
| fly | four | found |
| gave | girl | give |
| going | good | got |
| green | hand | have |
| head | help | home |
| house | how | jump |
| keep | know | last |
| left | let | live |
| long | man | many |
| may | men | mother |
| Mr. | never | next |
| once | open | own |
| play | put | ran |
| read | red | room |
| round | run | sat |
| saw | say | school |
| should | sing | sit |
| soon | stop | take |
| tell | than | these |
| thing | think | three |
| time | too | tree |
| under | us | very |
| walk | white | why |
| wish | work | would |
| | year | |

FIG. 6.3 **Dolch word list.**

| | | |
|---|---|---|
| Absorption | Acceleration | Acid |
| Activity | Alkali | Animal |
| Atom | Base | Carbohydrate |
| Cell | Change of state | Combustion |
| Conservation | Crystal | Current |
| Decomposition | Density | Digestion |
| Diffusion | Electrolyte | Electron |
| Enzyme | Equation | Evolution |
| Fat | Fertilization | Food chain |
| Force | Gas | Genetics |
| Heredity | Hormone | Interference |
| Invertebrate | Ion | Kinetic energy |
| Liquid | Mass | Metal |
| Molecule | Momentum | Non-metal |
| Osmosis | Parasite | Photosynthesis |
| Plant | Potential energy | Power |
| Pressure | Protein | Reaction |
| Reflection | Refraction | Reproduction |
| Salt | Saprophyte | Solid |
| Sterile | Synthesis | Temperature |
| Velocity | Vertebrate | Vitamin |
| Wave | Work | |

An extensive research exercise, on behalf of the Royal Society (1980), resulted in the publication of *Understanding of Non-technical Words in Science*. The introduction to the report states:

Perhaps what students find difficult about chemistry is not the subject matter itself but our way of talking about it. What words do pupils understand? Which words cause difficulty at certain ages? In teaching and examining chemistry which words should we be cautious about using?

The report covers the understanding of selected words in both the secondary and tertiary sectors of education. The secondary exercise involved some 60 schools and approximately 15 000 students; the tertiary survey included 12 establishments and 800 students. The report can be obtained from The Royal Society of Chemistry.

> Use the DES word list to check your own understanding of the scientific vocabulary expected of a 16 year old. You might then better understand the demands we make on our students.

## *Writing resources*

There are a number of reasons why teachers resort to the time-consuming practice of writing their own resources. Perhaps the most often argued reasons are that there is no published material totally suited to a teacher's own requirements or to the needs of a particular group of students, or that available published material is too costly. Chapter 5 of ASE (1979a) discusses the writing of resources in detail under the following headings:

(a) planning;
(b) writing guidelines:
  headings
  summaries
  vocabulary
  sentences
  instructions for experiments
  questions
  diagrams and illustrations
  graphs and titles
  layout and typographical considerations.

A valuable guide, *How to Produce Better Worksheets*, written by Robin Lloyd-Jones (1985), an adviser for Fife and lecturer on worksheet production at a resource centre, provides:

tips on how to make worksheets look appealing;
practical suggestions on presentation of written material;
advice on how to construct worksheets for different ability levels;
guidance on how to assess the effectiveness of worksheets;
about 40 sample worksheets which may be photocopied without permission.

There is little doubt that DIY worksheets, experiment descriptions, problem sheets etc. should be more closely related to the needs of a particular situation, but the reality is often very different. In a report by DES (1978), HM Inspectors described many of the worksheets they saw as unattractive, technically incompetent, unchallenging, lacking academic edge etc. Perhaps the situation has changed since then. However, if the main advantage of home-produced resource material is that it should be more closely related to a particular situation, then our previous warning must be repeated. Particular situations do change and, if the main reason for writing individual resource material is that of suitability, then the material should also change. But, having in mind the large amount of time which must be committed to this kind of exercise, how many of us are prepared to rewrite our favourite texts at the beginning of each new year? The growing availability of word processors in schools should, at least, make this task less painful!

Before ending this section on acquisition of resources something should be said about copyright. Until recently, the situation was far from satisfactory and ASE (1979a) summarized the legal situation as it then existed. In brief, the

Copyright Law of 1956 specified four main groups of material which are protected by copyright. They are:

1 Literary works. Virtually anything in words irrespective of 'literary merit' and including tables, science textbooks, letters etc.
2 Dramatic works (plays etc.) and music.
3 Artistic works. These include charts, graphs, diagrams, maps, drawings and photographs, all irrespective of artistic merit.
4 Sound recordings, films, broadcasts and published editions (the typographical layout of a literary, dramatic or musical work).

The copyright law provides its protection by listing those acts which are the exclusive right of the copyright owner to exercise. So far as the teacher is concerned, the most important act is that of reproducing in any material form. Before any type of material may be copied the permission of the owner of the copyright must be obtained. Much photocopying of published material which occurs in schools is, in fact, illegal.

The Whitford committee, set up by the Government to look at the application of the Law of Copyright, suggested that education should have the right to copy and record all types of protected material in return for which the copyright holder would be entitled to remuneration. Following negotiations between a newly established Copyright Licensing Agency (CLA) and the local authority associations, agreement on the introduction of a licensing scheme for photocopying copyright materials has been reached. In a twelve-month period during 1984–5, a percentage of schools throughout the country were sampled to assess the extent to which photocopying was taking place and the level at which the licensing fee charged to LEAs should be set for future years. A licensing system of this nature will do much to regularize the position in schools and will also provide some recompense for the efforts of the copyright holder.

## Deployment of resources

The science department of any secondary school will have under its control a vast array of many different kinds of resources. Some will consider their apparatus to be the most important aid to teaching, but no laboratory can function efficiently without a readily available supply of 'bits and pieces'. In discussing the deployment of these resources in the department we shall, once again, make the arbitrary distinction between apparatus and materials, and books.

### 1. Apparatus and materials

In many schools the three main science subject divisions (biology, chemistry and physics) are each responsible for their own apparatus and materials. Clearly physics teachers (and, to a growing extent, biologists and chemists) need their 'magic boxes' of electronic instruments; microscopes continue to be part of the stock-in-trade of biology teachers and chemists depend upon their bottles,

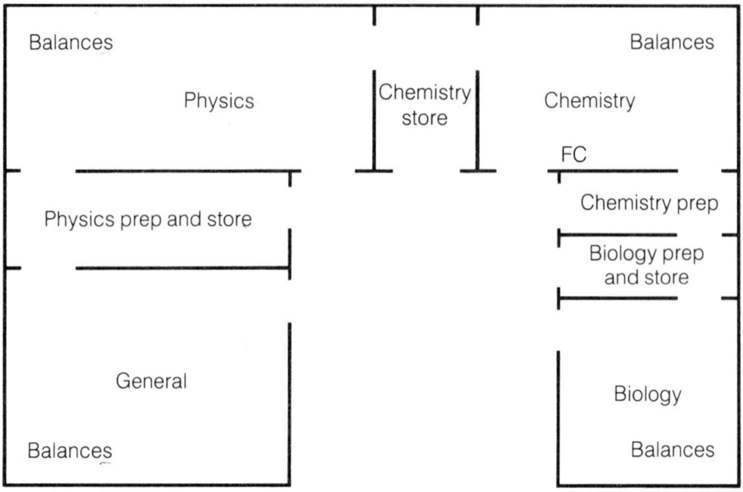


(a)

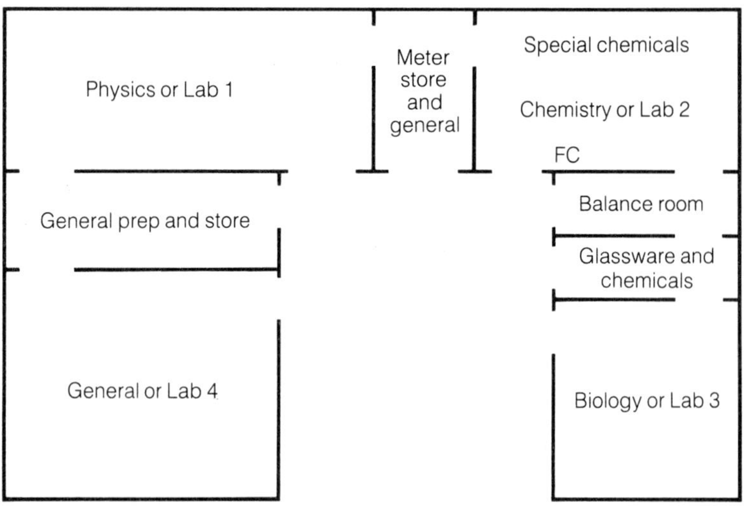


(b)

FIG. 6.4 **Laboratory layout**

beakers, bunsens and the like. There are items of apparatus which are used particularly, and almost exclusively, by an individual subject department, but what about equipment that is commonly used by all sections of the science department? Electrical measuring instruments, top-pan balances and glassware come immediately to mind. In the case of expensive pieces of apparatus, it is often unnecessary to have duplication in more than one laboratory or section of the department. Some schools have organized access points for apparatus like expensive balances, electrical measuring instruments, general glassware etc. These are held 'in stock' by the department but are available for the use of all members of the department. Such central control may be less easy to organize when separate and autonomous subject departments have individual charge of deploying their own resources. Who, for example, provides for an integrated science course under such circumstances? Further breakdown to yet another separate department would seem neither economic nor administratively sensible.

Expendable materials might be considered under three main headings:

chemicals
other materials
stationery

It will be argued later in this section that these should be held as joint departmental stock – probably under the control of the head of science or a head of subject and (where appropriate) the senior technician – whatever the form of internal organization. Individual subject divisions might have special requirements for chemicals and other materials specific to their own teaching needs but, in general, it is suggested that expendable stock should be centrally controlled. This method will not only assist the teaching of interdisciplinary subjects, but may well promote good housekeeping by avoiding unnecessary duplication and over-stocking.

The practical organization of this kind of system will depend largely upon the facilities available and upon the kind of organizational structure within the department, but flexible use of rooms will facilitate the use of centralized resource units. Figure 6.4 shows two different arrangements for the use of a suite of rooms belonging to a science department. Figure 6.4(a) probably reflects a 'subject division' orientated department, while the arrangement shown in Figure 6.4(b) would be more acceptable to a group of science teachers working in a more interdisciplinary fashion. Whatever system is used for the deployment of apparatus and materials, each individual item needs to be:

purchased (ordered);
recorded on delivery;
stored;
made available when required;
kept in good repair;
replaced as necessary (especially if consummable).

Although each of these steps is dependent on the others they will be considered separately in this chapter.

## Ordering new equipment

In state schools, different LEAs will have their own system of ordering new apparatus and equipment. Some give a great deal of freedom to individual schools and to members of staff within a school; others have a more heavily prescribed arrangement – which often leads to difficulties in individual circumstances. In some LEAs permission must be obtained for the purchase of a single piece of equipment costing more than a specified amount. As with much in the world of education, there are wide variations in practice. In the view of the authors, flexibility in procedural terms and the placing of responsibility at school and department level lead to positive benefits for teachers and their students.

Whatever procedure for ordering resources is acceptable in the school and LEA it should include:

keeping a record of orders placed and of goods received;
providing information for future reference, e.g. details of guarantee;
recording up-to-date information on the financial details of the order;
updating stock records on delivery.

## Recording the ordering and delivery of equipment

Records of ordering and delivery should contain much of the following information: company, date of order, order number, departmental order reference, catalogue reference number, catalogue price, estimated cost of order, date of receipt, invoice total, total final cost of order. Official (LEA) order forms are likely to be used, but the science department should keep its own records and these must dovetail into any school/LEA mechanism. The system shown in Figure 6.5 was used in a particular situation; it contains all (or most) of the information listed above but could be modified to suit individual circumstances. The official order will be supplied to the school.

In addition to the usual information required, it is useful to give each order a departmental reference which indicates the supplier, the order sequence for that supplier and the accounting year in which the order is placed. The reference shown in Figure 6.5 – PH/1/84.85 – provides this information in a compact form (no prizes for guessing the supplier — and no favouritism implied in its choice).

Figures 6.6 and 6.7 have the same format and are used to record the sequence of all orders placed by the department and the orders placed with a particular supplier. The departmental orders list enables a quick assessment of the total (estimated) cost of all orders placed at a particular time during the year; the company orders list is useful in discussing the state of any order with a company representative, since Column 6 will not be entered until the order is complete. The original proformas were printed on cards, but a loose-leaf A4 page format

LEA ..................................... Official order no. XYZ 12345

School .................................. Department ref no. PH/1/84.85

Order from Philip Harris Ltd ............ Date 1 April 1984 ....................

Deliver to ...............................

..........................................

| Cat. no. | Item | No. req. | Total cost |
|---|---|---|---|
| C17020/6 | Beaker tall form with spout 600 $cm^3$ | 36 | 28.26 |
| | Total | | £317.60 |

FIG. 6.5 **Official order form**

| Dept. ref. | Official order no. | Order date | Total order cost (est.) | Running total (est.) | Complete date | Invoice total | Running total invoice |
|---|---|---|---|---|---|---|---|
| PH/1/84.85 | XYZ 12345 | 1.4.84 | 317.60 | 317.60 | 7.6.84 | 346.20 | 346.20 |
| GG/1/84.85 | XYZ 12346 | 1.4.84 | 1537.60 | 1855.20 | 12.6.84 | 1800.00 | 2146.20 |
| RS/1/84.85 | XYZ 12347 | 3.4.84 | 56.70 | 1911.90 | 7.4.84 | 56.70 | 2202.90 |
| PH/2/84.85 | XYZ 12348 | 5.4.84 | 526.17 | 2438.07 | 3.7.84 | 572.30 | 2775.20 |

FIG. 6.6 **Department orders**

| Dept. ref. | Official order no. | Order date | Total order cost (est.) | Running total (est.) | Complete date | Invoice total | Running total invoice |
|---|---|---|---|---|---|---|---|
| PH/1/84.85 | XYZ 12345 | 1.4.84 | 317.60 | 317.60 | 7.6.84 | 346.20 | 346.20 |
| PH/2/84.85 | XYZ 12348 | 5.4.84 | 526.17 | 843.77 | 3.7.84 | 572.30 | 918.50 |

FIG. 6.7 **Company orders**

would be equally suitable. With the ever-increasing use of computers in schools, it should be possible to program this kind of system on to a micro.

Figures 6.8 and 6.9 represent the front and reverse sides of a card which is used to record the delivery and stock situation of individual items of apparatus and materials. In Figure 6.8, the date of delivery of an item is recorded and space is left for one or more deliveries of the same item from the same order. This is especially important when dealing with large orders, parts of which might be delivered on more than one occasion. The reverse of the card identifies the stock position of an item, also locating where in the department the stock is held. It has the salutory effect of pin-pointing the equipment hoarder at the end of each year.

Whatever system of accounting is used, the final responsibility for sanctioning

| BEAKER, Tall form with spout, 600 cm$^3$ | | | | | | | | | |
|---|---|---|---|---|---|---|---|---|---|
| Order no. | Date | No. ordered | Received | | | | | | Order complete |
| | | | Date | Quant. | Date | Quant. | Date | Quant. | |
| PH/1/84.85 | 1.4.84 | 36 | 6.5.84 | 30 | 7.6.84 | 6 | | | ✓ |

FIG. 6.8 **Stock card (front)**

| Year | Stock at beginning of year | New stock received during year | Stock held end of year | | | | | | | Stock used during year |
|---|---|---|---|---|---|---|---|---|---|---|
| | | | Lab 1 | Lab 2 | Lab 3 | Lab 4 | Prep 1 | Prep 2 | Total | |
| 84/85 | 92 | 36 | 30 | 20 | 32 | 20 | 10 | 8 | 120 | 8 |

FIG. 6.9 **Stock card (reverse)**

expenditure of any amount of money, large or small, should be exercised by one person. This will usually be the head of science or, perhaps, the school bursar acting in consultation with the head of science. Where the science department is sub-divided into subject departments, it is important that full discussion should take place. This will serve not only to determine the needs of subject specialists but also to minimize the duplication of orders for the same commodity.

On delivery, the individual items must be checked carefully against the original order to ensure that:

the correct item has been delivered;
the correct quantity has been received, or shortages noted;
each item is in good condition and in working order.

The goods must then be stored in a suitable place.

## *Storing resources*

Much has been written about the storage of science equipment and useful ideas can often be found in *The School Science Review* (under Science Notes). ASE (1979a) illustrates practical ideas for storing individual items of apparatus. It lists the following general principles which should apply to the efficient storage and retrieval of equipment. The organization of resources and equipment should ensure:

a high standard of laboratory safety;
a rapid and efficient circulation of students;
a minimum of fuss and frustration for everyone concerned;

rapid and efficient checking and removal of equipment at the end of each lesson; the minimum risk of damage to equipment.

The report then offers practical suggestions under the following headings:

trolleys;
cupboards;
self-checking and the use of trays;
shelves;
gas burners/tripods;
circuit board equipment;
chemicals;
etc.

Much apparatus can be stored in DIY racks but, for those who wish to purchase commercial storage systems, there appears to be an ever-growing list of suppliers. ASE (1979a) lists almost 30 companies manufacturing storage systems. For more up-to-date information the reader should consult the advertising pages of SSR or EIS.

## *Lesson preparation – provision of materials*

We started this chapter with the statement: 'Good organization makes it possible for plans to become effective . . .'. This is of immediate importance in the planning of individual lessons. You may know exactly how you are to conduct the lesson, but it is equally important to have the right equipment and materials ready and available at the right time. Prior preparation ensures that the material:

is held in school stock;
is available in the right quantities;
is not required by another member of staff (especially important if items are required from another department or from a school resource centre);
will be readily available for the students you are teaching.

In some cases long-term planning will be required, especially if special apparatus has to be ordered or constructed. As a general rule, it should be a departmental requirement that requests for apparatus must be made at least before the end of the previous week. Such requests should be made, in writing, possibly using a large desk diary or a pro-forma system to indicate daily requirements. It should then be possible for the technicians to ensure that apparatus ordered the previous week will be ready and in position for a particular lesson. They should not be expected to meet requests made five minutes before a lesson is due to commence – except in cases of emergency.

The technical staff have a crucial role to play in the deployment of resources within the department. Both the quantity and the quality of technical assistance available varies greatly from one school to another and from one LEA to another. The ASE has made recommendations on the provision of laboratory assistance and these can be found in 'The Provision of School Science Technicians' (1976, pp. 14 and 15). Assuming that a school employs at least one trained and experienced technician – who probably will be the senior technician – this person could be responsible for the general supervision of resources. However, the ultimate responsibility must rest with the head of department.

It is highly likely that most secondary schools will have more than one laboratory and/or preparation room, each with its own basic provision of apparatus and equipment. Some resources will be particularly appropriate to a specific laboratory, others – such as glassware etc. – will be part of the stock of each laboratory. How can this be identified with its base? Some system of laboratory identification is needed. Colour coding is one method often used, initials (e.g. PL, CL, BL etc.) etched on the glass is another. The stock card shown in Figure 6.9 enables a check to be made, but this would normally be done only once every year.

The deployment of resources takes on even greater importance if individual learning schemes are employed in the school. In this context ASE (1979a), although somewhat dated, is a mine of information presented in an easily accessible manner.

## 2 Books and other AVA resources

The variety of resources which can be included under this heading has multiplied greatly during the last few years. Beswick (1973) defined a resource in the following way:

A resource includes anything which may be an object of study or stimulus for the pupil, including books, periodicals, newspapers, press cuttings, pictures, maps, charts, photocopies and microforms, worksheets, slides, filmstrips, filmloops, films, records, audio tapes, radio and television programmes, video tapes, slide/tapes and filmstrip/record combinations, multimedia kits, programmed material, models and realia as well as individuals and objects in the community.

To this list must now be added computer programs – probably the fastest growing resource category available to schools. From this list it would seem that every newspaper, textbook, magazine or pamphlet is a potential resource for use by an enterprising teacher.

The deployment of written and other audio-visual material within the science department is often complicated in many schools by the presence of centrally-based libraries and resource centres. School librarians are frequently loth to see their acquisitions scattered around the departments of a school. By contrast, science department staff usually see no reason why titles specifically applicable to their own disciplines should not be housed within easy reach of their own work centre. This is not an easy problem to solve and much depends upon the relationships which exist between the interested parties. One compromise is for the science department to hold, on semi-permanent loan, a restricted number of resources (especially books) which are specifically connected with the work of the department and which are in regular and frequent use by the staff of the department.

Just as we have recommended a departmental resource centre for apparatus and materials, so we would suggest that audio-visual material should be held in a central pool in the science department. Particular attention should be given to transporting heavy pieces of hardware (such as projectors, computers etc.) from one part of the department to another. Difficulties in this respect are often used as excuses for not employing such useful resources. Regular review of the resources held in this way will preclude the department from retaining the resource beyond the time when it is no longer necessary.

Issue of such resources to students requires the same necessary close control as is applied to teaching staff. Both depend largely on an efficient cataloguing system for the resources. Long-term loans (such as class textbooks) should be carefully recorded and their condition noted at the time of issue and on return. There should be a school policy for dealing with students who maltreat textbooks and other resources.

The most important issue in the deployment of this kind of resource is not storage but retrieval. How often is the cry heard, 'It is here somewhere'? Options open to the busy teacher are to store this kind of material:

under broad subject headings (e.g. biology, chemistry, physics);
under teaching content groups (e.g. magnetism, energy, respiration, etc.);
alphabetically;
by source (e.g. TES, SSR, book titles etc);
on computers.

Colour coding and reference numbers will help. One immediate problem is that some resources refer to more than one classification. Should multiple copies be filed under each group? The ultimate problem might be that more space is taken up in storing resources than is actually reserved for student activities.

## Management and maintenance of resources

Resources have been ordered, delivered, collected, stored and can easily be retrieved; what administrative structure exists for ensuring that they are in good working order when needed? The following guidelines describe the basic procedure which should be established in any science department:

Equipment and apparatus should be checked by the technician as it is collected together for a particular teaching period.

The member of staff should make a quick check on the apparatus before the start of the lesson.

Students should be encouraged to carry out their own check before using any apparatus. This will not necessarily detect faults but it will encourage the formation of good habits.

Apparatus should be checked by the teacher at the end of each period and before the students are allowed to leave the laboratory.
It might be necessary for the technician to re-check each item of equipment as it is returned to its storage position.

At each stage faults, breakages or damage should be reported to the appropriate person. Once again, there should be a school (or departmental) policy for dealing with minor breakages or damage by students – especially if these have been caused by misbehaviour.

School vacations are often the most appropriate time for technical staff to carry out a major overhaul of resources. This should be done on a systematic basis and the laboratory stock card (Figures 6.8 and 6.9) might be used to record the date of the last inspection. Emergency plans for dealing with hazardous situations (e.g. gas leaks, faulty electrical components, loss of radioactive sources etc.) should be a matter of departmental concern and there must be a clear understanding of these by all those using the laboratories and/or preparation rooms.

Facilities for the repair or replacement of apparatus and equipment will vary but, whatever the mechanism, they will usually require financing. Unless there are funds set aside specifically for this purpose, an allocation of money from the department's budget must be made at the beginning of each financial year. This might be part of a contingency fund (considered at the beginning of this chapter).

Procedures for the repair of equipment might follow a hierarchical structure, e.g.

repair by departmental staff (technical or teaching);
LEA central supplies departments;
return to manufacturer.

Before allowing departmental staff to attempt a repair it should be ascertained whether this will contravene any manufacturer's guarantee. Some teachers' centres have special apparatus repair facilities and, if good relationships exist, the staff of local FE, HE colleges and universities might be persuaded to give assistance.

## Using outside resources and professional support

Even in the most organized science departments there is often a need for assistance which can best be provided by agencies outside the school. In the first section of this chapter nothing was said about raising funds from outside the school. Parent teacher associations (PTAs) are often engaged in fund raising activities for a school but it should not be assumed that this is their sole (or even main) function.

Perhaps the first point of contact outside the school should be with the LEA science advisers, both in terms of the range of practical advice they are able to give – based on extensive contact with other schools and national agencies – and intimate contacts with local authority structures and resources.

Teachers' centres serve a variety of different purposes. Some exist principally as conference centres; others as a focal point for social activities; many provide extensive resource facilities. Whatever their function, it is important that all members of a science department are aware of their existence. The science adviser is usually a source of information about the activities of local teachers' centres. In addition, some authorities have specialist science centres.

Local and national bodies concerned with science education include the Association for Science Education (ASE) and the Science and Technology Regional Organizations (SATROs). The ASE, through its sub-committees, publications and annual meeting, engages in national (and international) activities and, through its 19 regions, provides a full programme of local activities. The SATROs are regional centres which develop active dialogue between schools, further and higher education, industry and commerce. At the time of writing there are nearly 40 SATROs, covering most areas of the United Kingdom, and between them offering a wide range of facilities. Further information about the SATRO movement can be obtained from:

National Liaison Officer
SCSST
1 Birdcage Walk
London SW1H 9JJ (Tel: 01-222 7899)

While it is impracticable, in a handbook of this nature, to provide a list of 'useful addresses' for science teachers, the following publications provide such information:

*Addresses for Science Teachers* (Archenhold *et al.*, 1983)
*Useful Addresses for Biologists* (Dixon, 1984)
*A Directory of Resource Physics Materials* (Bullet, 1985)
*Goldmine: Resources for Teachers* (Brown, 1985)

## Links with industry

In its policy document of 1979 ASE listed 'three perspectives from which the aims of science education should be viewed'. They were:

science as an intellectual discipline;
science as a cultural activity;
science and its applications.

Sir Denis Rooke, chairman of British Gas (and past president of the ASE) wrote (1982):

The preface to the ASE policy document declares: 'Science has important implications for all citizens and it would be disastrous if it were to be seen by our students as a difficult and esoteric pursuit, isolated from the rest of modern thought and endeavour and of no concern to the common man and woman'. This statement implies that science teachers should draw on resources outside the classroom. Industries like my own represent such a resource; their total viability depends on the successful application of scientific expertise. I firmly believe that these industries therefore have a responsibility to support and encourage science education, which can and should be regarded as an investment in the future success of the company. In my view the recovery of British industry – and in consequence the prosperity of the whole nation – will depend to a vital degree on the applied science capabilities of the next generation.

DES (1985) sets down ten principles which describe the provision of science education in schools. Phrases such as 'Teaching should also be closely related to everyday and industrial applications . . .' and 'Too many examples of the technological applications of science included in science courses and examinations reflect past developments rather than current ones' etc. confirm the continuing concern that schools and industry should be closely linked together.

There will be few science teachers today who would disagree with the above statement or with the often repeated claim that science teaching must be better related to the world outside school. 'Relevance' is the watchword. But how is this to be achieved? How do we make science relevant to students? It is quite clear that there is no single 'best way'. The broad range of activities which have been attempted by a wide variety of agencies include:

lectures;
conferences;
long-term secondment of teachers to industry;
visits to schools by industrial lecturers;
visits to industry by students and/or teachers;
production of resource material
  involving teachers
  written specifically by an industry;
short-term secondment of teachers to industry (sometimes resulting in the production of resource material).

Many industries spend large sums of money annually in providing help and assistance for schools. This takes many forms and often results in useful published material. The Department of Trade and Industry (DTI) has been at the forefront of many initiatives in this field and there are many other national bodies, such as the School Curriculum Industry Project (SCIP) engaged in similar activities. The *Physics at Work* project (McKim, 1985) is another example of the way in which science can be made relevant.

As an example of one type of industry/education liaison project (of the last kind listed above), *The GASS Book* project (Nicholl, 1982) listed the following as its objectives:

1 to provide the opportunity for teachers to become acquainted with the research activities of a major industry;

2 to encourage the participants to investigate how particular scientific applications found in the gas industry could be related both to the content of modern science teaching syllabuses and to the intellectual maturity and interests of the students;
3 to enable the participants to produce teaching materials related to the industrial applications they were able to investigate at the research stations;
4 to publish the collected materials in a form that would enhance the teaching of science beyond the immediate sphere of influence of the individual participants.

In achieving these objectives, it was hoped that teachers would:

enjoy the opportunity to look outside the classroom;
enrich their teaching through the knowledge and experience gained;
appreciate the potential of industrial applications in the teaching of science in schools;
understand more clearly the interrelationships between scientific principles and their applications;
be able to help students gain a better appreciation of the role of a science-based industry within the community;
be encouraged to explore opportunities to work with industry in their own locality.

As previously mentioned, the DTI has been a prime mover and financial pump primer for many of the activities falling within the sphere of 'links with industry'. Its journal *VIEW*

aims to act as a link between different organizations active in the field of schools/industry liaison and to spread the ideas being developed in various parts of the country as widely as possible in the hope that they may stimulate others to take action in their own area.

Those wishing to receive copies of *VIEW* regularly should write to:

VIEW (Distribution)
Central Office of Information
Hercules Road
London SE1 7DU

It would seem important then that science departments are both properly informed and make the most of opportunities and resources provided by agencies such as those noted above, as well as developing their own local industrial contacts. A useful strategy is for one member of a department to take particular responsibility for knowing about industry-related activities and resources. He/she can then disseminate appropriate information to particular individuals or sections of the departmental team.

## Legal responsibilities and safety

The question of safety in the science laboratory is dealt with more fully in Chapter 7. The following documents, which relate specifically to safety in the use of resources, are reprinted from the *Help for New Heads of Science* (ASE, 1986) for information. It is recommended that similar documents should be written for every school science department.

### Health and safety at work – science department policy statement 1.

**Fire**
Pupils must know the correct procedure in the event of fire.

**Accidents**
Accidents to teachers or pupils, other than the very trivial, must be reported to the head of department, and a written report made out.

**Breakages**
Broken equipment other than that of trivial items such as test tubes must be reported in writing to the head of department.
N.B. Cracked glassware should not be used.

**Hazards**
Any potential hazard, e.g. non-functioning fume cupboard, must not be used and must be reported to the head of department.

**Disposal**
Organic solvents, chemicals such as sodium, etc, must be handed to the senior technician for disposal. Broken glass must not be placed in wastepaper baskets but in a separate bin.

**Spillages**
The immediate area, or the whole room if necessary, should be evacuated in the event of a spillage of mercury, other toxic substance, concentrated acid, organic solvent, micro-organism, etc. The senior technician should be notified in order that he/she can deal with the spillage.

**Storage**
Records of the use and stocks of materials, especially of dangerous substances (corrosive, flammable, pathogenic, poisonous, radioactive, etc.) shall be properly kept and be subject to annual audit.

**Apparatus**
Apparatus, especially electrical equipment, must be connected and used in accordance with the manufacturers' instructions. Apparatus made in the school

must be tested, safe for use and provided with adequate instructions. Such matters as electrical safety of equipment shall be the subject of annual checks.

## Health and safety at work – science department

Rules for staff

1 Pupils must not be left in a laboratory, at work, except in an emergency.
2 Pupils must not eat or drink in a laboratory.
3 Laboratories should be kept tidy, i.e. unused equipment should not be left on benches; pupils' bags etc. should be stored out of the way.
4 Teachers and pupils must wear eye protection where the experiment demands it.
5 Pupils must be dressed in a reasonable way – coats off, cardigans buttoned, long hair tied out of the way, etc.
6 Spillages of water etc. must be mopped up immediately.
7 Fire-fighting equipment must be accessible and regularly checked.
8 Pupils must not be allowed to use mains electrical equipment until it has been checked by the teacher.
9 Excessive quantities of chemicals should not be supplied for an experiment. This applies in particular to metals like sodium and magnesium, flammable liquids, caustic chemicals and acids.
10 Bunsens should be turned off or to a low, luminous flame when not in use.
11 Particular care should be taken when using the following, and safety screens must be used where necessary:
high voltage equipment;
radioactive materials;
laser;
compressed gases and vacuum equipment;
microbiological colonies;
concentrated acid or alkali;
flammable liquids;
metals like sodium;
white phosphorus;
mercury.
12 Experiments which involve the production of unpleasant or hazardous gases must be carried out in a fume cupboard or under a fume hood.
13 Pupils must not be allowed to insert glass tubing, thermometers, etc., into corks or rubber bungs.
14 Safety spectacles and mains electrical equipment should be checked at regular intervals by the senior technician.
15 Staff must ensure that no apparatus, chemicals or materials are removed from the laboratories by pupils.

> Discuss these two sets of instructions with members of the science department, noting any omissions and any which you would wish to change.

In this chapter we have discussed a number of organizational practices which have proved to be of value to science teachers. But there is no unique 'best' method of organization and each department must devise a pattern which suits itself. The main requirement must be the improvement of the learning processes available to the students – not the development of a 'perfect' system.

## Bibliography

APU, 1982, *Science in Schools Age 15*, Report No. 1 (HMSO, London)

Archenhold, W. E., Jenkins, E. W., and Wood-Robinson, C., 1983, *Addresses for Science Teachers (2nd edition)* (Centre for Science Education, Leeds University, Leeds)

ASE, 1979b, *Alternatives for Science Education* (Association for Science Education, Hatfield)

ASE, 1985, *Choosing Published Primary Science Materials for Use in the Classroom* (Association for Science Education, Hatfield)

ASE, 1986, *Help for New Heads of Science* (Association for Science Education, Hatfield)

ASE, 1979 (June), 'The Provision of School Science Technicians', *Education in Science* (Association for Science Education, Hatfield)

ASE, 1979a, *Study Series No. 14, Resource-based Learning in Science* (Association for Science Education, Hatfield)

ASE, 1980, *Study Series No. 16, Language in Science* (Association for Science Education, Hatfield)

ASE/EPC Survey, 1984 (January), *Education in Science*, p15 Issue no. 106 (Association for Science Education, Hatfield)

Beswick, N. W., 1973, *Schools Council Working Paper No. 43*, School Resource Centre (Evans/Methuen, London)

Brown, D., 1985, *Goldmine: Resources for Teachers* (Epistemology, 62 Newland Road, Worthing BN11 1JX)

Bullett, P., 1985, *A Directory of Resource Physics Materials* (Association for Science Education, Hatfield)

Bulman, L., 1985, *Teaching Language and Study Skills in Secondary Science* (Heinemann Educational Books, London)

Carrick, T., 1978, Problems of assessing the readability of biology textbooks for first examinations, *Journal of Biological Education*, 12 (2), 113–220 (Centre for Studies in Science and Mathematics Education, Leeds University, Leeds)

Davies, F., and Green, T., 1980, *Reading for Learning in Science* (Schools Council/Nottingham University, Nottingham)

DES, 1977, *Curriculum 11–16*, Working papers by HMI (HMSO, London)

DES, 1978, *Mixed Ability Work in Comprehensive Schools*, a report by HMI (HMSO, London)

DES and Welsh Office, 1985, *Science 5–16: A Statement of Policy* (HMSO, London)

Dixon, A., *Useful Addresses for Biologists* (2nd edition) (Association for Science Education, Hatfield)

Foster, J., 1978, *Assessing the Suitability of Books for School Use*, A paper presented at COSTA-EPC Conference 1978) (Educational Publishers Council, London)

Galliland, J., 1972, *Readability* (Hodder and Stoughton, Sevenoaks)

Hull, R., and Adams, H., 1981, *Decisions in the Science Department* (Schools Council/ASE, London)

Lloyd-Jones, R., 1985, *How to Produce Better Worksheets* (Hutchinson, London)

McKim, F. R., 1985, *Physics at Work* (Hobsons Scientific, Cambridge)

McNally, J., and Murray, W., 1962, *Key Words to Literacy and the Teaching of Reading* (Schoolmaster Publishing Company)

Newton, D. P., 1984 (December), 'Science textbooks and readability measures – a caveat', *The School Science Review*, 368

Nicholl, B. (ed.), 1982, *The GASS Book* (*Gas Applications for School Science*) (ASE/British Gas, Hatfield)

The Royal Society of Chemistry, 1980, *Understanding of Non-technical Words in Science*, a report of research done by J. R. T. Cassels and A. H. Johnstone (Royal Society of Chemistry, London)

Sutton, C. (ed.), 1981, *Communicating in the Classroom* (Hodder and Stoughton, Sevenoaks)

# 7 Special problems

- ★ Some of the significant issues which concern science teachers are discussed by individuals who have particular expertise in those particular areas.
- ★ The science department's task for physically handicapped students is to match provision in science to their 'special needs'.
- ★ The multicultural aspects of science and improved attitudes can make science more relevant for ethnic minorities.
- ★ A broad, balanced and relevant curriculum needs to include knowledge and skills from across the whole range of 'areas of experience'.
- ★ Increased knowledge and a proper attitude to risks can improve safety in the school laboratory.
- ★ The developments in the 14–18 view of the curriculum mean that teachers must take on a dual role as teachers of, and educators through, relevant science.
- ★ An awareness of any difference in attitudes to girls and boys helps ensure that girls get equal encouragement in science.

# (a) Students with special needs

**Alan Jones**

## Introduction

The title 'Science for students with special needs', if properly applied, covers a large proportion of the students in our schools. It would include the slow learners, remedial groups and those with handicaps which include the physical, mental, emotional and socially disabled. Science teachers have a major contribution to make to the education of all such students. The department's task is to match provision in science, set in the framework of the whole curriculum, to the 'special needs' of these young people. This part chapter concentrates particularly, though not exclusively, on science for students who have identified physical handicaps. It will be apparent that a whole complex of learning difficulties can accompany such disabilities. It might help in the discussion which follows if a rough classification is made of the kinds of institution which have been specifically established to cater for young people with special needs. This would include:

special units attached to ordinary schools;
ESN(M) schools – now designated as schools for students with specific learning difficulties. These are now admitting a much wider range of problems, taking in students with social and behavioural problems as well as the true slow learner;
schools for the physically handicapped.

The publication of the Warnock report (Warnock, 1978) and the Education Act 1981 drew attention to those young people attending these kinds of school. The

Act refers to the desire to integrate handicapped students into normal schools, whenever possible and feasible, in a way that is beneficial to all concerned and that does not create an imposition on the existing school, the handicapped students or the staff.

It is this emphasis on the integration of the handicapped into normal classrooms that will cause apprehension for many teachers – and especially to the teacher of science. Safety is likely to loom very large; the ordinary school laboratory is not usually designed to accommodate wheelchairs, calipers and the like. Yet the opportunity to participate in a wide range of activities has obvious appeal to most young people. The need for a balanced and realistic curriculum is paramount. This also must be true for any students not thought to be able to cope with the integrated situation and so therefore should remain in a special school. In both situations, a strong case can be made for the inclusion of science and technology into the curriculum of the student with special needs.

## Integration

Much has been written since the 1981 Act was formulated and its implementation on 1 April 1983. Johnson and Johnson (1981) thought the purpose of integration was to structure the learning situation in such a way that:

friendships are formed between handicapped and non-handicapped students;
the social skills of all students are promoted;
the self-esteem of all students is enhanced;
the achievement of all students is maximized.

This sounds a most laudable set of aims but it cannot be achieved by just placing a student in a classroom and letting life proceed as usual. Integration is just the beginning of a process and it contains the risk of failure (as do all educational experiences), as the child may be stigmatized, rejected, ignored or treated in an over-patronizing manner. But if things go well (says Johnson), true friendships and positive relationships may develop.

### Which children will be integrated?

It is probable that for integration to take place efficiently, the local education authority will have selected certain schools to take the majority of the students. The choice often is related to the existing buildings and access to the facilities. After discussion with parents, the young person concerned, teachers and advisers, those thought to be able to benefit from integration will be recommended to do so. These young people could have any of the following disabilities: partial sight, partial hearing, orthopaedically handicapped (cerebral palsy, spastic, muscular dystrophy etc).

Once the student's cognitive and manipulative abilities have been measured then he/she can fit into the normal teaching groups alongside any other student of similar ability. Often these students have missed a great deal of schooling, because of their constant visits to doctors and hospitals, so initially many might demonstrate low performance but may develop rapidly. Other students may have a disease which is progressive and their abilities will be declining, e.g. those suffering from muscular dystrophy. Some students, often those who are paralysed from the chest or waist downwards (spastic, cerebral palsy), have difficulty with perceiving diagrams in three dimensions and have a distorted understanding of what is meant by 'down' – since they cannot feel anything lower than the chest! Further advice on the exact difficulties of each student will be found in their notes from their previous school. It will not be easy trying to integrate these students into a normal classroom situation, but the effort will be well rewarded. Help and advice can be obtained from the local inspectors, and staff of local special schools are only too willing to be of assistance.

## Practical science courses

It is readily understood that most science teachers will be concerned about the problems to be surmounted when faced with the prospect of receiving a handicapped student into an otherwise 'normal' class. Yet many schools for the physically handicapped have a long tradition of teaching science – both to O and A level. It will be argued that they have special facilities and were specially built to cope with young people in wheelchairs etc. Perhaps the teacher in an ordinary school can learn something from their experiences. It was for this purpose that Leach (1985), a science teacher at Hephaistos School in Reading, wrote the article 'Practical examination science and physically handicapped pupils'. In his article, Leach describes some of the handicaps associated with specific medical conditions and the problems these present in practical science classes. In summary, these include lack of co-ordination, weakness in hands and arms, communication problems, impaired spatio-visual perception and inability to follow sequential instructions. On safety risks, the author writes:

Lack of co-ordination and muscular weakness both render the handling of glassware or reagents particularly dangerous. Wheelchair users cannot escape quickly from accidental spillages, bunsen flames, and so on, and anything running off the end of the bench will inevitably fall into their laps. The shoulder height of an average wheelchair-bound pupil is about 1 m, which raises problems regarding the shelf storage of reagents and heavy equipment.

Many science teachers have expressed concern for the safety of physically handicapped pupils in the laboratory and, indeed, for the safety of their able-bodied peers when wheelchairs are in the way. This has meant that physically handicapped pupils have been excluded from practical science classes in some schools.

One team of teachers has disputed the claim that science practical work is too dangerous to be performed by handicapped students. They have tried practical science, technology and problem solving with a large number of handicapped students and some of their findings are reported in Jones (1983). Further, the School Science Research Project (SSRP) at Trent Polytechnic gave some attention to this problem and has published some useful material for teachers (obtainable from SSRP, Department of Physical Science, Trent Polytechnic, Clifton Site, Nottingham). It was sometimes found that, as with many slow learners, the basic scientific understanding was often absent but that the motivation to do an experiment together with simple problem solving was immense. When the emphasis was placed on doing something useful, meaningful and worthwhile, then the activities improved vocabulary, drawing skills and manipulative skills. The sense of achievement of actually doing a science experiment for themselves was a good boost for their often flagging self esteem and peer group esteem.

## What science is suitable?

The science content of any course must be designed to be similar to the syllabus used with any normal student, but often the methods used might have to be adapted; a procedure accepted as normal when teaching other mixed ability groups. Science courses must be chosen to suit the young person's mental ability and that of the group in which he or she is taught, but each handicapped student will have his or her own specific limitations. This is also true with practical work, although it has been found that handicapped youngsters are often more careful and safe than the normal youngsters because they know their own manipulative limitations.

The SSRP consulted many practising teachers and together they scrutinized a number of currently available science schemes. They have tried the suggested activities with deaf, partially sighted and orthopaedically handicapped students. With only minor modifications in the majority of cases, the handicapped student could follow similar courses to students of the same mental ability. Often the handicapped student is provided with a 'helper' and this can be useful when particularly difficult situations arise. Science schemes which have been successfully used include:

Look;
Science Horizons;
Insight to Science;
Science at Work;
LAMP;
Open Science;
Science for Handicapped Children.

It has been found that a problem solving approach to science is suitable for those students who are constantly absent or hospitalized. They can continue thinking about the problem even when at home or in hospital.

## What happens if I get a handicapped student assigned to my class?

Few in the teaching profession have been trained to deal with handicapped young people. Yet the handicapped students entering normal schools are educationally the same as any other students and all that is needed is to apply the same common sense teaching principles. In no way can the following advice replace the wealth of experience gained from being trained to teach students with special needs, but it might help initially to overcome some of the day-to-day problems which might arise.

1 Ideally the student will already know something about the school – if not, arrange for a preliminary visit before regular attendance commences. Discuss the normal classroom procedures so that the toilet, medical or physiotherapy facilities can be visited easily. It must be assumed that if the school has been designated to accept handicapped students then wide toilet doors for wheelchair-bound students, Braille signs for blind students and a source of batteries for deaf aids for hearing-impaired students (as appropriate) will have been pre-arranged.
2 Talk to the young person (and his/her parents) privately, to see if there is a need for any special equipment and what must be done should immediate medical care be needed. This information should be communicated to all members of staff who are likely to teach the student.
3 Discuss with the student the safety rules of the school and the laboratories and arrange for one member of the class to act as a chaperone in the event of a fire alarm.
4 When writing timetables, try to keep the wheelchair-bound student, or the student with calipers, based in ground floor rooms. Ensure that his/her work station is easily reached – possibly near the door.
5 For laboratory work, try to arrange for a bench of a suitable height – even if this means cutting down the legs of an old table. Consider what apparatus will be needed, e.g. a heating mantle or hot plate might be more suitable than an exposed flame. Large plastic grips can be bought for some pieces of apparatus and non-slip plastic mats are also available (from Nottingham Educational Supplies (Aids for Handicapped), 17 Ludlow Hill Road, Melton Road, West Bridgford, Nottingham)
6 If visits or outings are planned, check that they are suitable for the handicapped student and ensure that the 'taxi' service, which often brings handicapped students to school is informed of a possible delayed arrival back at school.
7 If the young person has a muscular or neuromuscular complaint, movement and speech is sometimes affected. Prepare other members of the class so that they can be supportive and aid communication and confidence, rather than making ridicule of the problem.
8 Some young people are provided with microwriters or typewriters, tape recorders etc. to help them to communicate. These do not usually cause any disturbance to other members of the class. Teachers are sometimes asked to wear lapel microphones which feed into a deaf student's earpiece. All these devices are provided as aids to help the handicapped to integrate more easily into the life of the class. They should be accepted as part of the nor-

mal equipment of the teaching/learning situation and not as something of an oddity.

9 If partially sighted and deaf students are present in a class, it will assist their lip reading if you:

ensure that you face the class when talking;
stand in front of the class and do not wander around the room;
avoid standing in front of a window, or a bright light.

Prior to a lesson, list any new words which will be introduced during the lesson and, if a video or film is to be used, provide a summary of its contents for the student to read beforehand (assuming that he/she can read).

For blind students, tactile diagrams can be made or obtained. One simple method of construction is to imprint the message on a smooth polystyrene tile, ensuring that it is two or three times larger than usual (tactile senses are not as discriminating as the eye).

10 Instructions for experiments can be given on a sound tape. This can be time-consuming but well worth the effort. Other students in the class might be encouraged to assist in this work.

11 Some students with sensory deprivation have distorted views of simple things. A young person who is paralysed uses the words up/down, forward/backward, without fully appreciating their meaning, and this is often revealed in their conversation and written work. Numeracy and three-dimensional perception seems to be less developed in cerebral palsy youngsters. Often, muscular dystrophy students have been free and mobile at some period in the past, but are now progressively losing their muscle actions. This can be frustrating and sometimes causes depression. They usually end up in an electric wheelchair, but their mental capacities are still active and alert.

## Summary

Integrating students with special needs into the ordinary classroom is a daunting task. The science teacher must be concerned for the safety of all under his/her charge. However, Gerald Leach believes that the young person's fundamental rights to as complete an education as possible far outweigh the considerations of greater safety risk – a view which is often shared by the parents of handicapped children. It is the duty of every teacher to prepare his/her charges to take part in and derive satisfaction from the society in which they are to live – and this is particularly true for this special group of young people. It can be very rewarding – for both teacher and students.

## Further reading

Hofman, H., H., and Ricker, K. S. (eds), 1979, *Science Education and the Physically Handicapped* (National Science Teachers Association, 1742 Connecticut Avenue, Washington DC 20009, USA).

Hadary, D., 1978, *Laboratory Science and Art for Blind, Deaf and Emotionally Disturbed children*, A mainstream approach, (University Park, Baltimore, Maryland, USA).

Hegarty, S., and Pocklington, K., with Lucas, D., 1982, *Integration in Action* Case studies in the integration of pupils with special needs (NFER/Nelson, London).

Hegarty, S., Pocklington, K., and Lucas, D., 1982, *Educating Pupils with Special Needs in the Ordinary School* (NFER/Nelson, London).

Jones, A. V., *et al.*, 1981, 82, 84, *Science for Handicapped Children* (School Science Research Project, Trent Polytechnic, Nottingham).

Pankhurst, J., and McAllister, A. G., 1980, *An Approach to the Further Education of the Physically Handicapped* (NFER Publishing Co., Windsor).

Reese, K. M., 1981, *Teaching Chemistry to Physically Handicapped Students* (American Chemical Society, 1155 16th Street NW, Washington DC 20036, USA.)

Human Horizon series of books published by Souvenir Press, London. The series includes:
*Out of Doors with Handicapped People* – Mike Cotton (1981);
*Science for Handicapped Children* – Alan Jones (1983);
*Outdoor Adventure for Handicapped People* – Mike Cotton (1983);
*Behaviour Problems in Handicapped Children* – Malcolm Jones (1983).

A number of excellent publications from the Amercian Association for the Advancement of Science – Co-ordination for Handicapped Persons, Martha R. Redden, AAAS, 1776 Massachusetts Avenue NW, Washington DC 20036, USA.

Handicapped Persons Research Unit, Jim Sandhu, Newcastle upon Tyne Polytechnic, 1 Coach Lane, Newcastle.

SAVI/SELPH (Science activities for visually impaired and Science enrichment learning for the physically handicapped), Centre for Multisensory Learning, Lawrence Hall of Science, University of California, Berkeley, USA.

### Articles in British journals

Coleman, D. A., 1981 (September), Technology with the young disabled, *School Technology*, p. 2.

Jones, A. V., and Barnett, A., 1980, Science for the physically handicapped, *Special Education: Forward Trends*, Vol. 7, No. 3, p. 25.

Leach, G., 1982, Making science more accessible, *Special Education: Forward Trends*, Vol. 19, No. 1, pp. 13–15.

## Newsletters (specifically including science)

Occasional newsletters from School Science Research Project (SSRP), Physical Science Department, Trent Polytechnic, Clifton Site, Nottingham.

*Foundation for Science and the Handicapped Newsletter*, Editor: C. Keller, 236 Grand Street, Morgantown, West Virginia, 26505 USA.

*The Good Newsletter* by Dr Ben Thompson, Science for the Handicapped Association, Department of Education, University of Wisconsin, Eau Claire, Wisconsin, USA.

# (b) Science education and ethnic minorities

**Kabir Shaikh**

## Introduction

The publication in March 1985 of the final report of the Swann committee, 'Education for all', focused attention on the education of ethnic minority students. The investigation had been in progress for five years, during which time a number of LEAs had gone 'multicultural'. This reflected a need to provide education for a society which was fast becoming multicultural.

One broad aim of any such effort must be to promote mutual respect and understanding between people of different cultures, leading to a harmonious and peaceful co-existence. Science remains a vital and integral part of this education and cannot escape its share of responsibility and effort in achieving this aim. It must be understood, however, that science, by the nature of its approach in teaching, poses greater problems than most other subjects. This is due more to the perception of what science is than any limitations within the subject itself.

The terminology used throughout this section is 'science for a multicultural society', or 'multicultural aspects of science' rather than 'multicultural science'. The term 'multicultural science' often invites comments such as, 'How can a scientific principle or law be changed to make it multicultural?' Questions like this are quite genuine, but also reflect an understanding of science teaching as a transfer of a body of knowledge consisting of facts, principles, laws, equations and concepts, all of which are value-free expressions, and should be treated as such, irrespective of the ethnic origin of the learning group. This seems to be a rational way of looking at it but one which leaves an important gap, namely, relevance. It is the area of how science is delivered and in what human context it relates to the learning population which needs to be looked at closely. The current concern of science education about the relevance and context of what is taught provides a useful opportunity to explore the multicultural aspects of the subject, leading to a much wider appreciation of the human dimension of science, how it relates to various societies and what is their contribution to science – its developments and its applications.

## The problems of the minorities

Science does not always seem as easily accessible to the minorities as do some other subjects, partly because of the way it is presented. It sometimes appears to be about successful, technologically developed nations, full of apparently clever people. Scientific achievement is linked with progress, success and wealth; poverty, illiteracy and starvation (which are common phenomena in the home countries of many ethnic minority students) are linked with the lack of scientific knowledge and its industrial application. This has an alienating effect and results in a lack of enthusiasm for the subject. Science seems to be a subject in which they are not good enough to achieve any success, to which their societies have made little contribution and which, in some cases, conflicts with their religious and moral beliefs. Their overall reaction is of a complex nature and cannot be fully analysed, but the following seem to be some of the affecting factors.

## Language

Science is often expressed using difficult scientific terms and cumbersome statements of laws and principles. There are several notations and mathematical forms used to express ideas and these only add to the difficulty. This is a fairly common problem faced by all students studying science but it is cripplingly acute in students whose mother tongue is not English. It builds up a feeling of failure, affecting motivation, and the subject seems to be even more remote, difficult and inaccessible.

## Identity and association

Science, in its content and presentation, projects a Eurocentric image. The contribution to its development and study made by any other non-European society seldom gets a mention, thus reinforcing the belief that it is a subject for the more advanced and successful societies. To the minorities it seems a remote venture. There might also be a negative effect on the 'majority' students in that they might continue to look down upon the minorities as people with no contribution to make to a subject of human excellence in intelligence and sophistication.

## Religious and moral conflict

There is a basic difference of philosophy about science in the Eastern part of the world and the West. In places like India and China, where science was studied in great detail nearly 3000 years ago, good scientific practice related to health and hygiene, and medicine was incorporated into the religious beliefs of the time. It was regarded as 'folk-wisdom' and was passed on through generations without being questioned. It depended on observational and postulative studies. In the West, science developed at a very much later stage and was based mainly upon the experimental approach of people like Galileo (1564–1642). Galileo himself fell foul of the religious authorities of the time and this has led to the belief that Western science cannot be reconciled to religion – as it had been with the Indians, the Chinese and the Islamic people for many centuries. In its modern form, science appears as a series of cold facts and principles which often challenge religious and moral beliefs. For some minority people, sex education highlights this problem and such students are under strong pressure from their parents to 'guard' themselves against such training.

### Low expectations

The problem of identifying (or not) with science is also extended to teachers whose expectations from students from ethnic minorities is generally low. This problem has also been recognized in girls studying science. Low expectation leads to under-achievement. Students from ethnic minorities often lack the skill to express themselves in an articulate way. This is basically a language problem but it can often be misconceived as a lack of ability.

### Classroom organization and practice

Classroom organization does not always take into account some of the factors discussed above. Class discussions, student interaction, instructions – both oral and written – do not always show an understanding of the problems. Ideas and expectations of such matters as authority, self-discipline and social behaviour differ in different cultures and communities. A science laboratory can be quite different in its set-up and behavioural requirements from most other classrooms. It demands more discipline, less noise and an orderly framework of approach. Student interaction is sometimes restricted to co-operation in setting up and performing an experiment but little verbal exchange of a student's perception of what is happening is encouraged. Students from some cultural backgrounds find it too restrictive to learn effectively; others lack the confidence to contribute anything to classroom discussions because of the fear that what they might have to say would be seen as nonsense by the rest of the class. Such students often attach themselves to somebody who 'knows better' and copy results – often without understanding them. It is heartening to note that much current thinking increasingly recognizes the central role of discussion and debate in prompting effective learning in science.

### Relevance

Most introductions to new topics, examples and explanations in science come from the European culture. They fail to relate to the daily life, culture and societies from which the ethnic minorities originate. Perhaps a good example of this occurs in the 'food and nutrition' section of a syllabus. A very large proportion of Asian families still eat 'Indian' food at home. This is no less an example of a balanced diet than that which is prescribed in most textbooks and by most science teachers, yet items from this kind of diet seldom find their way into lists of acceptable foods. It must be added that this is often not due to a lack of interest on the part of teachers, but caused by a lack of such readily available information.

## What can be done?

(This section is taken from a discussion document submitted to the ILEA Science Inspectorate by S. Elia, M. Hollins and K. Shaikh.)

Science is widely thought to consist of such activities as enquiry, observation, speculation, prediction, confirmation, classification, testing, criticism, generalization, measurement etc. All these human activities contribute to a way of life and hence form an integral part of any culture. However, people from different cultures bring different, yet equally valid, values to their experience of these activities, which results in a diversity of perception. Science has the ability to provide a forum for the expression of this diversity and yet act as a uniting link. This potential role of science within the wider context of a multicultural education is important and needs to be explored.

The means of exploration, if they are to be of any use to teachers and to have any impact on the students, must be both enlightening and practical. It is very important to stress that there is no one correct method and, initially, it is necessary to put forward a range of materials, suggestions and practices which will help teachers to begin to explore multicultural aspects of science. Eventually, it should evolve into an integral part of any core syllabus and not just be tagged on to an existing course. It is also important to stress that it does not require any dismantling of existing courses.

There are two main areas where realistic and useful work can be done, which will be looked at in the following sections.

## Attitudes of students, parents and teachers

An increased awareness and understanding of the problems of ethnic minorities will bring about some positive changes in areas such as teaching strategies, classroom practice and the general approach to the teaching of science. A recognition of the contribution to science made by other societies, acceptance of experiences of students from different cultures as being equally valid and the treatment of the subject as a human achievement – as opposed to that of a particular society – will create an atmosphere where an anti-racist policy can operate effectively. Racism is not a problem in science alone, but science has a potentially important role to play in clearing up certain misconceptions about race, genetics and intelligence.

A study of the history of science and alternative technology will go some way towards producing healthy attitudes and positive images. The contribution made to science and its development – both in practice and in theory – by non-Europeans is immense. This includes a great deal of work in areas such as medicine, plant classification, surgery, numerology and mathematics. The numeral system that is almost universally used today, and which includes the number 'zero', is India's contribution to the world of science and mathematics. The basic foundations of astronomy, trigonometry and metallurgy are all examples of non-European achievement and excellence in science.

Chinese technology was well advanced when Stonehenge was begun in Britain. The skills of the Chinese in producing fine silk and drawing maps were unmatched; they used ploughs and studied astronomy. Paper, printing, the magnetic compass, gunpowder, kites, horizontal windmills and pyrotechnics are among China's gift to the rest of the world. Even today the Chinese have solved many of their problems in health and medicine with great originality and skill.

Islamic excellence in the field of science touches such areas as chemistry, engineering, medicine, astronomy, map reading, and a number of other fields, including mathematics. China, India and the Islamic nations are not alone in making significant contributions. In tropical Africa the science of metallurgy was an advanced skill from early times. Even today, many of these places show a skilful and sophisticated use of scientific principles in building simple but highly effective machines to solve important problems. Human ingenuity lies as much in its use of science to solve a problem efficiently and effectively using simple and inexpensive equipment and equally simple techniques, as it does in solving technological problems of great complexity, using highly sophisticated machinery. The area of alternative technology also presents the opportunity to adopt a problem solving approach in science teaching and to show the relevance of science in a human context. Students find a simple idea used 'cleverly' much more fascinating than a complex series of concepts which they cannot fully comprehend.

The history of science coupled with alternative technology can make a very interesting introduction to the study of science and provide students with a stimulating insight to its full breadth. It can make them appreciate its social implications and other matters such as the interdependence of societies and nations. It serves also to illustrate the role of science as a unifying link.

## Curriculum

Two major problems faced by any science teacher interested in the multicultural aspects of science are a lack of adequate resource material and the identification of those areas of curriculum into which such material might be inserted. It should be made clear that there is no need to look for new curriculum areas for this purpose. The present curriculum offers ample opportunity to explore the multicultural dimension. Biology offers greater opportunity than other sciences but it must be emphasized that no topic should be set aside specifically as 'science for a multicultural society'; integration with the normal curriculum wherever appropriate opportunity exists is the key. It can form an introduction to a topic or can be used equally effectively as homework or extension work, or even as a project. Approaches can range through practical activities to informal discussion.

Resource materials allow a fair range of activities and approaches. Appendix I shows an example of how a topic like 'salt' can be given added interest to both minority students and their peers. Other headings which offer similar opportunities include health education, nutrition, teeth, sex education, ammonia, soap, pumps, cooling and evaporation, distillation, mining, ores, purification, water, housing, cleaning, food and energy.

## Other areas

There are more subtle and indirect ways of raising the awareness of students and at the same time restoring the confidence of ethnic minorities by giving a much needed boost to their self-image in science. One of these is to have wall charts showing non-European contributions to science. There are many non-European scientists, spread all over the world, doing scientific work of great value. Information about them can be brought to students' notice through such charts. Rather than showing all non-European scientists and their achievements on one chart, it is better to choose a theme like light and energy etc. and to show how scientists from a range of ethnic backgrounds contribute to developments in the chosen field.

It is also worth looking critically at textbooks, which can offer obvious or subtle stereotypes. By the same token, care must also be taken in presenting written materials such as workcards, homework exercises etc.

## Resources

A series of booklets entitled *Third World Science*, written and compiled by Professor Iolo Williams and his team at the School of Education, University College of North Wales, provide interesting and useful resource material for teachers interested in this area. The list of units, now being published by the Centre for World Development Education, is given at the end of this section.

The India Office Library and Records (British Library), 197 Blackfriars Road, London SE1 8NG, has several books on the history and development of science in India.

H. T. Colebrook's enlightening works, *Translations of Brahmagupta 1817* and *Translations of Lilavat; 1869*, show the full extent of Indian excellence and achievement in the field of science and medicine.

The book *Islamic Science – An Illustrated Study* by Seyyed Hossien Nasr, published by the World of Islam Festival Publishing Co., throws light on the Islamic contribution to science.

Other bodies like World Development Education, 128 Buckingham Palace Road, London SW1W 9SH, and Oxfam, Education Department, 14 Brixton Road, London SW9, are also engaged in collecting material suitable for multicultural aspects of science.

*Science Teaching in a Multiethnic Society* (ILEA Science Centres) is a collection of short articles written mainly by London science teachers who have approached this issue in their classroom teaching, and in discussion within their departments and schools.

Finally, what can be done and how best it can be done still remains at the experimental stage. We have now reached a point where increasing action is needed. More and more information and resource materials will soon become available, as there are many groups, large and small, of teachers and educationists currently working on this major area of concern. Local authorities and other institutions are also concentrating efforts in this direction. As with much else in education, progress may be slow but the place of science for a multicultural society will be as an important and integral part of science education, to meet the needs of the minorities, but more generally to cope with the demands of society as a whole. In the process, it may well be that the science we teach will become more relevant and interesting to all.

### Third World Science

Units now available:

| | |
|---|---|
| Carrying loads on heads | Cement (in prep.) |
| Charcoal | Clay pots |
| Dental care | Diet and nutrition (in prep.) |
| Distillation | Energy converters |
| Fermentation | Food preservation (in prep.) |
| Fuels (in prep.) | Housing |
| Iron smelting | Methane digestors |
| Natural dyes | Natural fibres (in prep.) |
| Plants and medicine | Salt |
| Soap | Vegetable oils (in prep.) |
| Pupils' project from Zambia | |

Each pack contains information for teachers on science activities from the Third World for use in British schools. The aims of the materials are:

to make science teaching more interesting by providing novel illustrations of basic principles, drawn from the environment, traditional craft practice and modern technological developments in the Third World;

to contribute to development education by drawing attention to the skill, knowledge and expertise that men and women in developing countries already have, as well as their social, economic and technological needs.

## Appendix I. An interesting additional treatment of the topic 'salt'

Salt has always been an important commodity. This fact presents an opportunity for a problem solving approach to the topic 'How would you obtain salt without any salt mines or the sea?'

Few students will come up with the answer that it could be obtained by burning leaves, but this is the solution used in Ghana for many centuries. This leads to an interesting series of experiments:

1 Burning leaves and collecting ashes.
2 Dissolving ashes in water and filtering (a refreshing alternative to the salt and sand experiment!).
3 Evaporating and crystallization.
4 Flame tests to confirm the product.

The 'Third World Science' unit on salt provides some very interesting information on the topic.

# Appendix II. A framework for multicultural approaches to classroom science

| *Justification (aspects of the nature of science)* | *Multicultural approach* | *Possible curriculum development activities* |
|---|---|---|
| 1 Science is a cultural activity. | Emphasis on personal, subjective, pluralistic aspects of the practice of science. | (a) Use of 'Science in Society' materials.<br>(b) History and philosophy of science – simple stories for students, background material accessible to teachers.<br>(c) Open-ended, problem solving activities. |
| 2 Science is about understanding: | | |
| (a) the natural world. | Worldwide examples of natural phenomena – flora, fauna, climate, resources, geology, etc. | |
| (b) people | Anti-racist | Develop materials on genetics, species variation etc. |
| (c) the synthetic world (technology and medicine<br>(d) the domestic environment | Meeting the needs of different groups of people. | Use 'Third World Science' materials and explore development and under-development, e.g. foods, buildings etc. |
| 3 Science education must be appropriate to the students taught. | (i) Content must be motivating, with positive images for groups taught. | (a) Raise teachers' awareness of positive and negative images re. cultural groups.<br>(b) Provide information on cultural differences for teachers. |
| | (ii) Awareness of special needs. | (a) Language development – develop strategies.<br>(b) Compensate for shortcoming in previous education of recent immigrants. |
| | (iii) Awareness of under-achievement among certain groups. | Digest of findings for teachers, e.g. Rampton and Swann reports. |

# (c) Links across the curriculum

**Bryan Milner**

The links between science and other school subject areas are extensive and have deep implications for the curriculum. An examination of the overall aims of the whole educational enterprise is necessary to provide a sufficiently comprehensive context for a full exploration of the relationship between science and the whole curriculum.

## Overall aims of education

In our developed and democratic society, the needs of individuals living their lives in the context of that society, and the needs of the society for individuals who are adequately equipped to maintain it and develop it further, should be regarded as being of equal importance. It is the responsibility of schools – through both their curriculum and their social environment – to provide an education:

which offers youngsters, at all stages, experiences which are interesting, rewarding and worthwhile in their own right (thus not only making the realization of other aims more likely but also properly respecting children as children rather than treating them merely as adults-in-the making);

which will equip youngsters:

to make an active, responsible contribution to our society, yet be constructively critical of it;

to make the most of the opportunities afforded by our society.

A curriculum which is sufficiently broad, balanced and relevant to be capable of achieving these aims, and thus educating young people not only as unique, developing individuals, but also for citizenship, employment (or the lack of it), leisure, and as consumers, voters, parents etc., will need to include knowledge and skills, selected as being important for anyone, from across the whole range of 'forms of knowledge' or 'areas of experience'.

Chapter 1 of this handbook provided reasons for regarding science as a distinctive form of knowledge. It then went on to identify several important aspects or dimensions of science. Further analysis of these dimensions, in combination with reference to some of the general educational aims listed above, make possible the production of a comprehensive (and somewhat complex) set of aims for science education. At several points during this analysis, however, it emerged that knowledge and skills from science, while making an important contribution to the realization of some education aims, were not by themselves sufficient to achieve it; integration with knowledge and skills from other areas was also needed. To facilitate detailed consideration of this matter (a task deliberately deferred in Chapter 1) we shall attempt to provide a comprehensive categorization of the 'forms of knowledge' or 'areas of experience'.

## Areas of experience

An analysis of knowledge into distinctive forms as a means of resolving questions of balance and selection of content in school curricula was a task initially undertaken by Hirst. The idea was subsequently adopted, with a change in terminology – 'areas of experience' replacing 'forms of knowledge' – by HMI in DES (1977). This latter categorization has been extended in order to produce a set of areas of experience which is more comprehensive and hence more directly useful in curriculum planning. No attempt is made to provide a philosophical justification for this extension, any more than HMIs did for their modification.

It is suggested that 'education for all' should include – at appropriate stages and in a form suited to their abilities – knowledge and skills from the following areas of experience:

1 the communicative – the ability to communicate effectively (especially, though not exclusively, in speech and writing) and to understand, appreciate and critically evaluate what is communicated by others;
2 the mathematical – a precise and logical set of languages constituting an intellectual activity in its own right but also important both in everyday life and as a tool in science, technology, economics etc.;
3 the aesthetic and creative – involving both practice and appreciation in music, drama, literature and a variety of art and craft media;
4 the scientific – understanding the natural world and becoming able to use the processes by which that understanding is achieved and developed;
5 the physical – learning to use the body skilfully and to take good care of it;
6 the technological – appreciating and practising the integration of concepts and skills from science, craft, aesthetics and economics through which man shaped the world in order more effectively to meet his needs;
7 the environmental – understanding the complex interdependencies in the local, national and global environment; developing an awareness of the impact of man's technology on that environment and of the consequent need to protect the environment and manage scarce resources responsibly;
8 the social/political/economic – recognizing the interdependence of individuals and society; understanding how social, political and economic institutions function and change and how individuals both develop and operate within these institutions;
9 the ethical and spiritual – enabling young people to develop a coherent set of attitudes, values and beliefs which, in a pluralist and multi-racial society, should include the capacity to understand, respect and tolerate races, beliefs, world-views and ways of life other than one's own;

10 the inter-personal – the ability to relate appropriately to and interact effectively with other people in a wide variety of different situations;
11 the historical – an appreciation of how the human race itself, particular 'races' and nation-states, and all human activities and institutions have evolved through time;
12 the philosophical – explicit understanding of the distinctive features of different areas of knowledge and experience and of the contribution they make, separately and together, to our understanding of and practical activity in the natural and social world.

It is important to note that this categorization of areas of experience only partially matches the subject divisions normally encountered on the school curriculum. This does not necessarily imply that these subject divisions must be radically revised, though it certainly indicates the need for:

careful analysis, with respect to each area of experience, of the important dimensions of that area, and hence of the distinctive contribution it makes to a person's overall education;
detailed consideration of the contribution (if any) each school subject makes to each area of experience.

Science is one of the few school subjects which itself constitutes an area of experience; its distinctive features and hence the distinctive educational contribution it makes were analysed in Chapter 1. Science education will not, however, make its full contribution to youngsters' overall education unless it has taken fully into account:

that several other subjects incorporate a significant element of science (e.g. home economics, physical geography);
that education in science itself involves skills and/or knowledge from other areas of experience (e.g. the communicative and the mathematical);
that some areas of experience are inherently multi-disciplinary involving the integration of knowledge and skills from other areas of experience. (Chapter 1 identified the technological and the environmental as having an important science component);
that some areas of experience are essentially parasitic, i.e. they comprise a detached examination of the distinctive concepts and processes of other areas of experience. (The meta-scientific dimension referred to in Chapter 1 involves historical and philosophical perspectives on science.)

It is convenient to take each area of experience in turn, to consider its interrelationships, if any, with the scientific area of experience and to explore the implications of any such interrelationships for the curriculum.

# Science and other areas of experience

## 1 Science and the communicative

Language, in both its spoken and written forms, plays an important role in the teaching and learning of science (and other subjects). Analysis of the many aspects of language relevant to teaching and learning is far too complex and lengthy a task to be attempted here. It is, however, most important for schools (or, perhaps better, LEAs) to provide the framework within which an overall policy can be formulated.

Each subject area can then identify not only the particular contributions it makes toward the realization of the overall policy, but can also recognise the nature and phasing of the contributions made in other subject areas, and hence make some use of these. English departments might normally be expected to play the co-ordinating role essential for effective liaison across the curriculum.

Ways in which language is deployed or developed in science education will vary with context (in the sense of that term used in Chapter 1). Some aspects will be best promoted by tightly structured questioning and by recording work in a form that is both concise and precise. The speculative thought needed for the solution of technological problems or the formulation of views on complex environmental issues, on the other hand, demands much freer talk (often student/student rather than student/teacher) and the rough drafting and redrafting of ideas.

Of course language is not the only vehicle for communication. Frequently, it is not the most appropriate: in science, for example, diagrams or tables are often more effective at conveying how tasks are to be (or have been) accomplished.

## 2 Science and the mathematical

The relationship between science and the mathematical area of experience resembles that between science and the communicative area. Mathematics comprises a set of precise and logical 'languages', which not only lead to interesting activities in their own right, but can also be applied (or 'interpreted') in everyday life and used as descriptions or models in science, technology and other areas.

The curricular implications of the relationship between mathematics and other areas of experience is rather simpler than in the case of the communicative area of experience. At school level, mathematics is used as a tool primarily in science and technology and, to a lesser extent, in economics and geography. It does not, like the mother tongue, deeply permeate all other curriculum activities. It is nonetheless important to have a detailed set of aims and content for mathematical education, and for the relevant departments to know what mathematical concepts and skills are to be used, by whom and at what stage. Decisions can then be made about where responsibility for introducing various areas of mathematics will lie, and who will be using, consolidating and possibly extending concepts and skills already acquired. The co-ordination needed for effective liaison within a school might normally be expected to rest with the mathematics department.

Although space precludes any detailed consideration of the areas of mathematics which could and should be incorporated into science education, it is appropriate to make two points. Firstly, concern has been expressed about science teachers evading responsibility for contributing to children's mathematical education by omitting from their teaching material whose mathematical content is likely to prove difficult. A proper balance would involve science departments using science to help develop or consolidate mathematical competence (and, at the same time, refining the science) without creating negative attitudes towards science in topics where a qualitative understanding is itself of considerable value. Secondly, many science teachers feel that mathematics has, in recent years, been unduly pre-occupied with patterns, relationships and its own internal grammar, i.e. with 'maths for maths sake' rather than as a tool for use in everyday life or in science. Where such feelings exist they should become important items on the agenda when schools (or LEAs) are formulating their aims and content for mathematical education.

## 3 Science and the aesthetic/creative

The contribution made by science to various craft areas, for example, is primarily technological in nature (e.g. glazing in pottery). Aesthetic criteria also make an important contribution, alongside knowledge and skills from science and other areas of experience, towards solving technological problems in an environmentally satisfactory way. So far as science education is concerned, therefore, we can incorporate this area of experience into our discussion of the technological and environmental areas of experience. This should not be taken to imply that the aesthetic areas of experience make no significant contribution to a person's overall education.

## 4 Science and the scientific

The important features of the distinctively scientific area of experience are fully discussed in Chapter 1.

## 5 Science and the physical

The fact that human beings have bodies as well as minds gives rise to two important educational aims:

- the ability to use the body skilfully in a variety of contexts and for a variety of purposes;
- knowing how to treat one's body – a complex and finely tuned physiological mechanism – with proper consideration, and knowing how to maintain and repair it adequately.

Science has a contribution to make to both these aims: firstly, ensuring important manipulative skills are developed via practical work; and secondly, making an understanding of human physiology form an essential part of any adequate health education programme.

It should, however, be noted that the science component of health education is frequently taught in subjects other than science, e.g. in home economics or in physical education. The issue then is not the territorial question of whose right it is to teach health education, but rather of ensuring that, whatever options the students make, the opportunity to acquire important knowledge and skills is not missed and that the same material is not covered at much the same level in several different subjects. As already noted, in those curriculum areas where several subjects make a contribution, it is vital for the relevant departments to formulate a school policy, thereby avoiding either serious omission or fruitless repetition. The latter is particularly likely to happen when departments are making a determined effort to bring out the everyday relevance of their subjects. Sometimes the solution to this problem is for departments to combine their resources and expertise for the teaching of some units of work. On other occasions, one department might undertake the major responsibility; other departments can then refer in their own teaching to what they know has been learned elsewhere, thereby consolidating the work in an educationally profitable way, rather than simply repeating it.

## 6 Science and the technological
## 7 Science and the environmental

These two areas of experience have been bracketed together, not because their relations with science are less important than those of other areas, but rather because they are multidisciplinary areas of experience. They are, therefore, subject to similar problems as health education (discussed in Section 5 above). Similar solutions apply.

Technology, interpreted as in Chapter 1 so as to include, for example, horticulture and baking bread as well as constructing mechanical devices, involves combining scientific understanding with craft skills and making judgements of both an aesthetic and an economic nature. The relative importance of these aspects varies considerably with the product being made.

The environmental area of experience involves science in two different ways: not only do technological activities of a strongly scientific character have an enormous influence on the environment, but scientific knowledge and skills also make an essential contribution to understanding complex environmental situations. (Aesthetic, economic and ethical judgements are also involved in arriving at points of view or making decisions about environmental issues.)

Curriculum problems and their solutions in the technological and environmental areas are similar but somewhat more complex than those discussed for health education. Each area needs a comprehensive statement of aims and a detailed consideration of content similar to those provided for science in Chapter 1. When this has been accomplished at school level (or, perhaps better, at LEA level), relevant subject departments can plan their curricula to avoid the twin problems of omission and replication.

It should be noted that the technological area mainly concerns science, CDT and economics departments (though mathematics departments might also be involved in computer appreciation/microprocessor control.) The environmental area involves mainly science and the humanities (especially geography, economics and ethics). Without careful control in both areas of overall curriculum structure and specific course content, the potential for unjustifiable replication is quite enormous.

## 8 Science and the social/political/economic
## 9 Science and the ethical and spiritual

Knowledge, skills and perspectives from these areas are combined with scientific knowledge and skills in the technological and environmental areas discussed above. Little more need be added here, but comprehensive statements of aims for these areas, together with detailed considerations of content, are vital if young people are to be properly educated in these often neglected areas.

Though sociology, psychology, politics and economics are often regarded as sciences, they are more properly treated as the responsibility of humanities departments. Material from the more physiological end of the psychology spectrum, i.e. concerned with sensation and perception, is a possible exception to this principle. (The fact that *MACOS (Man a Course of Study)*, (see p. 281 for details) which attempts to place human behaviour and society in perspective via ethological studies of salmon, gulls and chimpanzees, is usually undertaken by humanities departments, is fully consistent with the demarcation suggested above.) What ultimately matters, however, is that important knowledge and skills are included in school curricula. By whom they are included is of secondary importance.

It is worth mentioning additionally that honesty and integrity are ethical principles of paramount importance in science. For example, recording the results actually obtained (and not those which the experimenter would have liked to obtain or which should have been obtained) underpins all experimental work whether at school or in the wider scientific community.

## 10 Science and the inter-personal

Education in science, as in any other area, involves social interaction not only between students and teachers, but also between students themselves. Different styles of teaching create different overall climates. Each of these make particular demands on students and promote particular styles of interaction. Carrying out practical assignments in pairs or small groups, for example, requires students to discuss and agree strategies and to share responsibilities. As a generalization, schools could usefully adopt a more positive and structured approach to the development of inter-personal skills and to the variety of context, including science, in which they might be practised.

### 11 Science and the historical
### 12 Science and the philosophical

The meta-scientific dimension of science education, an analysis of which is provided in Chapter 1, is not itself part of science. It involves historical and philosophical perspectives on the nature and development of science itself, and of the applications and implications of science.

It does not, however, follow that this aspect of science education should necessarily be taken on exclusively by humanities departments. What matters is that its importance is recognized, that overall aims are specified and appropriate content selected. Responsibility for teaching can then be negotiated between science and humanities departments, bearing in mind the interests and competence of teaching staff, the overall curriculum structure within which they are working and all other work the departments are expected to cover within their time allocation. Since these issues are of wider importance, they form the substance of the next section.

## Science within the overall curriculum

The question of selecting organizational frameworks appropriate for realizing the various aims of science education was raised in Chapter 1 and thoroughly examined in Chapter 2. The predominant message emerging here is the necessity for selecting appropriate organizational frameworks, not only at departmental level, to provide for all young people a broad balanced and relevant science education, but also at *school level* to provide for all young people a broad, balanced and relevant *overall* education.

This is a task of some complexity and magnitude, increasingly tackled at LEA level through the formal publication of both general and subject specific policy statements. Such statements, usually drawn up with the active involvement of practising teachers, provide a framework of aims and pointers to other aspects of curriculum structure and practice. A framework established in this way is not immutable, but subject to continual review. Within it, staff in individual schools exercise their own professional expertise and judgement in formulating curriculum policies appropriate to their own particular circumstances. Taking a whole curriculum view is likely to reveal the need to define a basic educational core which will be pursued by all students (albeit to different depths); options can then be selected to extend this core in a range of directions. Developments of this nature do, of course, have implications for examinations at 16+. It is of some regret that 16+ subject criteria are being formulated prior to any serious attempt to review the overall curriculum. (16+ criteria for the established separate sciences were even formulated before those for science!) There is then a serious danger that the opportunity to create an examination structure reflecting a truly comprehensive curriculum will be lost.

A further particular concern for science is the emerging 'orthodoxy' concerning the proportion of time which should be allocated to science during the years of compulsory secondary education. Such approaches attempt to ensure:

that all students receive an adequate education in science;
that no students over-emphasize science at the expense of other curriculum areas.

A variety of sources (e.g. DES, ASE and SSCR) propose a figure of around 20 per cent of total curriculum time as an appropriate allocation for science (with perhaps a little less time than this in the early years of secondary education).

Quoting hard and fast proportions for particular subjects in this way is, however, inadequate for two reasons. Firstly, time needed depends very much upon the outcome of the negotiations (referred to above) between science departments and other departments. Where a science department undertakes a significant responsibility for the mathematical, the technological, the environmental and the meta-scientific components of education, considerably more than 20 per cent of curriculum time would need to be allocated to science. Secondly, if a basic educational core is established, options, though reduced in number, really could be options – thus permitting a considerable science emphasis in a child's overall curriculum. The core science component would ensure that those not choosing extra science in Years 4 and 5 are not precluded from further study of science, though having done additional science would obviously facilitate such further study.

**Interactive questions**

1 Are members of the science department as fully aware as they need to be
   (a) of the work done in areas of the science department other than that for which they have a direct teaching responsibility?
   (b) of the related work done in other departments?
2 What procedures and/or designated responsibilities are there, at departmental level and at school level, to develop and maintain the necessary levels of awareness?
3 How far, if at all, does your time allocation for science differ from the DES recommendation? How would you want to justify any differences?

Finally, a brief comment about science in primary schools. Much of the foregoing discussion of the relationship between science and other curriculum areas is mainly of relevance to secondary schools. In the primary school, with a single class teacher, the problem of 'horizontal liaison' across the curriculum does not arise. Vertical liaison does, however, remain an issue. A view of what children have learned in the various curriculum areas in previous years, and what they are to learn in subsequent years is essential for proper continuity and progression. Liaison is then needed, both between teachers at different stages of primary education and between the primary and secondary phases of education. As science-based activities increasingly penetrate the primary curriculum, so too the need for effective liaison grows.

## Further reading


### 1 Overall philosophy

DES, 1977 *Curriculum 11–16*, Working papers by HMI (HMSO, London).

Hirst, P. H., 1977, *Knowledge and the Curriculum* (Routledge and Kegan Paul, London).

### 2 Science and the communicative

ASE, 1980, *Study Series No. 16, Language in Science* (Association for Science Education, Hatfield).

Bulman, L. 1985, *Teaching Language and Study Skills in Secondary Science* (Heinemann Educational Books, London).

### 3 Science and the mathematical

Cockcroft, W., 1982, *Mathematics Counts* (HMSO. London).

HMI, 1979, *Aspects of Secondary Education* (HMSO, London).

### 4 Science and the physical

DES, 1977, *Health Education in Schools* (HMSO, London).

Material from the Schools Council *Health Education 15–18* project.

### 5 Science and the technological

DES, 1977, *Curriculum 11–16*, Working papers by HMI (HMSO, London).

Schools Council, 1981, Schools Council Modular Technology; *Teachers' Master Manual* (Oliver and Boyd, London).

Pirsig, R. M., 1976, *Zen and the Art of Motorcycle Maintenance* (Corgi, London).

### 6 Science and the environmental

Solomon, J., 1983, *Science in a Social Context (SISCON)* (Association for Science Education, Hatfield).

ASE, 1979, *Study Series No. 15, What is Science?* (Association for Science Education, Hatfield).

ASE, 1981, *Science in Society* (Heinemann Educational Books, London).

# (d) Safety in school science laboratories

**David Tawney**

## Why is it seen as a problem?

Accidents occur in school science laboratories, causing damage to equipment and, more seriously, injury to staff and students. LEAs and school science staffs do consciously try to reduce their number. However, the number of accidents occurring and their severity is much less than is often supposed, an example of a common phenomenon of actual risk differing from the risk perceived by the public.

Four to five per cent of student accidents reported by secondary schools occur in laboratories, a proportion which does not seem to vary appreciably from LEA to LEA or from year to year. Many more accidents occur on playgrounds and in corridors and outside the school on the roads. The chance of a secondary school student being injured on the road is approximately five times as great as being injured in the laboratory and the injury is much more likely to be serious. Very few laboratory accidents require a stay in hospital.

It is worth considering why, despite these statistics, school laboratories are regarded as dangerous places. One factor must be that many accidents appear to be consequences of special 'laboratory' activities: slipping can occur anywhere but a splash of chemical in the eye only in a laboratory. (That many household chemicals are nasty and do get in the eyes is ignored!) We are more likely to excuse supposed lapses in student surveillance similar to those a parent might make than those attributable to professional failure.

In addition to the esoteric, specialist nature of laboratory accidents, two other factors cause their seriousness to be exaggerated: sometimes they are spectactular, for example the results of igniting the jet of hydrogen issuing from apparatus before all the air has been flushed out, and sometimes their cause is unseen and so sinister. Two examples of supposed unseen causes are ionizing radiations and mercury vapour.

## Causes of laboratory accidents

When laboratory accidents do occur, they can sometimes only be attributed to sheer bad luck. More often, they can be considered due to one or more of four 'lacks': lack of awareness, lack of control, lack of knowledge, and lack of the right attitude.

Lack of awareness and control of student behaviour is a problem encountered by many inexperienced teachers. Here it is appropriate to point out only that the consequences of the problem can be serious in the laboratory, particularly if exacerbated by a lack of control of an experiment. No more will be said about the first two lacks, apart from observing that senior staff need to be on the look out for their appearance wherever they occur and be prepared to help.

Before more is said about knowledge and attitude, the legal aspects of laboratory accidents will be discussed.

## The law and laboratory safety

Teachers sometimes fear that the Health and Safety at Work Act 1974 renders them liable to prosecution in a criminal court and possible imprisonment if a student is injured or, more unjustly, if the small print of some obscure regulation is infringed. While legally possible, nothing is less likely. Factory inspectors prefer to persuade and educate rather than prosecute. Should this fail, their next step would probably be to ask the employer, that is the Local Education Authority for a teacher at a state school, to take some action, perhaps to arrange different teaching or extra training. Prosecution of an individual employee is likely only in cases of extreme irresponsibility.

Of course, it has long been possible for the parents of an injured student to sue a teacher for damages in a civil court, almost certainly suing the employer as joint defendant in case the injury was attributable to his failure. (Employers have more money, anyway!) Teachers should insure against liability for third party injury and it is worth reminding science teachers that membership of the Association for Science Education automatically provides substantial cover.

A common misconception is that many materials commonly found in laboratories and many practices are controlled by national legislation. In fact, few are. It is sometimes supposed that, with the coming into force of the Health and Safety at Work Act 1974, Factory Act legislation such as the Highly Flammable Liquid Regulations 1972 now applies to schools. This is not so. Also, later legislation, introduced under the Health and Safety at Work Act, needs to be examined carefully for relevance to schools: for example, the Packaging and Labelling of Dangerous Substances Regulations 1978 and 1981 apply to suppliers not purchasers.

However, these acts and regulations can be of use to LEAs because they suggest ways of dealing with problems which, if intelligently applied to schools, can be extremely helpful. Applied rigidly to the letter and not in the spirit they can do more harm than good.

Legislation is seldom the direct concern of employees. The Health and Safety at Work Act lays on the employer the duty of forming a safety policy and establishing codes to control the practices of its employees, and it is these which a teacher must follow. There have been some cases where a regulation of one LEA has seemed unreasonable compared to those obtaining elsewhere, leading teachers to complain and to consult bodies such as the ASE, CLEAPSE or SSSERC. However, while an LEA regulation is in force, a teacher is obliged to obey it. Many LEAs have produced fairly general codes of practice, referring for detailed recommendations to booklets such as the DES (1978) *Safety in Science Laboratories*, and use circulars to update the codes and to draw attention to particular problems.

## Knowledge

Two groups which lack knowledge of laboratory hazards are inexperienced teachers (including student teachers, probationers and those teaching outside the area in which they qualified) and unqualified laboratory technicians; the latter, being appointed to wash up and fetch and carry, can easily and unknowingly encounter hazards. In addition to the problems that the lack of knowledge possessed by these two groups may cause, there are those due to changes in knowledge resulting in reassessments of hazards. Over the last few years there have been many reassessments.

Thirty years ago, eye protection was not seen in school chemistry laboratories and no one bothered to clear up the mercury from a broken thermometer. Now, not to wear eye protection for most chemical operations is regarded as irresponsible and care is usually taken to clear up mercury spills in order to keep the vapour level as low as possible.

The duty to inform the inexperienced of hazards and all staff of reassessments of hazards falls on employers and on those to whom they have delegated responsibility. Training and the systematic circulation of information is needed, also the careful printing of reminders in course outlines, on containers and on apparatus. For example, a warning to check the safety valve should be attached to the base of a steam engine.

However, information varies in its reliability and it is important for science teachers to be sceptical of newspaper reports, even those appearing in the so-called quality papers. 'Mercury – one lab in three polluted?' reported the Times Educational Supplement (4.3.77): 'Ignorance and uncertainty about mercury poisoning are widespread in schools. DES guidance is still awaited.' Measurements by CLEAPSE in 6000 science rooms confirm that the headline is totally misleading: while mercury vapour can be detected in many rooms, in almost all cases the level is far below that considered to present a hazard and even that at which action should be taken. Information derived from hearsay or the press should be checked before action is taken, with the LEA science adviser or bodies such as CLEAPSE, SSSERC or the ASE.

The first source of safety information of a science department must be that circulated by its employer, usually an LEA. Second are the books listed in the Further Reading section. School science laboratory safety news appears regularly in *Education in Science* published by the ASE and in the bulletins of SSSERC and CLEAPSE. Almost all of this safety information takes the form of recommended precautions or alternatives, not bans: its messages is usually 'how' not 'don't'. Although a list of precautions can seem daunting, with practice it can become second nature. Having to observe the 'Highway Code' does not deter many from driving.

Two principles should guide the amount of attention devoted to the prevention of a particular accident, the likelihood of its occurring and its seriousness. Table 7.1, derived from the accident reports submitted in 11 LEAs over a two to three year period, provides examples. 'Chemicals entering the eye' is fre-

TABLE 7.1 **Accidents to students and staff categorized**

| *Category* | *Number* | *%* |
|---|---|---|
| Chemicals on the body: | 388 | 43.4 |
| In the eyes | 177 | 22.8 |
| Elsewhere | 161 | 20.6 |
| Cuts | 158 | 20.3 |
| Burns caused by flames and hot objects: | | |
| Scalds | 113 | 14.5 |
| Dropping, falling, slipping, knocking, lifting | 57 | 7.3 |
| Chemicals in the mouth | 32 | 4.1 |
| Inhalation | 29 | 3.7 |
| Animal bites | 22 | 2.8 |
| Explosions | 12 | 1.5 |
| Fainting | 12 | 1.5 |
| Electric Shock | 5 | 0.6 |
| Total | 788 | 99.9 |

quently reported and so eye protection should be worn more often than it is. 'Electric shock' is seldom reported but, because its consequence can be serious, care should be taken to avoid it.

The data in the table have consequences for First Aid training: as many laboratory staff as possible should have practice in washing eyes and in rescuscitation, and periodical drills in these skills are desirable.

## Attitude

The general attitude of school science staff to safety is excellent, as the accident statistics bear witness. However, within a satisfactory general picture there are extremes. An example of a disregard of precautions is allowing the mouth pipetting of liquids as toxic as oxalic acid and as corrosive as molar caustic soda. An example of a valuable demonstration omitted because its hazards are exaggerated or the precautions necessary considered irksome is the setting up of a mercury barometer.

Some of the consequences of extreme attitudes are obvious, others less so. Insufficient care can lead to injury of students and staff and all that entails and, less important, damage to equipment; it can also produce undesirable student attitudes. Overcarefulness can waste time and money and reduce student experience; it can also deflect attention from real to imaginary hazards and produce undesirable student attitudes.

Extreme attitudes are also exhibited by some LEAs. Typical examples of a disregard of precautions are insufficient maintenance of gas and electric fittings and the tardy replacement of loose floor tiles. At the other extreme, there is the total banning of a substance, such as benzene, which is no more hazardous than many others successfully handled in school laboratories. Some LEAs seem to favour safety precautions which demonstrate that care is being taken and money spent on safety rather than less dramatic ones which are carefully directed at the real hazards. Eyewash bottles, for example, make a greater show of concern than a rubber tube attached to a tap but are harder to use and maintain.

## Conclusion

The main danger of extreme attitudes to hazards is the effect they have on the attitudes of our students. Risks are not confined to the laboratory but are part of living, so that safety in the laboratory should not just be regarded as a chore, to be got over as quickly as possible – like the copying of rules on to the front page of science notebooks, but an opportunity for education in one of the social aspects of science.

Eye protection is not just for the laboratory but for spraying apple trees and for rust proofing under the car. Toxic and highly flammable liquids are found in the home as well as the laboratory. Electric shocks can be experienced in the kitchen and cultures of micro-organisms will grow there as well as in laboratory incubators.

Students need to develop a proper appreciation of risks, including the realizations that many human activities have some risk associated with them but are considered acceptable, and that real and perceived risks are different categories. They must begin to appreciate our hypocrisies over risks, our different attitude to those we consider to be imposed on us and those we readily accept because they are convenient, like motor transport, or gratifying, like smoking tobacco. We do not evacuate Aberdeen, for example, despite its higher-than-average background radiation. A sensible attitude to risks is essential to a full life and safety education in the laboratory, as well as serving immediate ends, can make an important contribution towards it.

## Further reading

### 1 Essential

ASE, 1981, *Safeguards in the School Laboratory* (8th edition) (Association for Science Education, Hatfield)

DES, 1978, *Safety in Science Laboratories* (3rd edition), DES Safety Series No. 2 (HMSO, London)

Schools Council, 1974, *Recommended Practice for Schools Relating to Use of Living Organisms and Material of Living Origin* (Hodder and Stoughton, Sevenoaks)

### 2 Essential reference books

ASE, 1982, *Topics in Safety* (Association for Science Education, Hatfield)

CLEAPSE/SSSERC, 1981, *Hazards* (CLEAPSE, Uxbridge)

Muir, G. D., 1977, *Hazards in the Chemical Laboratory* (2nd edition) (The Chemical Society, London)

SSSERC, 1979, *Hazardous Chemicals – A Manual for Schools and Colleges* (Oliver and Boyd, London).

## 3 Other useful reading

Armitage, P., and Fasemore, J., 1977, *Laboratory Safety – a Science Teachers' Source-book* (Heinemann, London).

DES, 1977, *The Use of Micro-organisms in Schools*, Education pamphlet 61, (HMSO, London).

Everett, K., and Jenkins, E. W., 1980 *A Safety Handbook for Science Teachers* (3rd edition) (John Murray, London).

Gaston, P. J., 1964, *The Care, Handling and Disposal of Dangerous Chemicals* (IST, Aberdeen)

Nichols, D. (ed.), 1980, *Safety in Biological Fieldwork – Guidance Notes for Codes of Practice* (Institute of Biology, London)

## 4 For the pupil

ASE, 1982, *Safety in the Laboratory (leaflet)* (Association for Science Education, Hatfield)

# (e) Science in the 14–18 Curriculum

**Giles Job**

## The emergence of the 14–18 curriculum

1.1 In 1972 when the school leaving age was raised to 16, two-thirds of 16 year olds left school. Of these, about half became apprentices or received part-time training in employment. The other half went into unskilled work and received no further education or training.

1.2 Today, approximately the same proportion leave school at 16 but only about 10 per cent of them now find employment. The openings in both apprenticeships and in unskilled jobs have fallen dramatically. Jobs in the service industries have increased, and there is a continuing growth in demand for technician-based rather than craft-based skills. The majority of those who leave school at 16 now take part in some form of training scheme (most often the Youth Training Scheme) before moving on to permanent employment – or further unemployment.

1.3 Increasingly, 18 is being seen as the lowest realistic age for – with luck – entry into permanent employment. Thus, although the statutory school leaving age has not changed, full-time education and/or training to the age of 18 is, for most young people, an effective reality.

1.4 One obvious impact on schools of this shift in employment pattern has been a devaluing of traditional 'separate subject' academic qualifications at 16 as passports to successful employment. Exhortations to work hard to obtain better grades can ring hollow if those grades have no employment currency: In general, the uncertainty about prospects beyond 16 leads to increasing demands for the school curriculum to be *seen to be* responsive and appropriate to the personal, social and economic needs of young people faced with this uncertainty, and also to the fast changing needs of industry and commerce. (This summary, like much of this part-chapter, draws heavily on YES (1985), which provides a detailed and thought-provoking summary of the issues, while taking a positive view of possible development.)

1.5 The last two years of compulsory schooling are increasingly seen as the start of this transition to social and economic adulthood, rather than as a culmination of education based on the study of a range of chosen subjects.

1.6 Alongside, and to some extent associated with, these shifts in the economic background, there has been since the late 1970s an increased concern with and involvement in the school curriculum by groups outside the traditional educational sector. Since Callaghan's Ruskin speech of 1977 calling for a 'great debate' on the curriculum, and accountability for it, the agencies of industry and commerce have increasingly confidently staked their claim to a say in the development and outcome of the school curriculum. The most obvious outcome of this pressure has been the spectacular intervention of the Manpower Services Commission, an organ of the Department of Employment, in areas which have been traditionally the preserve of the educational service. The YTS and TVEI schemes, and the responsibility of MSC for much work-related non-advanced further education, are examples of this intervention.

1.7 These are part of the web of influences that have led to a dramatic growth of interest in the 14–18 age range as a clearly definable phase for which coherent provision of education and training is needed. Also important have been changes within the educational system itself, not least the impact of falling student rolls on school and college organization, and on the financial viability of the examination industry. Thus the '14–18' lobby brings together a spectrum (some would say an unholy alliance) of agencies, interests and motivations possibly unprecedented in English education. It is not surprising that there often appears to be confusion and inconsistency in the discussion of the 14–18 curriculum.

## The 14–18 framework

2.1 This confusion is well illustrated by the phrase 'pre-vocational education', which is usually seen as the key element of the 14–18 curriculum. This phrase can be interpreted as that broad, general education to which all students are entitled, as the basis from which they prepare to develop their own vocational interests. Others would interpret it in terms of giving students sufficient vocational experience to allow them to develop aspects of their general education through their preferred vocational area, preparatory to specific vocational training in that area. (At the time of writing, there is no accepted 'correct' interpretation, although the consensus lies closer to the latter than the former.) Ironically, although there is great dispute about the *purpose* of the 14–18 curriculum, there is a large measure of agreement on the desirable *processes* to structure within it. These are typified by the requirements in the Certificate for Pre-Vocational Education (CPVE) for:

(i) a more experience-based and practical mode of learning;
(ii) planned work experience;
(iii) constant guidance and counselling;
(iv) negotiation of learning objectives;
(v) a system of profiling through which the young person's competences, qualifications, experiences, interests and achievements might be recorded.

The emphasis throughout is on *learning how* rather than *learning facts*.

2.2 Given all the reservations expressed above, it is possible to make some generalization about the characteristics of courses so far developed in response to this 14–18 thinking. Typical features of such courses are:

(i) pre-vocational focus – providing a basis of skills, experiences, attitudes and knowledge for progress to further education, training and work;
(ii) experience-based learning – experience determining what is to be studied rather than vice-versa;
(iii) learning from the work place – an integration of work experience into learning;
(iv) problem solving – arising from problems seen by the students as their problems;
(v) personal and social development;
(vi) negotiated curriculum and contract learning;
(vii) guidance and counselling;
(viii) modular course design and graded assessment – a move towards self-contained units of work with clear, short-term objectives, that allow for flexibility in course structure;
(ix) profiling – both as a learning tool and a source of detailed information to users;
(x) community involvement;
(xi) residential experience;
(xii) a core content – to be integrated into the course rather than studied as a series of separate subjects.

(The work of the Further Education Curriculum Review and Development Unit (FEU), directed by Jack Mansell, has been highly influential in this area. See particularly its seminal paper on a core of pre-vocational education (FEU, 1979). Later versions of this, and the CPVE core, specify a core role for science and technology.)

## The implications for science education

3.1 Science has a somewhat ambiguous role within 14–18 thinking. On one hand, it has a *vocational* role in providing the skills and qualifications necessary for progression into and through many routes of vocational studies, particularly in the technical field. This is a relatively familiar role, involving the teaching of familiar subject skills and content. However, the blurring of school and FE boundaries and the growth of modular curriculum and assessment structures are requiring school science teachers to look afresh at the structuring of their specialist courses, and to come to terms with the more modular, centre-based and vocationally oriented assessment traditions of, for example, B/TEC and CGLI.

3.2 On the other hand, a more fundamental challenge to science teachers lies in realizing the potential of science in the *central education* for all students in the core of 14–18 courses. (This central role to general education of a broad and balanced science education is stressed by DES (1977) ASE (1981) and more recently in the DES (1985) policy statement – all writing, ironically, with a 5–16 or 11–16 perspective of the curriculum.) The British tradition of science education obviously has valued many of the characteristics described in paragraph 2.2 and should have much to contribute especially in terms of *experience-based learning*, *problem solving* and, possibly, *negotiation*.

3.3 Of particular relevance here is much recent work in primary science (for example, science 5–13), and several secondary projects which have deliberately avoided 'subject context' (e.g. Nuffield Secondary Science project, the ASE's LAMP project and a project which overtly incorporates nearly all the principles listed above, the Nuffield *Working with Science* project). All of these stress the use of scientific processes in practically tackling problems which are directly relevant to the students' perceived needs and interests.

3.4 Although these materials and traditions have much of value to contribute to core 14–18 programmes, their practical implementation can easily be limited by the lack of a suitable curriculum framework to which science teachers can effectively contribute, overwhelmed as they often are by their involvement in meeting the more specialist, vocational demands of the curriculum. (One of the striking features of the early TVEI initiatives has been the lack of involvement in their curriculum innovation of school science departments – and LEA science advisers. Science has largely featured, if at all, in a 'service' or 'vocational' capacity (Benson, 1984.))

3.5 Another area of potential confusion in the 14–18 debate lies in the area of 'science and technology'. This phrase occurs frequently, but with little consensus on the definition, in its own right and in the context of the curriculum, of technology and its relationship to science. That the two are closely related is clear, and this is reflected, for example, by the British School Technology programme which encourages the joint teaching of technology courses by science and CDT teachers. Certainly, technology is more than applied science, and institutions need to come to a working definition of technology (e.g. that area concerned with controlling the environment in order to meet human needs) before its place in the structure of the curriculum, and the appropriate contribution of science expertise to it, can be effectively achieved (APU, 1981; Black and Harrison, 1985).

## Conclusion

4.1 The developments in the 14–18 view of the curriculum are far-reaching and fast moving. At the time of writing, it is not easy to predict to what extent these views will result in a radical restructuring of the educational system and its curriculum framework. It is certain, however, that many of the issues raised will not go away, and teachers of all subjects will have to come to terms with changed perceptions of the purpose of schooling, and the nature of teaching and learning. Science teachers in particular will have to come to terms with their dual role as teachers of science and educators through science, and they will have to respond rapidly to changing views of the relevance of science if their subjects are not to follow Latin along the road from vocational requirement to status symbol to irrelevance.

## Further reading

ASE, 1985, Curriculum and assessment for the 14–18 age range, *Education in Science*, No. 111. A report of the ASE Education Conference 1984, summarizing the political and institutional influences.

*The Certificate of Pre-Vocational Education Part A*, 1985 (The Joint Board for Pre-Vocational Education, 46 Britannia Street, London WCIX 9RG).

FEU, 1979, *A Basis for Choice*, and subsequent FEU publications.

Hargreaves, D., *Improving Secondary Schools* (ILEA).

## Bibliography

APU, 1981, *Understanding Design and Technology* (HMSO, London)

ASE, 1981, *Education through Science* (Association for Science Education, Hatfield)

Benson, P., 1984, A position for science in pre-vocational education, *Education in Science*, Nos. 108, 109

Black, P., and Harrison, G., 1985, *In Place of Confusion: Technology and Science in the School Curriculum* (Nuffield-Chelsea Curriculum Trust, London, National Centre for School Technology, Nottingham)

DES, 1977, *Curriculum 11–16*, Working papers by HMI (HMSO, London)

DES, 1978, *Safety in Science Laboratories* (3rd edition), DES Safety Series No. 2 (HMSO, London)

DES, 1978, *Special Educational Needs* (*The Warnock Report*) (HMSO, London)

Educational Development Centre Inc, Cambridge, Mass., 1970, *MACOS (Man a Course of Study)* (Curriculum Development Associates, Washington D.C.)

DES and Welsh Office, 1985, *Science 5–16: A Statement of Policy* (HMSO, London)

FEU, 1982, *Profiles* (Department of Education and Science, London)

Johnson, R. T., and Johnson, D. W., 1981, 'Mainstreaming handicapped students in science', in *Teaching Handicapped Students Science* (edited by M. E. Corrick), (National Education Association Production)

Jones, A. V., 1983, *Science for Handicapped Children* (Souvenir Press, London)

Leach, G., 1985, Practical examination science and physically handicapped pupils, *The School Science Review*, 66 (No. 236)

Swann, 1985, *Education for All* (HMSO, London)
YES, 1985, *The 14–18 Curriculum: Integrating CPVE, YTS, TVEI?* (YES, 14 Frederick Place, Clifton, Bristol BS8 1AS)
*Education Act 1981: The Law on Special Education*, a summary compiled by the Advisory Centre of Education (Advisory Centre for Education, London)

# (f) Girls and science

**Linda Scott**

Education has long been one of the most decisive of our life-chances, the key to equal opportunity and the ladder to advancement, since men [sic] first learnt that literacy and communication in the hands of a few meant power, government and the control of many. Without education, and especially without equal education experiences or skills and qualifications, men and women alike of certain classes and social groups have over the years been condemned to inferior lives in their personal developments, in their choice of work, as citizens, and in their power to influence government, leadership and the national decisions which affect their local lives. (Byrne, 1978, p. 14)

## Introduction

The Sex Discrimination Act came into force in December 1975. It was intended to eliminate discrimination on the grounds of sex and in doing so provide the opportunity for women to achieve social and economic equality with men. The legislation has had limited success in generating equality for our pupils. Though desirable, it is not possible to remove prejudices and eradicate differential treatment of boys and girls in the space of a few years. Many of the ideas held about the 'traditional' role of women are based on historical domestic situations and have little justification in today's society. (In the days when the life expectancy of the average woman was 40 years, during which time she bore six children, there was obviously little opportunity for a role in the advancement of science. Today, the average 'career gap' for a woman in order to bring up children is only seven years, giving therefore about forty years in which to pursue a career.) Furthermore, national statistics (General Household Survey) indicate that only about 5 per cent of our households now consist of two-parent families with a full–time 'housewife'. There is a great need for women to be scientifically literate and have a basic comprehension of technology. This is valuable within the home because of their close relationships with young children during their early formative years and equally necessary outside the home in order to achieve equality of opportunity within the job market.

## The problem of stereotyping

It is still the case that young girls experience a great deal of pressure to conform to the stereotyped female role promoted by romantic fiction and which is in direct conflict with social and economic reality. These pressures come from society from early childhood, when toys, for example, are selected according to the sex of the child, and are continued throughout the development of the young person. Adolescent boys are frequently steered towards science because it is viewed as being appropriate for them and likely to be of use in their future career. Adolescent girls have to break the traditional barriers. 'Option' time normally occurs when the pupils are about fourteen years old. This timing coincides with the period of rapid maturation for the majority of girls so that they are acutely aware of their sexuality and are still coming to terms with all the implications, physical and psychological, of their femininity. Boys 'conform' by selecting science, girls who select science at this stage in their adolescence have to possess above average determination and self-confidence to cross the traditional barriers. By being aware of these additional hurdles for the girls, and by providing a non-threatening environment in which the girls can discuss the alternatives open to them, science teachers can help girls to make curricular decisions based on their interests and aptitudes rather than allowing them to follow traditional routes without questioning them.

## Girls have lower career aspirations

At the moment, girls have a restricted image of their future, and suffer badly because they are less career-orientated than boys. Teachers have a responsibility to encourage girls to treat the question of developing a career much more seriously. The solution lies not only in lobbying for more and earlier careers education for pupils, but also in the promotion of careers awareness within daily lessons. It could be argued that this happens at the moment, every time a real-life context is provided for some topic, e.g. a farmer wants to grow... or a pilot flies due north at... etc. However, in the absence of explicit examples of girls and women in careers or engaged in pursuits outside the home, by default, a large majority of readers will assume that the worker is male. Did *you* visualize a male or female farmer and pilot in the examples given above? Admittedly, there are many more male farmers and pilots around, but the actual numbers are determined more by tradition than by capacity to do the job. These situations, and many thousands more like them, will remain unnecessarily sex-stereotyped unless teachers make the effort to stress the particular aptitudes and qualities needed in an occupation and avoid or challenge the traditional assumptions about the gender of the person concerned. This has the dual effect of suggesting to the girls that this could be a possible future for them, and of alerting the boys to the fact that they do not have sole rights on certain occupations (neither are they precluded from others), because of their sex.

It is relatively easy to prepare worksheets etc. which promote the image of women taking part in activities which are at present classed as 'non-traditional' for them. It is much more difficult to incorporate these ideas in our everyday teaching because it can feel unnatural and even uncomfortable at times. It requires a great deal of mental agility to edit every sentence before it is spoken – and to make running alterations to one's supply of examples or anecdotes. Most depressing is the response from the pupils – they may well not appreciate the new emphasis immediately and appear unresponsive, or worse, hostile. This is to be expected if they have already been strongly influenced by pressures from the media and the community, and provides all the more reason for persisting with the exercise.

## Girls 'opt out' of science

One of the greatest impediments to the realization of equal opportunities for girls within science is their own reluctance to participate in the science lessons which are provided. It would be wrong to suggest that the adoption of a 'science for all' policy within a school will be sufficient to rectify the situation. At the moment the majority of girls move away from science, physical science in particular. This is a gradual rejection of the subject, highlighted at 'option' time. Compelling pupils to attend science lessons in years four and five has questionable educational value, if the science on offer is a continuation of the theme which turned them off in the first place. (This point is equally applicable to the significant number of boys who, at present, study no science or unbalanced combinations of science.)

It must be stressed that girls are not incapable of coping with the intellectual demands of the study of science but generally they do not relate to the framework of contexts and applications which form the traditional vehicle for the teaching of the subject. The vast majority of the science principles which are introduced at school level have been developed by men, described by men with a male audience in mind, and are taught by men. E.g. a male colleague was attempting to make calculations involving the equations of motion more interesting by providing a physical context for each example. One calculation involved the flight of a Phantom travelling at 200 metres per second. He knew that the question related to an aircraft, and so did the boys in the class, but a girl who had no background knowledge of military aircraft was trying to make sense of a question apparently about a high speed ghost! Faced with this sort of adverse environment it is understandable that many girls label science as a masculine domain, reject it, and allow themselves to retreat to other subjects where they believe they have more chance of success.

## What can we do?

### First steps to tackling the problem

There are some relatively simple strategies which can reduce the disadvantages experienced by girls, and a few of the major ones are outlined below. However, the complete solution lies not merely in developing the girls' self-confidence but in reappraising science and providing alternative presentations which are more relevant to the girls and more appropriate to their needs. The work of the Children's Learning in Science (CLIS) team has lead to recommendations for teachers to explore the views and experiences of all their pupils before embarking on a new topic – so that the learning environment can be constructed to follow on from the pupils' present beliefs.

Tables 7.2 and 7.3 below were compiled from information gathered during the APU Science study. They illustrate the differential experiences and interests declared by the boys and girls questioned. The majority of courses in use at the moment are based on assumptions about the previous experience of the pupils which are clearly valid only for the boys and a very small proportion of the girls. By taking account of information such as this, and by talking more to the pupils

TABLE 7.2 **Differences in the percentage of eleven-year-old boys and girls who have 'quite often' engaged in particular activities out of school. (From 1984 APU national survey data)**

| Activity | % pupils boys | % pupils girls |
|---|---|---|
| Make models from a kit (Airfix) | 44 | 7 |
| Play pool, billiards or snooker | 62 | 31 |
| Play with electric toy sets | 46 | 17 |
| Create models using lego, etc. | 51 | 24 |
| Take things apart to see inside | 41 | 20 |
| Go fishing or pond dipping | 32 | 14 |
| Watch birds | 31 | 28 |
| Sow seeds or grow plants | 33 | 37 |
| Look after small animals/pets | 54 | 60 |
| Collect/look at wild flowers | 9 | 29 |
| Weigh ingredients for cooking | 30 | 65 |
| Knit or sew | 5 | 50 |

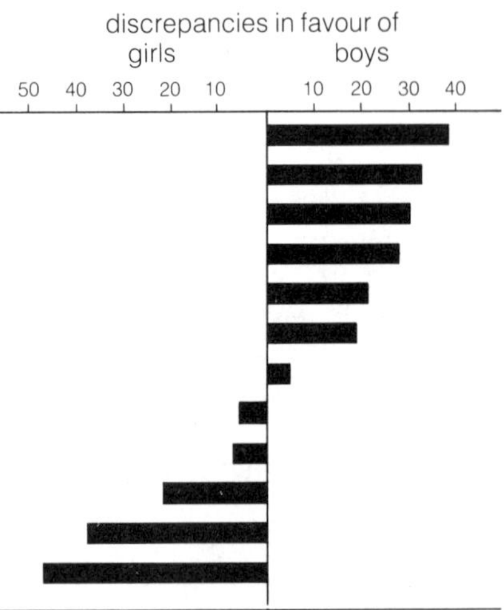


TABLE 7.3 **Differences in the percentages of eleven-year-old boys and girls who have used particular measuring instruments out of school. (From 1984 APU national survey data)**

| Measuring instrument | % pupils boys | % pupils girls |
|---|---|---|
| Compass | 68 | 46 |
| Microscope | 48 | 33 |
| Stopwatch/clock | 66 | 52 |
| Spring balance | 30 | 20 |
| Hand lens | 69 | 60 |
| Metre stick | 22 | 16 |
| Thermometer | 52 | 49 |
| Measuring cylinder | 65 | 70 |
| Weighing scales | 75 | 81 |

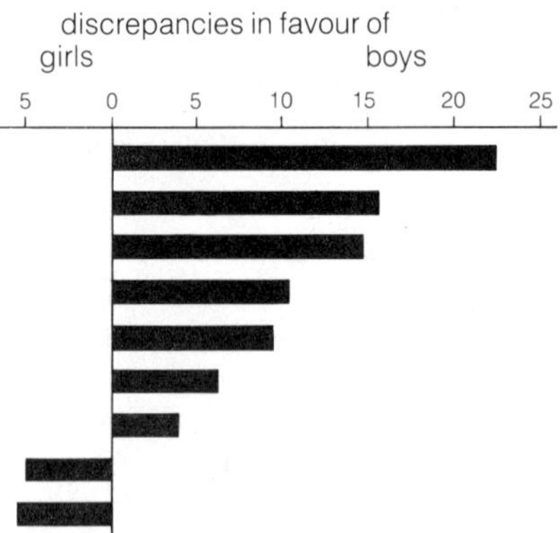

about their hobbies etc., courses can be devised which are more balanced than the present ones.

## Redressing the balance

The most obvious way in which girls are disadvantaged is in their comparative lack of experience in tinkering with simple machinery and in the use of basic tools. The type of manual dexterity developed by building scale models or using construction kits is of more direct relevance to future work in science than that developed by the girls through needlecraft or cookery. Their observation of the boys' extra confidence in certain aspects of practical work often leads the girls to make the unjustified assumption that the boys are inherently better at the tasks. Similarly some of the hobbies more common to boys such as playing snooker, darts, or variations on ball games, help enhance their spatial awareness. Again this generates a distinct advantage for the boys, particularly when dealing with physical science or technology areas of the syllabus.

It is important therefore to allow more time for girls to become familiar with equipment and/or situations which are new to them. From a classroom management point of view this may be built into individualized learning schemes or operated as a girls' science club designed to provide a range of compensatory experiences. The Secondary Science Curriculum Review (SSCR) is in the process of reviewing materials available in this field and details will be available in the SSCR 'Equal Opportunities' report.

## Confidence and self-esteem

Possibly related to the previous item is the difference in attitude displayed by boys and girls whenever they experience setbacks. The boys generally have a more positive self image, being able to shrug off problems, to attribute blame to circumstances – faulty equipment, lack of time, or to suggest that they could have performed better if they had applied more effort. Girls, on the other hand, are more likely to feel personally responsible for any setback. They underestimate their capacity to cope with a situation and are much more likely to play down any success which they experience, claiming that they were 'lucky'.

"I could be good at Maths if I wanted, but it's boring how they do it at school" (12-year-old boy).
"I don't think I'm good at Maths, it's just that the maths they give us at school is easy" (12-year-old girl).

(E.O.C., 1984, *An Equal Start*)

This optimism on the part of the boys may be unjustified on occasions but it does help them to be resilient and more prepared to speculate about the outcome of experiments, for example. These characteristics are valued within science, again creating a situation in which the boys have the advantage over girls. Skills such as communication and self-expression are not given the same prestige – the excuse being the time restraints imposed by the examination syllabus, but the reason often being the science teachers' lack of experience in managing classroom discussions and informal group work. The illiterate scientist has been a bad joke for decades. Now that the importance of giving pupils time to relate to the science and to appreciate and discuss some of its social, political and economic implications has been acknowledged, the new teaching styles needed will be considerably more 'girl-friendly'. Again, support for developing new teaching styles will be available through the structure of the SSCR.

## Providing role models

A good way to promote science for girls is to provide examples of women who are happy and successful at their work in some field of science. Local women who can actually visit the school and discuss their work and their training (through science lessons or at the invitation of the careers staff) are best. The women need not be outstanding intellectuals – young apprentices, when you can find them, can often relate really well to the girls, although they will probably need more support in preparing the visit. (This type of visit was popularized during WISE year, it may be that a list of local speakers has been drawn up for your area. Check with your local teachers' centre or SATRO.) The provision of these examples of successful women scientists and technologists is equally important for the re-education of boys. There is much evidence that boys can be particularly obstructive to girls who show an interest in what the boys regard as their own territory. It is not only the girls' attitudes which are moulded by society – many boys believe, without any justification, that they are better than girls at Maths and Science, merely because they are male. This belief is carried into the classroom and it can have serious adverse effects on the boy-teacher and boy-girl interactions.

## Classroom interactions

Several studies have highlighted the fact that in mixed classes the boys dominate the teacher's time. This has been challenged both by the teacher involved and the pupils, but confirmed whenever the recording of the lesson is analysed. Even teachers who have been made aware of the imbalance in time allocated to male and female pupils have difficulty giving the girls more than 40% of their time. Spender (1982) reports that when the amount of teacher time spent with girls reached 42%, the teacher was adamant that the figure was in fact closer to 90%: 'the girls were uncomfortable and the boys were rioting'. A recent report by the Commonwealth Schools Commission (1984) contains the following comment:

> Unlike their teachers, pupils indicate that they are aware of the male domination of classroom dynamics (Stanworth, 1981). However for the most part they regard this as proper – hence the girls' discomfort at receiving more than the usual allocation of teacher time. Girls who challenge the norm by being verbally active are branded by both teacher and peers with labels of 'loud', 'aggressive', 'bossy' and 'unfeminine'. Pressure on pupils to conform to the norms of the peer group is very strong. Teachers hesitate to encourage girls to violate the norm for fear of exposing them to negative sanctions and ridicule.

This is a sensitive area in which there is no single solution, each situation depending entirely on the personalities of the pupils involved. The teacher must declare firmly his/her expectations from the pupils and be prepared to change the balance of the classroom interactions with encouragement, chiding, or a combination of the two.

One area in which teachers are often guilty of making judgements, based purely on the sex of the pupil, is in their attitudes towards the appearance of written work. Teachers are much more tolerant of untidy work from boys because of the unwritten rule that girls are neater workers (often they are, but then, they do get more encouragement in that direction, since neatness is still regarded by many as a feminine virtue!). This is an example of double standards in which the boys are the losers, not just because their work is less attractive than it could be, but because, by being permitted to hand in work which is less than their best, they are losing an opportunity to develop self-discipline. There is also the danger that this preferential sympathy from teachers is directed towards boys when the quality of their work is being assessed. If a statement from a pupil is incomplete or partially correct, there is evidence to suggest (Margaret Goddard Spear, Inst. of Educational Technology, Open University) that teachers are more inclined to look positively on the work of a boy, 'reading between the lines' or drawing out the remainder of the answer. (By implication, the teacher believes that the boy knows more information and for some reason this has not been presented, whereas the girl has done what she can, and is evidently wrong, or has a partial understanding of the subject.) This is carried over into the marking of written work where the knowledge of the sex of the pupil can affect the teacher's judgement and influence the allocation of marks. This and other similar evidence suggests that many teachers have different expectations of their male and female pupils – a fact which does not go unnoticed by the class and which has a depressive effect on the motivation of the girls.

## Bias in written materials

Sex bias pervades every aspect of the materials we use and indeed underpins many teaching schemes, both commercial and 'in-house' products. The style and content of the texts continually implies a male audience. This shows up in all aspects of the work – the choice of applications, the type of hobbies assumed, the areas of interest assumed. Whenever attempts are made to balance the examples with ones of female interest, they are often heavily stereotyped. Such prescriptive 'boys' and 'girls' examples act to widen the gap in the science experiences of the pupils rather than to draw them together. There is a marked predominance of male characters in the illustrations, which gives out the message that the author of the materials considers that the science is primarily the concern of boys, which is yet another source of alienation for the girls. See Table 7.4 (overleaf).

Redressing the balance is not merely a question of making half the he's into she's and having a 50% representation of females in the examples – the choice

TABLE 7.4 **Analysis by sex of photographs, drawings, text and examples in *Nuffield Combined Science* activity books. (From Smail, 1984)**

| | | *Photographs/Drawings* | | | | *Text and examples* | | | |
|---|---|---|---|---|---|---|---|---|---|
| **Activity Book** | **Topics** | **Total people illustrated** | **Male** | **Female** | **Indeterminate** | **Total people mentioned** | **Male** | **Female** | **Indeterminate** |
| 1 | Exhibition Measuring Separating, Sourness | 28 | 25 | 1 | 2 | 31 | 24 | 1 | 6 |
| 2 | Movement, Forces Heating Things | 105 | 86 | 10 | 9 | 15 | 13 | 2 | 0 |
| 3 | Reproduction | 42 | 19 | 20 | 3 | 0 | 0 | 0 | 0 |
| 4 | Air Pressure and Composition | 61 | 54 | 3 | 4 | 13 | 12 | 1 | 0 |
| 5 | Electricity | 2 | 2 | 0 | 0 | 5 | 5 | 0 | 0 |
| 6 | Water | 52 | 42 | 5 | 5 | 7 | 5 | 2 | 0 |
| 7 | Small things | 35 | 31 | 4 | 0 | 3 | 2 | 1 | 0 |
| 8 | Earth, Cells and Eggs, Oil, Metals | 16 | 12 | 1 | 3 | 2 | 2 | 0 | 0 |
| 9 | Insects | 5 | 1 | 2 | 2 | 0 | 0 | 0 | 0 |
| 10 | Energy | 49 | 38 | 9 | 2 | 7 | 7 | 0 | 0 |
| All | | 395 | 310 | 55 | 30 | 83 | 70 | 7 | 6 |
| % | | 100 | 78.5 | 13.9 | 7.6 | 100 | 84.3 | 8.4 | 7.2 |

of context must be of interest and relevance to the girls, and girls and women must be represented in a favourable light. Too often in the materials in print at the moment, the 'token' female is in a domestic situation, or in a subordinate role, or merely looking decorative! It is necessary to challenge these stereotypes by explicity involving the women in non-traditional roles and, more significantly, taking care to show men participating in caring, nurturative activities. Similarly it is important to make clear that the values and perspectives which girls hold, whilst different in some respects from those of the boys, have as much validity and can be incorporated into the fabric of the science.

The monitoring of one's own lessons to check for bias and innuendo is always possible (e.g. by recording a lesson and analysing the transcript). However, the adoption of an 'Equal Opportunities' policy across the department (or better still, the school) is more satisfactory because of the scope for identifying common problems and sharing ideas and resources. The departmental finances may not stretch to the replacement of offending text books but it is possible to avoid making the same mistakes in 'in-house' materials and to compensate for the existing bias in the course of the classwork.

Girls and boys do not receive equal opportunities in their science education at the moment and this results in the large scale avoidance of science, physical science in particular, by almost half of our population! The problem is not a trivial one and it is difficult to tackle because it has so many facets rooted deep within our cultural heritage. I hope that this article has provided some useful information and that it acts as a stimulus to practicising teachers who were perhaps unaware of the scale of the problem, or not sure how to deal with it. There have been many papers and books written on the subject but I have restricted the list of Further Reading to articles which are addressed specifically to teachers. (The enthusiastic reader will find more exhaustive lists of references by consulting these articles.)

## Resources

Many examples of careers information which highlight opportunities for girls are available. Some Education Authorities have an Advisory Teacher for Equal Opportunities who will be familiar with the range of materials related to science; otherwise there may be copies available for loan or consultation at Teachers' Centres or SATROs. Many of the larger manufacturing companies and service industries have produced booklets which feature women at work and which include short biographies of the women featured. These have the advantage that they are normally free and available in reasonable quantities. Until recently, these publications concentrated on the graduate employees, but there is a growing number of materials of more direct relevance to pupils of average ability.

There are also a variety of films and videos aimed at informing pupils about jobs which require some scientific background. The more recent ones have taken care to promote the image of the female scientist or engineer. Again these are normally available for loan from Teachers' Centres or SATROs. The school careers staff may have access to materials, and may be willing to discuss liaison with you to help raise your pupils' awareness of the range of applications of science.

The Equal Opportunities Commission has produced a large range of materials concerned with education and careers. A list of their publications can be obtained by writing to: Equal Opportunities Commission, Overseas House, Quay Street, Manchester M3 3HN.

## References and further reading

Byrne, E., 1978, *Women and Education* (Tavistock Publications, London)

CDSS, 1985, *Time for Change? (The Girls' Education in Mathematics, Science and Technology (GEMSAT) Project)* (Curriculum Development Support Service, Notts)

CSC, 1984, *Girls and Tommorrow – The Challenge of Schools (Report of the Working Party on the Education of Girls)* (Commonwealth Schools Commission, Hanborough)

DES, 1980, 'Girls and Science' *HMI Matters for Discussion Series, 13* (HMSO, London)

EOC, 1984, *An Equal Start* (Equal Opportunities Commission, Manchester)

EOC, 1985, *Breaking the Mould - Equal Opportunities Initiatives and Careers Education* (Equal Opportunities Commission, Manchester)

EOC, 1985, *Do You Provide Equal Opportunities?* (Equal Opportunities Commission, Manchester)

EOC, 1985, *We Can Do It Now!* (Equal Opportunities Commission, Manchester)

Harding, J., 1983, *Switched Off: The Science Education of Girls* (Schools Curriculum Development Council, London)

Joint Physics Education Committee of the Royal Society and the Institute of Physics, 1982, *Girls and Physics* (Royal Society, London)

Kant, L., and Brown, M., 'Jobs for Girls?' (*Schools Council Pamphlet 22*) (Schools Council, London)

Kelly, A., 'The Construction of Masculine Science' *British Journal of Sociology of Education, vol. 6, no. 2* (Carfax Publishing Company, Abingdon)

Kelly, A., (Ed), 1981, *The Missing Half – Girls in Science Education* (Manchester University Press, Manchester)

Kelly, A., Smail, B., White, B., 1984, *Girls into Science and Technology (GIST) Project – Final Report* (Department of Sociology)

Millman, V., Weiner, G., 1985, *Sex Differentiation in Schooling: Is There Really a Problem?* (Schools Curriculum Development Council, London)

Smail, B., 1984, 'Girl-Friendly Science: Avoiding Sex Bias in the Curriculum' *(Schools Council Program 3)* (Longman, London)

Spender, D., 1982, *The Invisible Woman: The Schooling Scandal* (Writers and Readers, London)

SSCR, (in preparation) *Equal Opportunities Report* (Secondary Science Curriculum Review, London)

Stanworth, M., 1981, *Gender and Schooling: A Study of Sexual Divisions in the Classroom* (Women Research Resources Centre, London)

White, J., 1985, *Gender, Science and Technology In-Service Handbook* (Schools Curriculum Development Council/Longman, London)

# Glossary

AEB: Associated Examining Board
APU: Assessment of Performance Unit
ASE: Association for Science Education
BTEC: Business and Technician Education Council
CGLI: City and Guilds of London Institute
CLA: Copyright Licensing Agency
CLEAPSE: Consortium of LEAs for the Provision of Science Equipment
CLISP: The Children's Learning in Science Project
CLS: Curriculum Led Staffing
CPVE: Certificate of Pre-Vocational Education
CSE: Certificate of Secondary Education
DARTS: Directed Activities Related to Texts
DES: Department of Education and Science
EOC: Equal Opportunities Commission
ESN schools: Educationally Sub-Normal schools
FEU: Further Education Curriculum Review and Development Unit
GASS: Gas Applications for School Science
GCE: General Certificate of Education
GCSE: General Certificate of Secondary Education
GEMSAT: Girls' Education in Mathematics, Science and Technology
GIST: Girls Into Science and Technology
ILEA: Inner London Education Authority
JMB: Joint Matriculation Board
LAMP: Less Academically Motivated Pupils
LEAs: Local Education Authorities
MSC: Manpower Services Commission
MUF: Maximum Utilization Factor
NUT: National Union of Teachers
PTR: Pupil Teacher Ratio
SATIS: Science and Technology in Society
SATRO: Science and Technology Regional Organization
SCDC: School Curriculum Development Committee
SCIP: School Curriculum Industry Project
SCISP: Schools Council Integrated Science Project
SEC: Secondary Examinations Council
SISCON: Science in Social Context
SOCET: Social, Economic, Environmental and Technological elements of a course
SSCR: Secondary Science Curriculum Review
SSRP: School Science Research Project
SSSERC: Scottish Schools Science Equipment Research Centre
TAPS: Techniques for the Assessment of Practical Skills
TVEI: Technical and Vocational Educational Initiative
WISE year: Women In Science and Engineering year
YTS: Youth Training Scheme

# Index